THE NEW VILLENEUVE

THE NEW VILLENEUVE

The Life of Jacques Villeneuve

Timothy Collings

BLOOMSBURY

First published in 1997 by
Bloomsbury Publishing Plc
38 Soho Square
London W1V 5DF

This paperback edition published 1998

Copyright © by Timothy Collings 1997

A copy of the CIP entry for this book is available from the British Library

ISBN 0 7475 3103 X

10 9 8 7 6 5 4 3 2 1

Typeset by Hewer Text Composition Services, Edinburgh
Printed and bound in Great Britain by Clays Ltd, St Ives plc

CONTENTS

ACKNOWLEDGEMENTS

This book would not have been possible without the generous help and cooperation of many people, particularly those who gave up precious time to recount the part they played in, or observed of, Jacques Villeneuve's life.

All of the following, in no particular order, contributed to the research and writing of this book: *Autosport* magazine, *Motoring News*, *Motor Sport*, *F1 Racing*, *F1 News*, Frank Williams, Patrick Head, Rickard Rydell, Bernie Ecclestone, Andrew Cotton, Jon Noble, Richard Hart, Mandeep Sanghera, Dan Layton, Tim Tuttle, David Tremayne, Alan Henry, Nigel Roebuck (and his book *Gilles Villeneuve*), Maurice Hamilton, Christopher Hilton (and his book *Jacques Villeneuve, In His Own Right*), Sid Watkins (and his book *Life at the Limit*), Gerald Donaldson (and his book *Gilles Villeneuve, The Life of the Legendary Racing Driver*), Bruce Jones (who edited *The Ultimate Encyclopedia of Formula One* and wrote for *Autosport*), Oliver Holt, Ray Matts, Bob McKenzie, Andrew Benson, Tony Dodgins, Adam Cooper, Doug Stark of Ontario, David Letterman, Bruce Martin, Virginie Merlin, Jacob Richler, David Peevers, Gordon Kirby, Warren Hughes, Barry Green, Toni Toomey, Tony Cicale, Bruce Martin, Alan Docking, Tom Kristensen, Massimiliano Angelelli, Mika Salo, Eddie Irvine, Kuomisan of Toyota, Dan Layton, Alberto Antonini, Giorgio Piccolo, Henry Morrogh, Marc David, Pierre and Yula de Meyer, Fauso Martinelli, Jacques Villeneuve Snr., Eric Silbermann, the FIA Press Service, Simon Mills, Richard Williams, Angelo Rosin, Carlo Marzetti, Julian Thomas, Luca Badoer, Mark Skewis, Simon Arron, John Watson, Ben Edwards, Tim Clowes, Nick Harris and *ICN*, Stan Piecha, Derick Allsop, Ted Macauley of the *Daily Mirror*, Jean-Jacques Delaruwière and Christine Marquilie for the Renault Sport press service, Bernard Dudot, Damon Hill,

Acknowledgements

Gerhard Berger, Bob Constanduros, Richard Grundy, David Brown, David Coulthard, Johnny Herbert, Tyler Alexander, Jock Clear, Michael Schumacher, Adrian Newey, Jean-François Robin, Jean-François Caubet, Ann Bradshaw, Christiane Lorey, Kunihiko Akai, Johnny Rives, Anne Giuntini, Jeff Hutchinson, Hideaki Machida, 'Lord' Fred Petersens, Joe Saward, Paul Treuthardt, Jochen Mass, Alain Prost, Mike Doodson, Derek Wright, Heinz-Harald Frentzen and Tony Jardine. Special thanks must go to Sarah Prest for her patience and editing skills, to Kathy Rooney for coming up with the original idea, and to Ruth Collings for putting up with a grumpy husband working against the odds and the inevitable deadlines. Thanks, also, to the Rothmans Williams Renault team for their kindness and hospitality despite often strained circumstances in a competitive Formula One year. Finally, I acknowledge and thank the photographers who supplied the photographs used in this book, in particular Mario Luini and Hiroaki Matsumoto, and I apologize to anyone whose help has been overlooked.

Timothy Collings, October 1996

Introduction

July 26 1996, Hockenheim. The familiar sounds of a Formula One paddock late in the afternoon: buzzing traffic, a few helicopters, racing cars droning through the forests of the fast Hockenheim ring circuit in southern Germany and Formula One's top engineers and drivers hurrying from media commitments to debriefs in their air-conditioned transporters. It was a hot afternoon, the sun was high overhead and there was little shade to hide in on the asphalt stretch between the gleaming motorhomes and the trucks.

Close to the southern end of this ribbon of activity, a small, dishevelled and bespectacled figure in jeans and T-shirt scurried towards the rear of the Rothmans Williams Renault team transporter. Jacques Villeneuve, son of the legendary Gilles Villeneuve, was easily identifiable by his wispy hair, his slight hunch, his fashionably 'grunge' appearance and his slightly rolling walk as he aimed through the crowds towards the sanctuary of his workplace alongside the engineers. For anyone wishing to speak to him, albeit briefly, it was a good opportunity. His manager, Craig Pollock, to whom he seemed so closely attached that it was suggested, in jest, that they were held together by an invisible umbilical cord, was absent.

Villeneuve, however, while remaining perfectly civil, made it clear he did not want to talk. Nor to be interviewed. Nor did he wish to discuss his life, his personality, his career or his philosophy with the author of this biography. Nor did he want to help in the supply of anecdotes, or facts, or dates, times and places; not even to confirm them; there would be, quite simply, zero cooperation.

It soon became clear that this supremely talented champion of motor racing was a strong, complex character of kaleidoscopic nuances, subtle changes of temperament and stubborn outlooks that, at times, turned him perversely in on himself and, at other times, made him a light, engaging and delightful companion. It had to be remembered also that at that time he was under pressure, struggling to match his ambitions in the Williams Renault FW18, learning the fastest way around the high-speed Hockenheim track and coping also with the presence in the paddock, at the Williams motorhome, of his girlfriend and her mother. At 25, also, though he could display remarkable maturity at times, he appeared sometimes to be young and very immature in many ways. More than anything, he had two very forceful managers in Pollock and Julian Jakobi, the latter having distinguished himself by working simultaneously, quite properly, for Alain Prost and Ayrton Senna at the height of their rivalry in the late 1980s. The words that came from him may have echoed the thoughts of these men, the commercial calculations of the agents and the percentages. And this was, after all, the man who had said a year previously that he did not 'believe in being nice to someone just because you want something from them. Life isn't just about business and making money.' This, of course, echoed the famed honesty and directness of his father.

Villeneuve was a highly focused (a nice way of saying self-centred, but used only for sports people) and ambitious driver with but one thought, one goal, in his mind at that time: victory in the German Grand Prix. His powers of concentration, famous in America where he won the Indycar World Series and the Indianapolis 500, were rightly acclaimed, but they existed at the expense of an ability to enjoy the company of the varied and amusing people who attend Grand Prix racing. He admitted he hated talking about himself, loathed revealing inner truths and being open.

'I hate those questions, I hate just talking about myself,' he said. 'I don't like to be open. As far as that is concerned, I am quite shy. Okay, in the car my strength is maybe to be relaxed, which is important to keep the head cool, to know what to do when, when to be aggressive, when not to be. In my personal life . . . I don't know – just being happy and content with what I have, just being normal, that's good.'

It may be overstating the case to say that he seemed confused, but it is difficult to find another way of describing the conflicts of a man who consistently rejected any links between his own racing career and that of his father, yet raced still, and who attempted to project the image of a cool young guy with hardly a care in the world, yet who was so calculating that he knew his value in time and hard cash to a degree which would surprise many observers and fans.

'I don't like to be in the paddock just to be in the paddock,' he said. 'I am here to work, so I work. If I have nothing to do, I go. If I wasn't racing, I would not want to be in the paddock. I am sure that if I stop racing, I wouldn't be around any more, just coming to races and walking around. The race track is more or less my office. If everything is clear and finished, I go. Somebody doesn't stay in the office when his work is finished.'

Alas, for most people the race circuit is not an office, but a venue of dreams and joys. Racing so cleanly, so fast and so beautifully is a God-given talent and opportunity, which most drivers relish. This talent, however, has carried him into the realm of public adoration and fame and that, with its attendant duties and chores, is what makes him a public figure and an attraction for the commercial opportunists. Like most who saw Jacques Villeneuve arrive, shine and blossom in Formula One, there was understanding for his position; all his life, he had suffered from those who wanted a slice of his action. Why should he not wish to make sure he kept every slice to himself?

His own uncertainty, in my view, came directly from the loss of his father, at the age of only 11. It meant that, like Damon Hill, his Williams Renault team-mate of 1996, he had to redefine his life, his future, his values. He withdrew, became introspective and reserved and planned his life in minute detail. He had to do something for himself, for the memory of his father from which, in so many ways, he was always escaping each day of his life. He had to race, but he had to race in his own way, in his own style, with his own identity as Jacques Villeneuve. He needed to find his own hero inside himself to fill the void, to maintain the thread of the Villeneuve tradition and to satisfy himself and end the search. In the most blunt terms, it was a search for individual happiness, peace and contentment.

'I am just being myself,' he said. 'I don't care what people think. No, that's not correct. You do care what people think. You don't want people to think negatively about you. But I think the most important thing is to be yourself. If you want to be happy, you have to be yourself. If you are trying to be someone else, you are not going to be happy. And the most important thing is to be happy. And you do everything possible to make yourself happy.'

It was a speech of clues, an admission of seeking happiness. But why in racing? 'There are two things. I love competition in everything; it does not have to be in cars, it can be elsewhere as well. And the second thing is the speed. Not the speed in the straight line, it is the speed with the edge, with the limit. Always pushing the limit, and doing it better and working on it to end up more on the edge, feeling it, gives you a high. It is a feeling that is impossible to describe.

'It is something that is very personal. No one else can feel it, only the other guys in their cars – but maybe they feel it differently. Knowing that you are doing something special and that if you make a mistake you will have a bad accident, but you can control it . . . That gives you a big rush.'

Gilles Villeneuve, his father, died at Zolder, in a massive accident in a Ferrari during the practice session for the Belgian Grand Prix in 1982. He was, some said, a high-wire artist who performed without a net. Jacques, the son, clearly prefers a net in place, but wishes also to prove that the truly heroic thing is to do tricks and stay alive. Let us hope he finds that hero in himself and mellows afterwards to become one of us, another man in the paddock sharing the crack, the buzz, the jokes and gossip and thrills of Formula One. It is, after all, the environment in which he grew up; the place in which his father parked his camper, where his mother cooked her famous hamburgers, where Gilles lit a passion and blazed a trail; and the place where this, his story, begins.

Chapter One

Silverstone:
Made of the Right Stuff

There was no question about it. Bernie Ecclestone was right. Rothmans Williams Renault were right. Frank Williams and Patrick Head were right. Jacques Villeneuve was made of the right stuff. Accomplished, fast and manifestly perfect for Formula One, he looked the part. From head to toe, he oozed composure, ability and speed. The question was not about his talent, his ability, his future team or the cost . . . it was simpler than all that. It was when. On that hot afternoon of August 15 1995, barely 48 hours after the German Grand Prix at Hockenheim, less than 48 hours after struggling home 10th in the Michigan 500, Villeneuve proved himself on the first day of his first test in a Formula One car. He did it again on Wednesday August 16, his second day, and again on Thursday August 17. On the same Silverstone circuit where his father Gilles had made a hugely dramatic impression in July 1977, driving for McLaren, young Jacques, just 24, did the same by different means in a Williams FW17B. There was less of the rash, banzai attacking style and more of the smoothness of a quiet, but quick student; but the same goal was achieved and the many observers present murmured in appreciation as he accomplished his task with the minimum of fuss on a day when his car was often parked alongside that of another son of another famous driver in the Williams garage. Damon Hill, the son of Graham, hardly acknowledged him.

'I think he is the only guy that can give Schumacher some stick,' Ecclestone, the president of the Formula One Constructors' Association (FOCA) and a vice-president (for commercial affairs) of the Federation International de l'Automobile (FIA), had claimed in advance. Renowned as a shrewd judge of young talent and the commercial potential of importing north Americans to the European-based Formula One circus, of which he was the ringmaster, Ecclestone knew his opinions were both respected and quotable. 'He comes out of the Schumacher–Senna mould,' he said. 'Any team manager who has a chance to sign him, but doesn't, will live to regret it.'

These were bold assertions. They carried a powerful weight and Ecclestone knew he could guarantee a crowd for a mere test session at the old Northamptonshire airbase, if he crowed loud enough. There was a school of thought that he wanted to gain something in return for losing Nigel Mansell to America back in 1992 shortly after the moustachioed Englishman had seized his first and only Formula One world crown. 'When I said Schumacher was world champion before he came into Formula One, people blinked at me,' Ecclestone added, in explanation, on the third day of what proved to be an impressive test debut. 'But I am saying the same thing about this guy. He is something special, super-sensitive, and he can set up cars. I think he is a bit special. He's only been here three days and he is driving a car very different from those he knows, but he has got very close to Damon and there is no doubt about his ability to put in a few quick laps.'

No one argued. Few ever did, anyway, when Ecclestone spoke. But Villeneuve's talent was easy to see, his casual and controlled demeanour easy to note, his speed manifestly obvious from the stop-clocks and time-sheets from the very first day. It was a debut to remember. No wonder Villeneuve, in his unmarked white fireproof suit, who had driven in an unmarked car, smiled. No wonder his manager Craig Pollock smiled. No wonder Frank Williams and Patrick Head smiled on one of those occasions when both attended a test session. Not since Michael Schumacher had blitzed round the same Silverstone track in a Jordan in 1991 had a new boy left such an astonishing first impression.

Villeneuve had hardly had the best preparations. After racing in Michigan in one of the toughest of all oval races over 500 miles at high speeds, he had travelled via an overnight 'red-eye' to London for talks with Ecclestone and a negotiating session, and seat-fitting, with Williams at his team headquarters at Didcot. That was Monday. The following day, he was in the car and at it, carving such an impression out of the sultry summer air that even Hill, still burning with indignation after his second lap exit while leading at Hocken-heim, was impressed. 'I didn't follow him that closely out on the track, but from what I did see, and from his time, I am obviously very impressed. It looks as if he has got what it takes, doesn't it?'

It certainly did. The *Daily Mail*, of London, a sober newspaper not prone to over-sensationalisation in its sports reporting, said that Villeneuve left the Williams Renault team 'with their mouths ajar' on the first day of the test. 'Villeneuve, 24, who had never driven a Formula One machine and had never seen Silverstone before, was only eight-tenths of a second behind Hill's 1 minute 29.14 second lap . . . and then complained the car was too slow.' In *The Times*, Oliver Holt wrote that 'Jacques Villeneuve had blazed a trail as bright as a comet' while the *Daily Telegraph* reported that he 'looked every inch a Williams driver as he sat, half-smiling, in the corner of the team motorhome . . . surrounded by an admiring media corps'. Unfortunately, owing to their contractual obligations, none of the Williams staff were free to talk on the record and in an official capacity about their driver for this book. Even the team's long-serving and loyal press officer, Ann Bradshaw, was, she explained, shackled by the same binding restriction. Nonetheless, enough members of the team did talk, some off the record, some to colleagues and friends, others to intermediaries, to provide sufficient evidence to prove that Ville-neuve's first impression was as emphatic within the garage as it appeared to be from without. And this, of course, has been supported by the views of former team members and other qualified observers who were present at the time.

His father Gilles had made a spectacular first test in a Formula One car and had followed it up, in his first Grand Prix, by matching the pace of the leaders while driving a two-year-old car himself. It was that memory, a story passed down the years, which had drawn the old and the young in equal proportion to Silverstone. They wanted to see something like it again. In the end, however, though he was swift and assured, he was not the quickest. David Coulthard, the Scot whose place in the Williams Renault team was most under threat from the arrival of the French-Canadian, was more than a second faster than Villeneuve on the final day when a carefully planned showdown, orchestrated, it seemed, for the media as much as for anyone else, was wrecked by the new boy's inexperience.

The team had set up this unscheduled contest in the heat that day by supplying both men with new tyres and preparing them for it with light fuel loads. The laps of both men should have been as scorching as the sunshine which had left a bedraggled media corps seeking the shade, the tea urn in the garage and the cool of the darkness around the edges of the team garage. It was hot, exciting and tense for everyone. Each man and woman there knew that Coulthard's future, whilst not dependent on the outcome, remained in the balance. It was so still, so sultry, so warm; every wasp could be heard buzzing ever closer as the sun began to fall.

Villeneuve, if appearances are to be believed, seemed the coolest man around. Yet it was he who forgot the most fundamental part of his job, as Andrew Benson, reporting the test for *Autosport*, described: 'Villeneuve, showing his inexperience in an F1 car, forgot to switch on his electric fuel pump and coasted to a halt halfway round his warm-up lap. "Hell!" said a frustrated David Brown, Villeneuve's engineer on the final day, who had been looking forward to that final sprint as much as the British and foreign media gathered around the Williams pit. "I don't believe it." His thoughts reflected those of most of the sizeable crowd of onlookers, attracted to Silverstone to see exactly what Indycar racing's hottest prospect could do.'

If the outcome was inconclusive, if the contest did not really happen, it seemed not to matter. Villeneuve had been quick enough. At the end of his first day, he had been just nine-tenths of a second off the pace set by Hill. That, of course, was his first day in a Formula One car and his first day of driving at Silverstone in a car in which he was patently not too comfortable. 'The seat was terrible and I was moving around a lot,' he explained. At the end of his second day, he was just six-tenths off Hill's pace and progressing smoothly on the kind of path his admirers had dreamed of seeing. At the end of the third day, with Coulthard arriving to take over from Hill, he was to finish a second and more down, but only after he and his engineers had altered his gear ratios experimentally in a vain bid to improve things. For close Villeneuve-watchers, this was the first indication of his independence, his keenness to do his own thing and go his own way, sometimes in direct defiance of advice from older and much more experienced colleagues.

'I really enjoyed myself,' said Villeneuve at the end of it all, back in the cool, air-conditioned calm of the Williams motorhome. 'For a first experience of Formula One, testing with Williams in one of the top cars, is great because it means it's well set-up and enjoyable to drive.' This first assessment of his test, his ability and his potential came at the end from the man himself after he and his manager, Craig Pollock, had agreed that the best way to satisfy the needs of the media, hungry for a story about the F1 baptism of the son-of-Gilles, was to hold one communal meeting in a casual and relaxed atmosphere. This, too, was to be a signal of the way things were with Villeneuve; while other Formula One drivers would be happy to sit, or stand, and chat with anyone as for long as was reasonable to get the job done, the boyish newcomer was not. The 'By Appointment Only' signs were there from the start.

David Brown, the highly respected engineer who had worked in his time at Williams with Nigel Mansell, Alain Prost, Ayrton Senna and Damon Hill, was reluctant to be drawn into too many irrevocable statements. As he reflected on what had been an intriguing three days' test-work and on the ability of 'the kid', he withdrew into himself. Never one for taking the glory, or taking risks in relation to the Williams team's public relations machine, Brown was as circumspect as usual. Then, in summary, he revealed the essential truth he felt about Villeneuve when he said: 'He is capable of becoming a top driver. He had good feedback, and every time he changed something on the car, he went quicker. But he was also a nice guy, who was easy to work with.'

In three days at Silverstone that week, while he charmed those he worked with and impressed those who watched him from a distance, Villeneuve set an example for flawless progress from learner to master of his cockpit and his surroundings. He never hurried. He never attempted more than he could cope with and he spun off only once, at about 150mph, in the Becketts complex, without damaging his car. Ecclestone, a 100 miles away in his offices in London, must have grinned from ear to ear. His move to act as broker of the Canadian's transatlantic transfer was looking like a good piece of business – both on the track and in the headlines of his favourite British newspapers.

It seemed Jacques had been saying all the right things, too, even down to suggesting gently at the end of the first morning, that the Williams was not that special a car to drive for the first time. The Formula One aficionados, expecting him to be impressed by its speed, its cornering ability and its braking power, were stunned at this. 'It felt a lot lighter than an Indycar,' said Villeneuve before lunch on the first day. 'It feels slower in a straight line and it accelerates slower, but it handles much better in the corners.' Twenty-four hours later, he revised this opinion. 'I may have underestimated the difference between an F1 car and an Indycar yesterday,' he admitted. 'These are much quicker in the corners.'

And so by the end of the final day, when we all sat in the motorhome, he had still more to say, in his deliberate, carefully weighted manner in which he reserved his views on many questions and allowed Pollock to answer for him on many others. 'I knew the car was going to brake harder and that the cornering speed was going to be faster than an Indycar, so that wasn't a surprise. The car is lighter, so it's normal that it's going to be more driveable. You can get a little bit sideways and drive it a little bit easier than an Indycar. And the shifting on the steering wheel is great – that makes life much easier.'

It was technical stuff. It proved that he knew what he was talking about. But there was very little on a human level, about him, his father, his family and his future that any self-respecting hack could really hang his hat on. Of course, this was deliberate, but there were a few comments that helped illuminate his personality. Asked how he found working with the Williams team, for example, he responded, as he shuffled in his seat and swept his hair off his face, by saying: 'I had a great time. We worked well and had a few laughs too – I think it's really important when you work with people not to be serious all the time. This was a true test and that doesn't just mean going out and doing fast laps. It's for the team to see how a driver will work with them and vice versa – to see if there is a compatibility of characters.'

Questions about his father and his feelings for him were answered in much the same way as always. 'I am sorry to disappoint you,' he explained. 'But I never think about my father when I race. I have always been different, always my own person. I know what people would like to hear, but I don't say it. People have told my mother: "What is wrong with your son, have you heard what he is saying about his father?" Well, I am super-proud to be his son, but I am racing for myself. Mostly, having my father's name has been an advantage, but people expected me to be on the pace right from the start, so I didn't have time to learn. It was a big help for sponsors. Still, once you go in, they wanted results right away, or people would have said "he is not as fast as his father" and they would have thrown me in the garbage.'

It was not just what he said, but how he said it, which so impressed those sitting listening to him that evening in the Williams motorhome. He was the epitome of young, cool and anything-but-callow youth; an old head on young shoulders; an introspective child with the articulation of a man much older and much wiser and more experienced; his words were weighted carefully, he was calm, level-headed, self-sufficient, self-absorbed, showed touches and flashes of a light humour; he obviously knew what he wanted and was intent on getting it; and, all the time, he had his manager, Pollock, with him to meet any awkward questions about contracts, money, teams and any other leading subjects with a smooth, calm and charming manner. Pollock, a former teacher and ski instructor, who first met Jacques when he worked with him at a boarding school in Switzerland, is a Robert Wagner type of man, a clean-cut diplomatic sort with blue eyes that could sparkle, or cut like a laser, as and when required. He is a long-standing confidante of Villeneuve's with great influence on him. Together, they were a formidable verbal double act that evening, Villeneuve talking lucidly about racing, about cars and about the inside of the Williams team, while his manager intercepted trickier questions, deflected difficult ones, distracted the interviewer away from his prey and offered a shield when needed.

But there was plenty of laughter too. It was not all grey stuff, statistics, G-forces and contractual gobbledygook. Villeneuve in full flow (which is not the sort of flow that deserves comparison with such erudite predecessors, to whom he was unfairly compared, as Ayrton Senna or Alain Prost) was as eloquent as could be expected from someone brought up in a series of different countries, who began racing in Italy and then Japan, before spending three years in the United States. But it was not his use of English that we were to appreciate; it was his thoughts on racing. In these areas he was supremely confident, when allowed to speak freely.

For example, he was asked if he thought he could win races in Formula One in 1996. His pithy reply, intelligent, accurate and lacking any kind of sentiment, was direct. 'Any driver will always feel that he's capable of winning, so you'd better ask other people about that.' There was the impression of a shrug. Not a smile. No effort was made to win over his audience with charm. There was a total reliance of confidence and ability. It was almost as if the rich lifestyle he had enjoyed throughout his life, his assumption that he could travel first class wherever and whenever he wanted to, was sufficient cause for him to feel he was automatically right in everything he said. The confidence, in one so young and so inexperienced, bordered on arrogance; but it was fresh, welcome and revolutionary in a Formula One scene that had been dominated for far too long by the same talking heads and the same crash helmets.

Had he gained enough information, he was asked, to make an informed decision about his future? This meant did he want to abandon Team Green, where he had been so successful in Indycar racing, winning the drivers' championship and the Indianapolis 500, and move to Williams. 'I think so,' replied Villeneuve. 'If it had been three bad days, no. But it has been three good days, so I got a lot of information and feel. A race car is a race car and whatever series it is, once you're on the limit, it's hard work to go quicker. The desire is there, but it's not the desire to be in F1. It's the desire to be with a top competitive team.

'My ambition has always been to be a professional race car driver and to win races and, if possible, championships; not to be in F1 at any cost. I went to north America in the first place because at the time it was a better opportunity for me, a better career move. F1 and Indycars are the top of racing. F1 is bigger, international, and Indycar is north America, so it'll always be different. You can't really compare the two.'

It was a strange feature of this evening meeting, before Villeneuve and Pollock rushed away from Silverstone to have dinner with Ecclestone at San Lorenzo's restaurant in London, that the assumption that he was to be joining Williams and racing in Formula One was there in everyone's mind long before the first question was asked or answered. Rarely can such certainty have existed in such a manner at a test before, particularly when an existing Williams driver, Coulthard, was performing with so much obvious vim and pace.

Villeneuve, however, persisted in suggesting that he might remain with Team Green in Indycars even if he were to go on, as he did, and win the drivers' title. 'With the season finishing so early in the States, the teams have to know what you're doing too,' he said. 'You just cannot push it later and have them wait. I could make up my mind, but the F1 teams might not make up theirs and then I'd probably stay in north America.'

He added that it mattered little if he won the 1995 title or not, to add to his major success in the Indianapolis 500. 'That's not the key element,' he said. And when money was raised as a topic, he forced his way into the conversation to give an answer before anyone could intervene. 'Money is good on both sides. It is important, but it depends on a lot of things and it is not just up to me. It is up to the teams involved and then there are things like performance, personnel, contracts and money. But you also have to be able to win.'

It was said at the time that Villeneuve was earning slightly more than six million dollars in Indycar racing that year, 1995, with Team Green, thanks in large part to his success at Indianapolis in May. It was, therefore, reasonably simple for anyone to deduce that Williams would have to match that sort of earning power, or improve on it, to ensure that they signed him. 'I guess I am closer to Williams after this test than to anybody else,' he admitted. 'But, as I said, I am not going to drive in F1 at any cost.'

While Villeneuve prevaricated, if only briefly, there were plenty of observers, some with real experience of his predicament, who were only too willing to offer him advice. Michael Andretti, for example, the last driver from north America to try his luck in Formula One, made it clear that he felt that Villeneuve had to take the opportunity immediately. In a brief interview with *Autosport*, he did not say he should do it at any cost, but it was tantamount to a perfect contradiction of the French-Canadian's own cautious outlook. 'My advice to him is, if he wants to do F1, he should act now instead of waiting five years,' said Andretti, whose father Mario had been one of the few men to have won titles in both championships while remaining both popular and widely acclaimed for his skills. 'Do it right now – the younger the better.'

Andretti had been a married man with a long track record in

Indycar racing before he had joined McLaren for what proved to be a near-disastrous 1993 season. He had decided to commute to Europe for the races and what little testing he was required to attend and he recognised, with the benefit of hindsight, that this approach was wrong when asked to appraise the Villeneuve situation at the time of his impressive Silverstone test.

'I think Jacques has a couple of advantages over me that will help him in F1,' he explained. 'He hasn't been in Indycars that long, so he hasn't developed a real style for these cars yet. He's also younger than me, so he may be able to adapt a little better to something new. Being younger is a big help. When I got into F1, I'd been racing Indycars for ten years. Take the braking distances for example, it was hard to tell yourself to do it another way after you've been doing it a certain way for so long. But it was coming; I think I just needed more time.

'If Jacques does do F1, with Williams, and the team keeps up chassis-wise with what they've been doing in the past few years, that will be a great situation for him. Unfortunately, I joined McLaren on a downswing. Timing and hitting the right team at the right time is a key factor. In this test, Jacques did more laps in three days than I did in three months with McLaren before the season started. He wouldn't get that luxury once he got into the new season, going to new race tracks each weekend. That will be a bit of a problem for him. But I'm sure he can handle it. He's a good driver. He probably won't win races right away, but if you can win races in Indycars you're going to win races in F1, eventually.

'Still, I'd be surprised to see him driving a Williams next year, unless he comes down on what he wants for a retainer compared to what he will get in Indycars for 1996!'

This was the kind of straightforward advice that went straight to the point, based on experience. Others were equally enthusiastic for Villeneuve to make the move to Formula One. Emerson Fittipaldi told *Autosport*: 'Jacques is very, very talented. I think he has the same natural ability that Gilles had, but with much better control. I also think that Formula One and Indycars now are much closer to each other in feeling than they used to be, so I don't see any problems for Jacques. As long as the team is behind him, and supports his possibility of doing the job, he's going to do a very good job.'

Villeneuve's then race engineer with Team Green in America was equally convinced that the Silverstone test only confirmed what he had suspected: that the young driver had the ability to succeed. 'One thing Jacques is very spectacular at is learning,' said Tony Cicale. 'Not just new tracks, but new systems. Explain something to him once and that's it. So, I didn't think he'd have any problems with the shifting or the clutch on an F1 car. He's also a very, very late braker in Indycars, so since the braking is quite a bit better in F1, I thought he'd do quite well. He's a funny character. He does have a pretty thick skin, so I think he will survive in the F1 environment.'

This thick skin was to serve him well in many ways, but also worked against him later the following year once his Formula One career had begun. Initially, however, it was useful. It impressed the media gang, it added to the image created by the sparkling blue eyes, the intelligence and calculation, the down-to-earth approach to work and public relations. It also impressed some of the team who had to work around him and he left a good taste in the mouth of Patrick Head. 'We expected him to be pretty good,' he said. 'And he obviously is pretty good. Villeneuve's had four races in the last four weeks; then he's flown over the Atlantic and had three days here at Silverstone in extremely hot weather. It's a real test of stamina and he's done a good job. His lap times have been excellent and obviously he has given us something to think about.'

Asked if Williams had seen Villeneuve's full potential in the Silverstone test, Head was cagey. 'It's probably a bit over-simplistic to suggest that. There are a whole load of factors. A driver who is already in a team might be prepared to risk going off the circuit a bit more than someone who's having a test drive and is aware that the team is looking not just at their ability to do a lap, but also whether they throw the car off the circuit. So, you don't really know until doing a winter's testing.' The vastly experienced

Williams technical director, a man who has worked with all the team's great champions including Alan Jones, Keke Rosberg, Nelson Piquet, Nigel Mansell and Alain Prost, was clearly being as accurate in his comments as he possibly dared, but without drawing too many conclusions. He was certain, however, as he told Benson in *Autosport*, that Villeneuve was fully capable of doing a top-line job in Formula One. 'I'm sure he is,' he said. 'But it would be a very difficult decision for a team, and quite a hard task for him, to leap straight from Indy racing to a team right at the front of Grand Prix racing. It's something that ourselves and any other team thinking of running him would have to consider quite seriously. Every circuit would be new to him and as well as that the atmosphere that surrounds F1 is rather more aggressive and commercial than Indycars. A driver has to get used to handling that.'

Underlying Head's remarks was the feeling that he had seen a man he knew could do the job of partnering Damon Hill in 1996, if, as expected, David Coulthard and Williams were to go their separate ways. Coulthard had been involved in some strained legal proceedings involving Williams and McLaren the previous winter and it had not left the Didcot team too impressed with the management around him. But Coulthard himself was nothing if not proud and confident and, after the test, he said: 'I am not worried about my own position in so much as I have my contract for the year and have confidence in what I am doing. I don't feel I'm a less good driver than Damon, even though I've not had the results yet this year. But if you think of Jacques as another driver in the market place, then it is more negative for me and Damon than it is for other drivers in other teams. I don't believe Williams would test him and then not have an option on him for the future, so I believe if he comes to F1 it will be with Williams. Obviously, if he does that then three people – or however many Frank is looking at – into two doesn't go. I can only influence this decision with my performances, so that's what I intend to do.'

Coulthard was right. Villeneuve joined Williams and he had to drive well himself in his remaining races with the team to secure a future elsewhere, with McLaren. It was a typical re-shuffle of drivers in the market place, a typical Formula One episode. It was said Villeneuve was earning around $6 million in Indycar racing that summer, in 1995, and expected to earn at least as much again, or more, if he moved to Williams. No one would confirm this, but it was an estimate that was not contradicted as the kid from Quebec disappeared into the Silverstone sunset. 'He enjoyed his test,' said Pollock, the manager. 'But he may not enjoy F1. We have got to sit down in the next couple of days and discuss all the issues. We hope to know where we're going by this weekend. He has the pick in Indycar, but that doesn't mean to say that he has the pick in F1. He would still have to prove his worth in F1, but it all comes down to what he wants to do in the future. He's a person just like anybody else and he has to have a life based around driving cars.'

Two other people had a part to play in the final jigsaw that slotted together and signalled the future for Jacques: his mother, in Monaco, and his Indycar boss Barry Green in America. After dining with Ecclestone, to discuss the prospects and details, he travelled down to Monte Carlo for a quiet weekend of thought and reflection. Green, who had given him his break in the United States, was also left to rue the position he was in. 'It'll change a lot of things if Jacques goes to F1,' he said. 'The question is, without Jacques, will I have money from Players? I have a deal agreed with them if Jacques is driving the car, but the team has been a pretty good part of Jacques' success and I would hope Players would still consider us strongly, even if Jacques wasn't with us.

'I think it is good that he has gone over there. Jacques has done a good job and he knows he can drive an F1 car. I hoped he'd go even quicker, to be honest, because then everyone would want him and he could tell them he would do another year here and see who wants to pay the best money. I've just got to sit and wait and hold my breath. I told Jacques he's got to make up his mind because the only way I'm prepared to work with him is if I think he wants to be here. If he didn't want to be over here, he would be a handful.'

Mulling it over in the Monaco sunshine, Villeneuve reached his decision easily. Williams made the right kind of offer, the deal was done and he decided to leave Indycars behind. Green had no need to worry about him being a handful any more. That he tested as he did and then chose as he did proved what everyone knew, but wanted to see confirmed: he was determined to do it his way. He was made of the right stuff.

Chapter Two

The Legacy:
Headaches and Heartache

Jacques Villeneuve inherited so much. The blazing trail left by his car-racing sideways-sliding father; the single-mindedness of the same man, whose death lifted him to martyr-like status; his cold concentration in the cockpit; the dreadful tragedy of his death; an itinerant childhood in Canada, France, Switzerland and Italy and much of the rest of Europe; the riches and the lifestyle of a famous Monaco-based family; the close-up knowledge of things he could see, smell and experience – but could hardly understand. The legacy of Gilles Villeneuve, racing driver of rare talent and raw courage, was an interwoven tapestry of depth, splendour and dangers.

Romanticised after death by his legend and those who embellished it, the life of Gilles Villeneuve has seemed always, from the outside, to have been more heroic than saintly, more singular than familial, more about his own ambitions, deeds and achievements than those of his forebears or successors. By all accounts, he enjoyed having his family around him – but for his pleasure and convenience far more than theirs. It was bitterly ironic, yet merciful, that after years of carrying them with him from circuit to circuit across north America and then Europe, that they were absent at Zolder, in Belgium, on the day he was killed.

Joseph Gilles Henri Villeneuve, born January 18 1950, died after crashing during qualifying for the Belgian Grand Prix of 1982. That Saturday, May 8, had dawned bright and uplifting in the pine forests of the Flemish corner of Belgium and it was a pleasant afternoon until the last few minutes of the session when it became clear that Villeneuve, in an effort to overhaul his Ferrari teammate Didier Pironi's best qualifying lap time, had taken one risk too many. Villeneuve, at that time, despised Pironi for failing to honour an unspoken code at their previous race, the San Marino Grand Prix, where he won, in the French-Canadian's view, improperly. Impassioned by this breach of trust and understanding, he was taking more risks than ever to prove himself at Zolder when tragedy struck as he went for that invisible extra gap on a set of qualifying tyres which were well past their best.

To his and Ferrari's fanatical supporters, Villeneuve was held already in near-legendary affection and awe. For the previous 12 days, however, his mind had been in turmoil at Pironi's audacious and hurtful victory at Imola. A deep gloom had descended on Villeneuve as he brooded and sulked. It affected his every action and thought and he had travelled to Zolder filled with self-centred pity and a thirst for revenge. He tried as hard as he could to improve his time, to overhaul Pironi, but as the minutes passed by it became ever more clear that he was not able to do it. The Ferrari team knew this and put out a signal to come in at the end of the next lap. He did not respond and he did not come back.

Halfway round his lap, he went through the chicane and sped up and over the hill which followed towards the next corner, to the left, and its successor, to the right. In the distance, he could see a slow car which he knew, by instinct, would be on his best line at the corner to the right; and so the question was: to brake or to power on, foot down on the throttle, and find the gap on one side or the other. For this man, there was no need to reflect or think. He always drove to the limit – that was why the *tifosi* loved him. He was a manifestation of their dreams, with his sliding, spectacular style and his purity and bravery. The *tifosi* have since given him mythological status among the pantheon of Ferrari drivers, mostly for this very daredevil quality.

He kept his foot down. Flat. The car ahead was a March, driven by Jochen Mass of Germany, a man Gilles knew from a brief acquaintance at McLaren, where he had started his Formula One career, and in the paddocks and the pit lanes of the world. They both lived in Monaco. Mass was coasting back towards the pits, having given his all in his qualifying run to secure his place in what was scheduled to be his 100th Grand Prix. Mass noticed a flash of red in his mirror and opted to keep to the right, a move designed to allow Villeneuve to pass on the left and have a better and more usual line for the turn. The French-Canadian, however, had decided that this would not happen and that a gap would materialise to the right, not the left, of Mass's car. He had selected to attack a non-existent space towards the right of the track and had not given himself any room, or time, for error. The left front tyre of his Ferrari touched the rear right tyre of the March and, quite literally, took off.

It was a sickening collision. The Ferrari of Villeneuve was airborne, to the right, and within fractions of a second was out of the range of the television camera stationed at the corner. Then it returned into view, nose-diving with great energy and force, before somersaulting horribly across the circuit again. The impact was such that the front of the car snapped away. Villeneuve's helmet was reportedly pulled off and the driver was hurled, like a doll, into the catch fencing, made of wire-mesh, at the side of the circuit, on the outside of the corner, still wrapped in his seatbelts, which were connected to a lump of sheet metal torn out of the chassis. It was a devastating accident and Villeneuve was immediately given mouth-to-mouth resuscitation by the first medical officer at the scene. Other cars stopped. When Pironi arrived, Mass, himself shaken terribly, led him away, barely acknowledging that he might have been crushed by the bouncing remains of Villeneuve's out-of-control Ferrari as he came through the corner and pulled up.

'As we got round the back of the circuit, bits of debris appeared and finally the empty wreck of the Ferrari,' wrote Professor Sid Watkins, Formula One's permanent chief medical officer, in his account of the accident in his book, *Life at the Limit*. 'I knew then it was Villeneuve and my heart sank, remembering his words when we first met: "I hope I will never need you." '

Watkins, who was always among the first to the scene of any accident in Formula One in the last 20 years, described the accident in precise detail. 'Gilles had been thrown right across the circuit and lay at the bottom of some catch fencing. As I got to him it was clear he was not breathing, so we intubated him immediately and without difficulty and we started ventilating him with an Ambu bag and oxygen. It had taken about two minutes for me to get to the scene, but the surgeon had been there within 35 seconds. My surgical colleague carried on "bagging" while I looked at Gilles. He was quite flaccid and his pupils were dilated. Generally, he looked otherwise uninjured, so we concluded he probably had a cervical spine fracture with high spinal cord injury.'

Watkins was right. After Gilles was moved from the track to the medical centre and then taken by large military helicopter to the University St Raphael Hospital at Louvain, it was confirmed by the x-rays that he had suffered a fatal fracture of the neck just where the spine meets the base of the skull. Watkins contacted Joann at the family home in Monaco, where she had remained that weekend to make preparations for Melanie's first communion. Once she had arrived in Belgium, following a long, frank and dignified discussion, she and Watkins sat together and bore the last minutes in silence. There was to be no prolongation of his life with the aid of a life support system. He died that Saturday night by the time the rest of the Ferrari team had packed up and gone home.

Watkins, perhaps the only man to have been close to virtually every driver in Formula One in the last two decades, confirmed a widespread opinion when he related that, in his view, Villeneuve had been a victim of the failure of one of his own favourite theories. In *Life at the Limit*, he wrote of Villeneuve that he 'once had the misfortune to meet him in the lobby of the hotel at Sao Paulo, where he offered me a lift to Interlagos. Madame

Villeneuve was with him so when we got to his rented car, I moved to sit in the rear, but Madame insisted that I sat in the front. Gilles in a road car was frightening and when I turned to speak to his wife she was not visible as she had taken to the floor. She indicated that this was normal for her and I soon found out why.

'Villeneuve believed in the "gap theory" – ie that there was always a space into which he could move when faced with a high-speed collision. He ignored all the red lights, gently bounced off parked cars or lamp posts, talking all the time and never pausing or hesitating in the traffic. On getting to the circuit, he asked if I wanted a lift back later!'

This same 'gap theory' was adhered to in all situations by Gilles Villeneuve. In its most basic sense, it was a sheer reliance on luck and the preservation instincts of other people. It showed little consideration for his passengers, let alone other road-users. According to Watkins, it nearly always resulted in his rented cars being returned to their owners in a battered and often virtually undriveable condition, bereft of clutch or tyres, or both. His methods used in flying helicopters were similarly outrageous and irresponsible. Watkins reported that he had been told by Trevor Rowe, a former Secretary of the Grand Prix Drivers' Association, that Villeneuve frequently took off with the fuel gauge at zero, flying in and out of power cables and pylons with cool aplomb.

To some, when it came, Villeneuve's death, though tragic and a great loss, was no surprise. 'At one part of the circuit,' said Watkins, 'he tried to get past Jochen Mass, but when he got there his own theory had failed disastrously – there was no gap. There was a big impact, a launch, and Gilles was thrown from the car with his seat and seat-belt restraints still attached to him – all having been wrenched from the car – so high was the energy. Whether his neck fracture occurred when he left the car or landed near the catch fencing will never be known, but I am sure he did not in any conscious sense suffer. His family and friends did, and still do, so revered is his memory.'

Jochen Mass suffered on with the memory of that accident

and its after-effects for many years and admitted, at the 1996 Hungarian Grand Prix at the Hungaroring, north of Budapest, only hours before Jacques Villeneuve drove to his third Formula One victory, that he remained haunted by it. His whole life had been overshadowed by it. 'When Gilles raced, I had been in Formula One for eight or nine years already so all the excitement and glamour was not new for me, but for him it was. But he did not let it change him too much; he had the kids with him most of the time and it was very easy-going around him in the beginning.

'The legend came with his death, really, and from his style of racing. He was very spectacular. When he died, he became almost like a martyr. Everyone went with him that way. All this must have rubbed off on Jacques, but perhaps not in a good way. I don't really know. It must have been difficult anyway to have had a larger-than-life father. Because of his attitude, he had to be number one or nothing. Nothing else mattered. Perhaps he over-did that eventually. He was always after acts of heroism, but I think Jacques knows that all that has to be coupled with a sense of security and safety.

'I think Gilles' reputation grew after his death, as such reputations often do. By comparison, Jacques seems to me to be a rather more intelligent and controlled kind of driver. He is not cut out for instant glamour. He seems to want to achieve something and win something in his own way. He is Jacques Villeneuve, after all; not just the son of Gilles. I think about him, of course. That accident with Gilles overshadowed my season, my career and my life. It still does. It made me stop racing. I've got a family and kids of my own and I thought a lot about Gilles' children. About Jacques and Melanie. It made me feel very guilty and I still feel it sometimes even though I know I did nothing wrong. It is just one of those things.'

All this tragedy, this bloody and horrific death, must have left an equally dark and indelible stain on the young mind of Jacques, only 11 at the time. His father had been a hero and, like all fathers, his hero. To many, he was a wonderfully great driver, fast, daring and full of thrills; and also a great man, direct, honest, plain-speaking and plain-living. There is no doubt that Gilles Villeneuve had inspirational qualities. It can be measured still in the reverence with which he is remembered by many modern Formula One reporters who were there, then, in 1982 and who had seen his legend grow. Keke Rosberg, with whom Gilles had many a rough but fair encounter on a track, said of him: 'In a race car, he was the hardest bastard I ever knew, but absolutely fair. Racing was a very pure thing for Gilles. He never put a dirty move on anyone in his life.'

Another former world champion, Alan Jones, who also raced against Gilles Villeneuve, told *Autosport*'s Grand Prix editor Nigel Roebuck that 'he'd never deliberately block you . . . if he thought you'd won the corner, he'd give you room – maybe only a foot more than you needed, but never a foot less – and consequently I'd do the same for him. A totally honourable racing driver.'

These track tributes from Gilles' contemporaries help to give some idea of the aura that was built up around the reputation of the French-Canadian during his time in Formula One with Ferrari. They certainly created a colossus of the circuit in terms of his standing among his fellow-drivers. And for his son Jacques, they provide some insight into the size of the legacy, in racing terms, that he was bequeathed. Nigel Roebuck, who became a good friend of Gilles Villeneuve, felt that he was 'the fastest racing driver in the history of the sport', a description applied to him first by his former Ferrari team-mate Jody Scheckter. 'There may have been greater, certainly in terms of success, but none with more freakish car control,' concluded Roebuck. One of his contemporaries, Jacques Laffite, recalling the gifted driver's performance at Watkins Glen in 1979, during first qualifying for the United States Grand Prix, remembered that Gilles Villeneuve had been 11 seconds faster than anyone else in the downpour which engulfed the circuit and his Ferrari T4. His team-mate Jody Scheckter was second fastest. 'He's not like the rest of us,' said Laffite. 'He's on a separate level.'

This sense of awe at Gilles Villeneuve's talent, his intuitive control of a sliding car, snow-mobile (the first vehicles he raced in Canada) or projectile of virtually any description, captured the imagination of a generation of Formula One fans in the late 1970s and early 1980s, at a time when freedom and self-expression remained the key themes for many who had grown up through the social revolutions of the 1960s and the 1970s. In his driving, Villeneuve symbolised something more than just wondrous speed and élan; he delivered an essence, an elixir, which left those who inhaled a draught feeling lifted, intoxicated and very fine indeed. But his sense of elation and excitement, which created the reverie and the reverence, was accompanied too by a sense of foreboding. Roebuck admitted: 'I became very good friends with Gilles, but it was almost with reluctance, for I always doubted he would survive this sport. Formula One was infinitely more perilous then than now, and they say that if you go to The Gates often enough, eventually they open. Gilles, always at the bitter limit, and frequently over it, would take one chance too many, which ultimately he did.'

In his biography of the driver, Roebuck reported on an early conversation with him when Villeneuve made clear his lack of fear of accidents. 'I don't have any fear of a crash,' he said. 'OK, on a fifth-gear corner I don't want to crash – I'm not crazy. If I feel I'm going to put a wheel on the grass, I'm going to lift a bit, like anyone else. But if it's near the end of qualifying, and you're trying for pole position maybe, then I guess you can squeeze the fear.'

Roebuck cross-examined Villeneuve about an accident he suffered at Monaco in 1978 and asked him if he had not been at all frightened. 'For me, no, for the car, yes . . . I thought, "bloody hell, I'm going to have a nice one here!" But you know you just go like this . . .' Apparently, he stuck out his arms, screwed up his face and pretended to brace for an impact as if it was all a big joke. After his early years in snow-mobile racing in Quebec, it was little surprise. 'Every winter, you would reckon on three or four big spills,' he recalled. 'And that meant being thrown onto ice at maybe 100mph. But I never hurt myself on a snow-mobile – not seriously. And I think accidents always look worse to spectators than they feel to the driver.'

This daring man was the father of Jacques Villeneuve and it is an impossible task to ascertain with any degree of truth and accuracy just what effect his death had on Jacques. As a father, it is said, he was flawed. Whilst he loved to have the family – Joann, his wife, Jacques, his son, and Melanie, his daughter – around him in the early years, it is understood that he grew less enthusiastic in certain other aspects of his role as husband and father as his fame and wealth grew. Like many Canadians, Gilles was said to have a singular and introspective side to his nature which could manifest itself in acts of extraordinary, blind selfishness. He could be so self-centred and ambitious, it would seem he was shutting out all other considerations. His risk-taking in the various mechanical toys, which his burgeoning bank balance allowed him to afford once he had joined Ferrari, was just one example of that. But those who loved him have deep-rooted and affectionate feelings and memories of him.

'Those who recall only the wildness sell him short,' argued Roebuck, writing for *Autosport* in March 1996, when comparisons between father and son were *de rigueur* following Jacques' spectacular Formula One debut at the Australian Grand Prix in Melbourne. 'Virtually throughout his F1 career, Gilles had uncompetitive cars to drive, which meant forcing them along faster than they cared to go, attempting to bring their ability up to his own, and his detractors overlook the copybook drives, like Long Beach in 1979, or most memorably of all, Jarama in 1981, where he calmly held off four pursuing cars all afternoon and did it without the wisp of a mistake.'

Another fine memory of Gilles Villeneuve was provided by his first victory in Formula One at the 1978 Canadian Grand Prix at the Ile de Notre-Dame circuit in Montreal, where 80,000 spectators turned out to see their nation's latest and potentially greatest sporting hero tackle the event in his relatively unwieldy Ferrari, and by his famous second place behind Alan Jones's Williams the following year. These were the sort of exhibitions of talent which created the folklore and for which the circuit was later to be renamed after him. In the 1978 race, Villeneuve collected his victory after the retirements of others, including that of the leading Lotus driven by Jean-Pierre Jarier, drafted temporarily into the team following the death of the great Swede Ronnie Peterson at Monza. 'Some time later, he told me he could remember nothing of it,' recalled Roebuck. 'He said it was all a blur. "It might sound crazy, but I felt kind of embarrassed, in a way. Everyone was on top of me, laughing and crying and slapping me on the back, yet somehow I didn't feel part of it, like someone else had won. On the podium, there was Pierre Trudeau (then Canada's Prime Minister) waving a Ferrari flag, and it just seemed unreal that this was all for me," he said.'

For everyone present at those bitingly cold races, run in the Canadian autumn in the early days, it was not the first but the second of the two which has etched itself in the memory. This was in 1979, when Scheckter won the drivers' title for Ferrari and collected his points with great caution, while his team-mate, Gilles Villeneuve, did his utmost to support him, working it all out with the same cavalier sense of individualism that characterised his racing career. James Hunt, the Englishman who won the 1976 world title and who died sadly in June 1993, recalled: 'It seemed to me that Gilles did everything possible not to win the title that year. There was no doubt he had massive natural talent and he was the out-and-out quickest driver on earth. But surely the main reason anyone goes racing is to win the world championship, isn't it?'

This was an interesting question. Villeneuve, it turned out, did not think highly of the world title as a prized ambition and, in his own maverick way, had evaluated race victories as being of higher standing in his personal register of achievements. 'For me, the thing is to win races,' he told Roebuck. 'And the way I look at it, if you do that enough, the championship will come along automatically. But cruising sometimes, looking for points . . . please! A title won that way would be nothing to me. Remember Stirling Moss and Ronnie Peterson never won it, and then look at some of the guys who did.'

At Monza that year, Villeneuve finished second behind Scheckter, whose victory removed all doubt that he would be champion at the season's end. He suggested later, when asked, that he might have been able to pass Scheckter, but elected not to and instead adhered to the rules and traditions of Ferrari which were later to be broken by Pironi and trigger the reaction which sent him to his death. 'I knew the rules, I'd given my word,' explained Villeneuve at Monza, where he had respected the team orders. Afterwards, at Montreal, of course, there was no need for orders any more and he could drive as he pleased, which he did.

This was a race weekend remembered as much for the dramatic retirement of Niki Lauda, after the first practice session, when he climbed from his new Brabham BT49, sought out Bernie Ecclestone, told him of his decision and then flew forthwith to Los Angeles. In the race, Villeneuve led from the start, but had to contend with the might of Jones's fleet Williams on his tail. At the end of lap 51, Jones attacked and passed at the hairpin, only to find that the dogged Villeneuve refused to concede. Jones told Roebuck: 'I thought, I've done it, and once I was into the lead, I built up a bit of cushion, three seconds or so. But as soon as I backed off a fraction, there was that bloody red shitbox in my mirrors again. Villeneuve was unbelievable like that – I mean he never gave up. I never felt bad about a win in my life, you know, but I couldn't help feeling a bit sorry for Gilles that day. It was his home race, and he just drove the wheels off the thing.' Villeneuve finished second.

Three years later, back in Montreal, there was no Gilles Villeneuve to stand and smile alongside Jones on the podium and the circuit itself had been renamed in his honour. The world was still stunned by his death and many were still mourning. In Italy and Canada, his death was felt most profoundly. 900 people attended the funeral, in Quebec, including Prime Minister Pierre Trudeau. Enzo Ferrari said losing him was like losing a son. He had lost a member of his own family. Pironi was still with Ferrari, of course, and the black duel between him and Villeneuve was by now famous the world over. Pironi, who had carried Villeneuve's helmet back from the scene of his fatal accident at Zolder to the Ferrari motorhome, took pole and dedicated it to the memory of

Gilles, but he could not shake off the heavy sense of foreboding that remained around him.

On race day, tragedy struck again. At the start, Pironi's Ferrari stalled. The following cars had to dive either side of his stationary vehicle, but one from the back, driven by Ricardo Paletti, crashed into him at an estimated 120mph. It was a huge collision and it was followed by flames. Pironi survived. Paletti did not. A cruel series of misfortunes which had apparently dogged Ferrari that year seemed to have continued by claiming another life and adding another chapter to the Villeneuve legend. And, it was not over yet.

A few weeks later, in Germany, another dark day arrived – and this time it was Pironi who was to be involved as he hurtled around Hockenheim, through the wet clouds that hang among the trees on days of high precipitation, in practice on Saturday morning. As ever in this sport, Pironi could not see through the plumes and explosions of spray and crashed into the back of fellow-Frenchman Alain Prost's Renault. The effect was an accident that mirrored Villeneuve's at Zolder: the Ferrari flew up and away, somersaulting in lurching and horrifying flips, down the track. The impact was massive, the carnage terrifying. Pironi shattered both legs, but was alive, having suffered other injuries. His world championship dream was gone. Ferrari had suffered another grievous blow; yet, the following day, Patrick Tambay, a great friend of Gilles Villeneuve, who had been hired to replace him in his car, number 27, went out and scored his first Formula One victory.

The romantics believe this was linked in some way to the Villeneuve legend and to the mystical qualities of car 27 at Ferrari and their feelings were raised again at Imola in 1983 when, a year after the Pironi victory at the San Marino Grand Prix, Tambay drove to triumph from third place on the grid amid scenes of extraordinary emotion. Villeneuve had started third the year before and when Tambay arrived at his place before the start he found an unexpected message: it was painted on the track, at position number three, and it was unquestionably a link with his late friend and predecessor. The message was in the form of a

Canadian maple leaf flag and under it was written 'Win for Gilles'. Tambay was so moved, he wept. He was no longer driving only for himself, but for the legend and those who were living through it.

The race itself was a classic scrap between Tambay's chasing Ferrari and the Brabham of Italy's Riccardo Patrese. Tambay passed him and won, but came to a halt halfway round his victory lap when his car ran out of fuel. The *tifosi* mobbed him and Tambay felt strangely removed from one of the greatest experiences of his career, if not his life. 'I was not alone in the car that day,' he told Adam Cooper several years later. 'It's kind of awkward, huh? I always feel that I'm a bit of a foreigner in my own career.' Tambay escaped the invasion of the *tifosi*, choked back his tears and telephoned Monaco to speak to Joann, Gilles' widow, the mother of Jacques.

'I said "venge",' he told Cooper. 'You know what I mean? Revenged. Now he can rest in peace. He had been robbed the year before and he was in peace now. And I had been talking to him through the whole race . . .'

To believers in the supernatural, it provided a welcome symmetry to a story of tragedy and vengeance; but it was not all. Pironi, who had stimulated so much of this tale with his win at Imola, was unable to recover sufficiently from his dreadful injuries to race again in Formula One and, instead, turned his attentions to powerboat racing. It was in this arena, in August 1987, racing in the Needles Trophy off the Isle of Wight, that he died when his boat flipped at 100mph as it crossed the wake of a tanker. Two crewmen perished with him. A few months later, his girlfriend gave birth to twin boys and named them Didier – and Gilles.

All this, then, belongs in the legend bequeathed to Jacques Villeneuve, who was just 11 years old when his father died. Jacques' many silences and brief answers to questions about his father have led numerous observers to speculate on his feelings, his state of mind and his relationship with his father's legacy. Gerald Donaldson, whose biography of Giles entitled

Villeneuve, has been acclaimed for its detail and accuracy, offered many telling insights. 'His regard for his father is high, there is big respect,' he told David Tremayne in mid-1996. 'But he insists that he isn't following in his footsteps. He doesn't like to hear people expect him to bring the legend alive again. He said that no matter what he does in F1, it will never surpass what his father meant to the fans around the world. He has been trying to emerge from his father's shadow all the time since he started racing himself.

'He was under the closest possible scrutiny from the very beginning, great pressure, and even though his father's name opened all the sponsorship doors and gave him opportunities to race, the pressure was much more than expected. He thinks that because of that pressure, his progress as a driver accelerated. He had to perform. He couldn't stand the usual formative years floundering around. He admits that he was awful then because he was crashing all the time, trying to live up to expectations. It was only in Japan that he really straightened out. Living on his own, he grew up a lot.'

All this came with the legend. So, too, came pain, heartache and headache. Gilles Villeneuve was often very critical of his son, when Jacques was just a small child. 'It was just a stage that they went through in the family,' Donaldson explained. 'Jacques was a normally rumbustious little boy, running around and getting into trouble, and his sister Melanie was a charming little girl. Because of her gender, she was more quiet and probably more likable. And Gilles certainly seemed to favour her and she could do no wrong in his eyes, whereas he was critical of Jacques. And Jacques reacted adversely to this criticism . . .

'His mother told me that at the dinner table Jacques would be so nervous of making a mistake and incurring his father's criticism that his hand would shake when he was drinking his milk. And sometimes, despite trying so hard, he would spill it. And then when he was watching his father race, he sometimes got severe headaches, which his mother thought were just nervousness. On a couple of occasions at Monaco, he had to leave the pits and go home. It's very significant to us now, when you look back. It probably was just a passing stage, but it may have had some bearing on forming the character of Jacques.'

Tremayne also revealed that the effects of the legend, the legacy of his father, had resulted in Jacques avoiding certain references to him, particularly when they were stimulated by his feats in motor racing. At Imola, for example, he learned that Jacques had been asked early in 1996 what he thought about the circuit. Jacques replied that he thought it used to be a great track, but that some modified corners now annoyed him. When pressed to identify them, he responded: 'The section before the hairpin at Tosa, whatever that's called.' That place is called Villeneuve after an accident which his father survived there in 1980. A memorial stands there to explain the name.

Why? Who knows. Jacques Villeneuve prefers, for his own reasons, not to show any of his own feelings, in public at least, about his father, his accomplishments, his achievements and his legendary status. When asked about this, he said: 'I'm very proud to be his son, because he accomplished a lot. But, on the other hand, I don't try to compare myself to him. I don't try to continue what he started, or to walk in his shadow. I race because I enjoy it myself. The one thing that annoys me is when people ask me a question that has to do with my father, and I give my answer, and they are very unhappy with the answer because that is not what they want to hear. That annoys me. They want to hear that I do it for my father.

'After Indianapolis, the first question somebody asked me when they put the microphone under my mouth was "so, do you have a special thought for your father?" And that's the type of thing that really surprises me, and I have a hard time coping with it, because it just doesn't happen. I know that a lot of people get annoyed, because a lot of people phoned my mother, asking what's the problem with your son? Why does he negate his father? Which I don't. It's just that I'm racing because I enjoy it.'

Chapter Three

Childhood:
Caravans and Snowmen

Jacques Villeneuve was born on April 9 1971, at St-Jean-sur-Richlieu, Quebec, Canada. He was named after his uncle Jacques, the brother of his father Gilles Villeneuve, because, it is said, he smiled and behaved well with him when he was just an infant baby in the hospital. Later, he became an active child, noisy, effervescent and energetic, always making it clearly known when he wanted something. At this time, his father was in the transitional stage of his racing career, working as a snow-mobile racer in the winter and planning to become a circuit racer in the summer, trying to make ends meet and giving his wife Joann (née Barthe) and young family a veritable challenge not just in staying warm and comfortable in the winter, but retaining their sanity amid all sorts of challenges throughout the year. His paternal grandparents were Seville Villeneuve, an itinerant piano tuner, and Georgette (née Coupal) Villeneuve, whose family had owned a small construction business. His maternal grandparents were much poorer and less secure; indeed, according to Donaldson's biography of Gilles, Joann's father had left her family virtually impoverished when she was only eight and her mother, who suffered a heart defect and worked only intermittently, faced a struggle. Joann went to a convent school run by strict nuns who ensured that she understood the virtues of piety and moral virtue, qualities she carried with her as mother to Jacques.

As one might have expected with Gilles, he met Joann on a blind date. A popular couple, they married in October 1970. It was a small ceremony attended by family and a few friends, who left the church in Joliette in a noisy straggle to follow the newly-weds in a borrowed, bright orange Boss 429 Mustang, to tour the streets with their horns blaring. A reception followed at a nearby hall before Gilles and Joann Villeneuve went off for their one-night honeymoon at a nearby motel.

Among those who knew Joann at around this time was a local French-Canadian who, for personal reasons, preferred to remain anonymous when asked to talk about Jacques for this book. This source met them for the first time in February 1971, shortly before a snow-mobile race. 'I think Joann was pregnant at the time,' he recalled. 'She was with Gilles and they were very close. They were very young. But he was an intimidating kind of guy because of his youth. Kind of different, very nice, very direct. I met them many times after that. Jacques was born in 1971 and as he grew up, while he was very little, I remember him being very gentle and kind with other children. He was a clever kid, caring with others, but he travelled a lot too. Even though he was very small, as a little boy, he was also very active, noisy and boisterous. If Jacques wanted something, he made sure everyone else knew about it!

'He used to fight like hell for his own way. Of course, they used to give in to him, like all parents in the end. And that meant Jacques was always getting his own way. That is how he grew up in those days, but it was not easy for them as a family because they were not rich or anything and they had not much security or money. But Jacques was happy. He was one-track-minded from the start. He went to the race tracks and he knew everyone. As a family, the Villeneuves were well known and very well liked. Jacques could go everywhere. He was free. He played with all the other kids in the paddock. And when Gilles came home with the kids, it was always like a big storm for everyone in the house.

They all just wanted to play and be crazy together all the time. Gilles and Joann were just like the kids, too. They all wanted to play!

'I think, right from the beginning, it was clear that he was intelligent. Very bright. One time, in California, I remember Jacques was afraid and did not want to go on one of the amusement rides. So, instead of Jacques going with Gilles, I went with him and, I tell you, I nearly died. Then, I came off it. Jacques had a go and when he came back he said he loved it and he wanted to go on the front this time. Not the back, behind his father. And, you know, he wanted the ride to go faster and faster and faster. He was only five or six years old. I was afraid all the time, when I was on it. But Jacques was smiling. He was not afraid at all.

'They were the same everywhere. I remember going in a car with Gilles and Jacques would just sit there with him and shout out aloud: 'Faster, faster.' He was really enjoying things with his father. They were such a pair together. Gilles was so confident. He forced Jacques to grow up like him, the same way. They are alike in the way they live. I don't think there is any way in which Jacques would ever have come to Formula One without having had Gilles as his father.'

In those early, formative years, Jacques' father was a massive influence on him, but the family suffered hardships as the brilliant racing-driver-of-the-future concentrated on utilising snow-mobile racing to provide an income and at the same time enhance his reputation as a man in utter control of any high-powered machine moving at speed in any conditions. His father was a speed freak and his equally brilliant racing-driver-of-the-future son was to be entranced by it. Speed flowed through their lives and dictated the conditions in which they lived. Since everything in Gilles' life was to do with speed and movement, he decided that his first home as a husband and father should also be moveable and so he made a down payment on a 72-foot-long mobile home, towed it away from the dealer and parked it on a two-acre parcel of land across the road from his parents' house near Berthierville. Jacques' father plugged in the utilities, which came built in, and then left his mother to prepare the home, such as it was.

They were not wealthy or comfortable in those days and Jacques and his mother were given an overturned oil drum instead of front door steps, before, after some protests, rudimentary steps were installed. It was also a cold place and since the mobile home had no proper foundations or any real protection against the Canadian elements, it was no surprise to learn that the water pipes froze up solidly in the winter. Donaldson said that on particularly difficult sub-zero mornings, Joann, then only 19 and both a young bride and mother, would be forced to crawl beneath the floor to thaw out the pipes with a blow-torch. 'On particularly cold days, the pipes would burst and the hard-pressed heating system malfunctioned, leaving Joann's blow-torch and all the clothes she could find for herself and Jacques as sources of warmth,' wrote Donaldson.

While his mother fought the cold, his father tinkered with an old yellow school bus which he named Big Bertha. He divided it into two parts – the front for sleeping in at race meetings and the rear for working on snow-mobiles at race meetings. Jacques' father had an early reputation for flamboyance on these wild, motorised contraptions which were effectively little more than two short skis, driven by a rubber belt, powered by an engine and controlled by handle-bar steering. As time passed, he became famous for his antics, his improvisation and style – and his results. Indeed, while Joann was snowed in at home, Gilles would be away sometimes for several weeks on end racing, racing, racing. It was tough for her and tough for Jacques and his baby sister Melanie, born on July 26 1973, but Gilles was not perturbed and pursued his racing career with the single-mindedness which later characterised his approach to life and many aspects of his son's. Jacques grew up without luxuries at this time, which may explain why, in later life, he showed little inclination to surround himself with the more orthodox trappings of wealth and success, even extending his puritanism to not bothering with beds or curtains at certain stages of his life, according to friends and acquaintances in Japan.

'Gilles,' said Donaldson, 'would think nothing of spending their last 20 dollars on a fuel pump, leaving her [Joann] struggling to find enough money to feed and clothe the children. Bills were run up at local schools, debts mounted, and Joann despaired at her husband's apparent lack of concern.' It seemed, at the time, that Jacques and his family were being left by their father to fend for themselves while he went off on lengthy racing tours that sometimes stretched his wife's patience to breaking point.

'Joann was without any means of transport and had to trudge through the snow to the shops in Berthier,' Donaldson explained. 'Sometimes a kindly neighbour took pity on her and shovelled a path to the road, but on one occasion Joann's plight reached a crisis point. She had arranged a doctor's appointment for Jacques and awoke that morning to find snow drifted high around the front door and lying deep between there and the ploughed road. A taxi had been called and was waiting so there was no option but to wade out through 100 metres of winter's worst. "Jacques was about two then and Melanie was just a few months old so I couldn't leave her behind. I had to carry both kids and their diaper bags and my bag and the snow was up to my waist. I thought, I'll never get there and I was calling to the taxi driver to please come and help me. He yelled back that he didn't have any boots on and I thought, "Oh, God, why does this have to happen to me?" '

If this gives some indication of the conditions in which the young Jacques Villeneuve grew up, it should also be reported that he came from a happy and musical family. His grandfather Seville was a piano tuner, his father played the trumpet and his sister was talented enough to turn to music as a career. She moved to New York in the 1990s to study music with ambitions to make her living from it. Her grandfather Seville, like all the male Villeneuves it seemed, had the power to influence generations. Of his son Gilles, Seville said: 'Gilles doesn't feel fear at all. He always drove very fast, at the very limit. He always made everything he drove go as fast as it would go.'

It might have been Gilles talking, if he had had the opportunity, of his own son Jacques. Just as Jacques asked Gilles to go faster and faster when he travelled with him as a toddler, so his father Gilles, introduced to speed by Seville, had said the same. 'Before his boys could see over the dashboard of the family Ford,' reported Donaldson, 'Seville let them sit on his lap behind the wheel. Gilles was to say, "I loved it when the tyres squealed. I can remember yelling 'Faster, Daddy, faster!' or 'Pass him, pass him!' Maybe that is why he was always being caught for speeding!" '

Speed was manifestly in the blood and it swirled all around Jacques in his childhood in Canada just as fiercely as the icy winds which came down from the north in the winter and the hot sunshine which beat from the south in the summer. Financial difficulties and tough decisions were also a part of his family life in childhood as his father Gilles fought tooth and nail to keep his own racing career on an upward trajectory. Gilles was so obsessed that by 1974, when he was lusting for an opportunity to prove his snow-racing skills could transfer even more successfully to circuit road car racing in the summer, he was prepared to sell his house to complete a deal.

According to Donaldson, Joann remembered it clearly. ' "He came home and said 'I sold the house to buy a car.' A rather one-sided domestic quarrel immediately ensued, but the deed was done. "It didn't make any difference to him because he had decided that was the way it was going to be. If you like it, fine, if you don't like it, scream if you want. That was the way he was."

'The mobile home was not really his to sell since the bank still held a substantial mortgage on it, but Gilles turned over a cheque to Kris Harrison right on schedule. And, of course, he had a solution to his family's immediate housing crisis: Joann, Jacques and Melanie would travel with him to the races across Canada in Seville's pick-up truck with the little camper on the back.' It was not ideal for anyone, least of all Jacques' mother Joann, who suffered a severe migraine attack after her first marital home had been sold in such circumstances and, with Jacques and Melanie around to provide the innocent solace that only children can, she stayed in bed, or close to bed, for the first six weeks of her husband's racing season.

This migraine attack may have had a decisive influence on Jacques as, later, he began to suffer them himself. Whether copied or genetic, it was clear that as a child, and as he grew older, he empathised with his mother's sufferings, particularly when his father was negligent, callous or unduly selfish or hurtful, often without realising it. Jacques, as a child, was close to his mother through all of this; but, of course, left also to wonder in awe at his father's achievements in racing and his growing reputation, a reputation that was to reach legendary status as an artiste in speed.

It all resulted in a nomadic childhood. After the sale of their home, albeit a mobile one, the Villeneuves lived variously (when not traversing Canada to follow the motor racing) in Berthier and in Joliette, swapping from one address to another, moving from rooms at the Seville Villeneuve home to accommodation in Joann's mother's house. It worked briefly, but led to much further misery for Joann and the children. By the autumn, Joann issued an ultimatum to her husband and his reaction, after renting a very small apartment near to his parents' home, was to take them with him once again to all the Formula Atlantic races in which he took part.

Jacques' early childhood, therefore, consisted of a fragmented family life, much travel, plentiful experience of life and an education on the road. His father, as well as being one of the most naturally gifted racing drivers of his generation, was also a shrewd negotiator and an honest man. But he was stubborn too and could turn a blind eye to those things he wished to ignore. As a result, his family were expected to support him wholeheartedly in all his racing ventures, an attitude which meant that Jacques and his sister had to travel thousands of miles to see their mother work as a time-keeper, or as a cook, cleaner and babysitter, while their father charged around race tracks in a cloud of dust. But the fearlessness in the father rubbed off on the son.

'Gilles told me that Jacques was a real daredevil,' said a family friend. 'Gilles always had Jacques behind him. Gilles was doing crazy things with cars and boats and other things with Jacques, like they would all be together in a car going at more than 100mph. That was normal and it was the same later when they went to live in Europe. Patrick Tambay told me once that when Gilles was travelling fast, whatever the vehicle, Jacques would call for him to go faster and faster. It was part of his life. He grew up in that environment.

'He didn't know anything else but the limit. It was a part of his life, just like it was for his father. But I don't think he grew up crazy that way like his father. From what I heard and knew, he was a natural leader at school and good at most things and became interested seriously in being a racing driver later. He did not take it too seriously from the start, but just wanted to enjoy himself. For Jacques, after that kind of childhood, it had to be natural to become a racing driver. I remember once, I asked his mother why she allowed him to drive a racing car and she said: "I don't have any choice. I don't want to see him in a race car, because of what happened to Gilles, but if I stop him now, he will find his way on to the track later on and then he will just be angry. So, I have to let him find his own way. If he wants to be a world champion, he will fight like hell and he will probably do it."

'The main thing to know about Jacques from his childhood and his early life is his determination. If he wants something, he will not let anything get in his way. I learned this about him before they went to Europe, but I have seen it again since then in Jacques. They were very close, Gilles and Jacques, when he was young, but it was hard to see it. When Jacques was born, Gilles was in the middle of his parents' place and always moving. He raced every weekend and he spent 24 hours a day at the tracks. He did not have enough money for mechanics because his racing team was a small one, a small operation. He raced on the ice, I remember, and it was very dangerous stuff. They were always very tight races, just 10 or 12 laps or something, all running very close together, but very dangerous. I think that is where he learned a lot and I think Jacques learned a lot from it too, and from skiing.

'If you are running first at the first corner, you can be alright. But if you are in the middle and something happens, at the first corner, you just don't know. You cannot see at all and you just go by the sound. It is a bit like motorcycles on ice with these snow-mobiles and you need a lot of courage and instinct. They reach 100mph on just two skis with an engine on top and no real protection at all. If you go off, you're going to get hurt and a lot of those guys do. It is a crazy thing, but I think it taught them a lot, those guys.'

Without much doubt, Gilles acquired much of his exceptional control and understanding of speed through snow-mobiles and these talents have been passed on to Jacques. He has grown up, after all, as happy on snow as on dry land and as adept at balancing himself on skis as on roller-blades or at the wheel of a racing car. 'They seemed to come from a very strange place,' continued the family friend. 'It was like people arriving from a different planet. His father did everything to do with speed and that is what made his name. For Jacques, it was a strange childhood, compared to normal kids, but he grew up travelling around, in Quebec, then in France, in Monaco, at school in Switzerland. He spoke different languages and he lost his father. I don't really think they changed too much, as they lived as a family, after they went to Europe, but Gilles maybe changed. He made a lot of money, he spent it. He bought the place in Monaco and it had a big garage and I think he wanted a divorce too, later on, when he met another woman. I think Joann accepted that, but it did not happen.

'All this had an effect on Jacques, of course. I guess he reacted like all kids do when their parents have trouble. It builds up over time and the children feel it. Jacques was at all the races, travelling with his mother. That was a good thing, I think. And when Jacques won the Indianapolis 500, his mother was there and I think he really appreciated it. In the end, they are pretty close after everything, but it is difficult for them. It is hard to imagine it. Jacques has had an extraordinary life, an extraordinary childhood first and then everything else and he is still so young.'

The young Jacques, however, back in his earliest days as a child in Berthierville, had a happy and contented life, if filled with a mixture of hardships and extraordinary pleasures initiated by the long journeys to the races in Big Bertha. Donaldson admitted: 'Gilles Villeneuve's passion for racing was so great that at times he seemed inconsiderate of his family's welfare. Yet, they were very important to him and as soon as the children were old enough to travel, he insisted his family should accompany him to the races.'

As his father's career picked up and he progressed successfully through Formula Ford and Formula Atlantic in the summer and better-paid snow-mobile teams in the winter, so Jacques was treated to more comforts. But even after the purchase of a purpose-built motorhome (paid for by Gilles' winter snow-mobile team, in lieu of any travel and hotel expenses) equipped with beds, a kitchenette, shower and toilet, they were still living like gypsies and travelling all over north America. Jacques' education was hardly scholastic at this time, but certainly his mind was being broadened by life on the road and it helps to explain why, in many respects, he had an old head on such young shoulders when he first ventured into motor racing himself.

Around this time as well, the family acquired a pet, an Alsatian dog named Princess, with whom they all played when the motorhome was parked in a vast race paddock at the weekends. When he was apart from the dog and his father, Jacques, from the age of four to six, would keep himself occupied by pretending he was a racing driver, pedalling his own three-wheel tricycle among the trucks and transporters, spinning the wheels as furiously as possible in the manner his father was beginning to use as his own trademark on the track. During the actual races, he would sit in the pits and help Joann with her lap charts and cheer for his father who was becoming more and more famous. Spotted by James Hunt, the 1976 Formula One world drivers' champion, he was recommended to McLaren, flew to Britain for a test at Silverstone, but actually made his mark by joining Ferrari. When the great Italian team moved to contract his father, it was, for

Jacques, a signal that his life was never to be the same again. The innocent nomadic existence of his childhood was to end.

On the signature of his contract, Gilles agreed, according to Donaldson, a fee of $75,000 and with it a special travel allowance of $15,000 for his family. This was unheard of at the time, as most Formula One drivers made no effort to bring their wives and families with them to the races, but Gilles wished to and negotiated the clause into his deal. It meant that the Villeneuves were able, to a limited degree, to maintain their gypsy lifestyle of their north American days when they began travelling around Europe. To make it easier, and less of an upheaval, Gilles shipped a 36-foot-long Globestar motorhome to the south of France for use at Grands Prix around the continent. It was a famous paddock landmark and an equally famous item of gossip in the villages of the Côte d'Azur.

But all this was to come, later, after the Canadian days when Jacques learned about speed on his father's knee, from the paddocks of the Formula Atlantic circuits, from the inside of the Big Bertha bus and from the various locations in which Gilles would tinker with snow-mobiles (he once created his own advanced suspension system for his snow-mobile to make it go faster) and parts of racing cars. Yet, Jacques denies all this is in his genes and has always stressed he did not feel born to race at speed. 'Not really,' he said, in an interview with *Arena* magazine in Britain in 1996. 'Racing isn't like a gene that gets passed down. But when you come from a family of racers, you learn at a very early age to get used to speed.'

Given the close togetherness of his early childhood days, as the family traipsed over and back across the United States and Canada, it is easy to understand how he felt. It was also a formative experience on other aspects of his life. Joann, his mother, had suffered a largely fatherless childhood so she was happy for them to be with Gilles as much as possible and she provided plain food, as demanded by her husband, at regular intervals. Meat and potatoes, hamburgers, steaks and the favourite family dessert of Canadian sugar pie were the staples of their diet (sugar pie is still one of the chief attractions for Jacques, it is said, when he revisits his mother at her home in Monte Carlo, now that he lives close by again).

Time passed slowly on the road for the family, and Jacques and his sister Melanie, together with Princess, the dog, would keep themselves amused with puzzles, games and toys. The geography of north America was their kindergarten and the frequent running repairs, carried out whenever possible by his father, were Jacques' introduction to the mechanics and science of automotive engineering. Gilles, apparently, delighted in performing his own repairs to a vehicle which was often damaged as a result of his over-enthusiastic treatment and handling of it. Jacques, therefore, quickly learned to understand that pit-stops were all part of life's rich tapestry and not to be frustrated at such pauses in progress on the road and on the way to another race circuit.

There, in the paddock, Jacques would be left with his fiery tricycle again, as Donaldson revealed. 'He pedalled furiously at all times. Inspired by a certain Ecurie Canada March, that tended to spin its wheels frequently, Jacques learned how to apply a burst of power so as to spin the large front wheel of his mount and he did so at every opportunity. When the real racing cars were out on the track, Jacques and Melanie wore adult-sized insulated headsets to prevent hearing damage. During the races, they cheered loudly for their daddy and it seemed to work . . . because he nearly always won.'

Friendships were also formed in these paddocks and when Gilles formed a close relationship with John Lane, an American racing enthusiast who was to have some influence on his future, it meant that the Villeneuve camp was enlarged by the arrival of another motorhome and family. The Lanes had two daughters and two dogs, and Jacques and Melanie – whose first tongue was French – learned to use pidgin English and pidgin French to communicate with the two younger American girls. Jacques also taught Courtney how to wheel-spin on a tricycle.

For a time, they travelled together in a carefree way, relying on Gilles' prize-money to pay their passages. This meant, for Jacques, an early acquaintance and affection for the beautiful, vast and open countryside of Canada was developed as they travelled across Quebec and Ontario, through forests, lakes and mountains. It was no wonder, when Jacques came to race in Europe, that he preferred to drive from Monaco to such Grands Prix as those at Barcelona or Monza, if he could.

But Jacques saw other things too. At Edmonton, for example, he would have witnessed the famous battle between Gilles and Keke Rosberg in a wonderful Formula Atlantic race. The race was described by Lane, according to Donaldson, as 'just a war . . . They were touching everywhere. The track was way out in the boondocks from Edmonton and there were only about 12,000 people there, but they were going insane.'

It was a magnificent tussle, a long way from the snow-mobile racing which had made Gilles champion of his class in Quebec back in 1971, the year when Jacques was born. It was another style of racing, a wild frenzy of speed and commitment, which showed that Villeneuve could translate his raw talent – a talent which had upset rivals and frustrated team bosses because of his proclivity to return his machines in a damaged and beaten condition so often – into success. Jacques, small, young and impressionable, had grown up around it all. He saw his father's famous sideways sliding cornering. He saw him race and win. He saw him retire. He saw him damage his cars and he saw him arrive home from Mosport one weekend with his left leg encased in plaster from hip to toe after breaking it badly in two places. He learned to understand the dangers, but also to share his father's lack of fear and his enormous courage and ceaseless desire to carry on racing. Indeed, when Gilles was told at Mosport that his leg was broken, his response was to say to Joann, who was translating the doctor's words from English to French, 'How can this be?'

By 1976, Jacques was five and his father's life was changing. The snow-mobile days were being left behind, the nomadic lifestyle was altering, winters were to become more settled and educational. Gilles joined the Ecurie Canada Formula Atlantic team to race a Skiroule-liveried March 76B and his first antics in his new surroundings not only lit up the tyres of his car, but also set alight his reputation for heated and irreverent behaviour at the wheel. British engineer Ray Wardell told Donaldson that, on one of his first meetings with Gilles Villeneuve at Georgia, he was in for a shock. 'I didn't yet know the bloke very well and on the second day of testing he drove me to the track in a rental car. There was a gate we had to open and I got out to open it while he drove through. I closed it and all of a sudden the right rear wheel of the car just lit up in smoke and he stood there and burned that tyre until it virtually burst. The whole place was full of smoke. I thought, Geez, this guy's a real cowboy.'

And, in many ways, yes, a cowboy he was. John Watson, the noted and eloquent Formula One television commentator who was also the winner of the 1982 Belgian Grand Prix, following the death of Gilles, believed that had his waywardness been harnessed properly in his racing career and his talent nurtured and disciplined (as Jacques' has been), then not only would Gilles have shaken off his image as a reckless stuntman of a driver, but he would have also had enormous success and may not have been susceptible to the emotions which contributed to his death.

But the young Jacques was not to know or understand all this until much later. His father may have gone on to establish himself as a romantic martyr of motor racing, a man whose very 'destructive powers' were praised by Enzo Ferrari for contributing to the improvement of his cars and an icon of his age, but to Jacques he was just a hero of his childhood, a figure of fatherhood and fun, travel and excitement. Yet, during those childhood days amid the caravans and snowmen, he picked up so much of his father's essence. After Ferrari had hired Gilles (in September, 1977), he said: 'When they presented me with this "piccolo Canadiense", this muscular bundle of nerves, I immediately recognised in him the physique of Nuvolari and I said to myself let's give him a try . . . He contributed a lot to us with his intense competitiveness and his talent for taking anything mechanical and utterly destroying it. He continually brought us face to face with our limitations, with the most extreme tests for our cars that our engineers had ever encountered and had to solve and he indulged in some of the most hair-raising acrobatics I have ever seen in the process. Transmissions, gearboxes, driveshafts – all were subjected to the utmost punishment. He was a high priest of destruction, but his way of driving showed us how much we had to improve those parts so they could stand the assaults of any driver.'

For Jacques, his father Gilles was none of this, but it must have rubbed off on him. Just as his uncle Jacques also had an effect, not only introducing him to racing in his later life, after his father's death, but also by being a racer himself. Uncle Jacques enjoyed a successful career in snow-mobiles, Can-Am sportscars and in Formula Atlantic and has kept a sage eye on his nephew's progress.

Back in Berthierville now, there is a Villeneuve museum. Originally built on the site of a former post office, it has been moved into an old transport warehouse. Each year, more than 5,000 visitors from more than 20 countries visit this museum, which is, in its own way, also a shrine to the memory of Canada's greatest and most famous sportsman. For Jacques, of course, it is also a reminder of not only his father, but his childhood. A place he once lived in, a time he once passed through. Jacques has often said that when he returns to Canada now, he feels more Canadian than ever before. But it is in Berthierville, in Quebec, and through the broad and beautiful countryside that he must feel it strongest. After all, it was a long journey from that old mobile home and that innocent childhood to the gilded streets of Monte Carlo.

Chapter Four

Growing Up in Europe:
Blue Sea, Hot Sun

The view from the French village of Plascassier, across the valley to Grasse and sweeping left towards the Mediterranean and down to Cannes, is one of nature's most delightful. On a fine day, the air is scented with a sweet tingle from the Alpes Maritimes, where snow-topped peaks can be seen in the winter, and carries the familiar noises of French life, games of boules, chatter-filled cafés and light-engined motor bikes, with the breeze. Anyone who has ever wondered why people move to the Côte d'Azur and hide themselves away in the hillsides inland, beneath the backdrop of those majestic European mountains, would find the answer here. It is a splendid place: simple, orderly and happy. A fine place to bring up a family and, understandably, the place that Gilles Villeneuve chose as home after his arrival in Europe and the place, rented for three years thanks to Ferrari's bankroll, that Jacques grew up in.

It was not, however, the first Villeneuve abode after leaving Quebec. Given little time between the Japanese Grand Prix of 1977 (when Gilles, driving for Ferrari, killed two spectators, standing in a prohibited area, at Mount Fuji in only his third Formula One race), and the start of Ferrari's test programme at Fiorano, the Villeneuves accepted a generous offer from Patrick Tambay, the famous French racing driver who befriended Gilles, and moved into his villa at Cannes. This first base gave Gilles time to learn the journey to Ferrari's Italian base (in a Fiat supplied for the purpose) and also to take his wife and young family into the hills inland from the Mediterranean to search for a house of their own. Eventually, they settled on Plascassier and rented a villa in an area that is now known as the Cartier Massoeuboeuf. They moved in, recalled one local resident, Jean-Pierre Mariani, around October that year and quickly became well-known members of the village community – and popular too. They are still remembered well.

On the wall at the Auberge St Donat, a short walk from the Villeneuve villa on the Chemin Castellans, are fixed two photographs of racing drivers. One is of Ayrton Senna, the great Brazilian ace who won the world drivers' championship three times, and the other is of Gilles Villeneuve. He is still held in the highest esteem at the bar of the Auberge, as much for the martyr status he achieved in the village following his death as for his easy-going personality, the charm of his wife and children and the fact, plain and simple, that he drove for Ferrari. Even in France, a Ferrari driver really is someone.

Jacques, then aged seven, attended the local school, further up in the village across the road from a playground and close to some shops and bars; a typical French village school where the headmaster Rene Guglielmero enjoyed the presence of a young, and tiny, celebrity with a novel Quebecois accent and an interesting background in his classrooms. 'Madame Villeneuve always walked the children up to school, or nearly always,' explained Mariani. 'She was a good woman and a good mother and the children were well behaved. No one in the village knew anything different about her than that. She came, lived and was part of the people.'

For Jacques, more used to the extreme climate of Quebec, the snowdrifts in the winter and the blizzards which made coming home from school in Berthier such fun, the change to the warmth of the Mediterranean with its hot summers and mild winters came as a pleasant surprise. He could scurry around outdoors more easily for longer hours in better weather throughout the year and he could revel in the open spaces that gave him more of his first opportunities for speed on wheels, yet there were also many things that Jacques missed. It was difficult to adjust quickly to such a violent change of surroundings.

'It was difficult for the kids because we were kind of isolated up there,' recalled Joann in conversation with Donaldson. 'They had to find their way around a new school. They adapted quickly and soon made friends, but there was quite a culture shock, at first for all of us. We had to get used to little things, like the phones not working so well, the fact that the milkman didn't come to the door and the stores were closed from twelve to three. It took a few months to find out where to buy certain foods and some, like peanut butter and chocolate chips for baking cookies, we had to have sent over from Canada. But there was no real problem shopping for Gilles, no matter where he went in the world. He was a steak-and-potatoes person and that was that. For him, eating was a waste of time, something he had to do.'

Gilles told Donaldson that he felt, at this time, that in France they did not have quick snacks, 'just big meals. The bread is as hard as the table and the only thing they have to drink is water or wine.' Already, of course, Jacques was a sought-after image for photographers, along with his sister and his parents; but this had started the year before after his father's first race for Ferrari, in a car number 21, at Mosport, as Donaldson related.

'Journalists,' he wrote, 'wanted to know more details about the driver . . . and they chased down his wife in the Villeneuve motorhome parked in a corner of the Mosport paddock. They kept a cautious distance from a rather fierce-looking Alsatian standing guard near the door and questioned the sweetly smiling young lass with two cute kids by her side. Why were they camping out here in the boondocks instead of staying in the posh hotel room reserved for them by Ferrari? "We don't like hotels," Joann replied. "We like the motorhome. It's a nice warm place to stay. I can cook here and it's much better for Jacques and Melanie. I'd rather eat my own cooking and Gilles is happy as long as he gets a steak. Sure, we live like gypsies. But we like it and I don't think we'll change. We may have a bit more money from now on, but we aren't going to change our lives." '

Gilles' accident in Japan did nothing to enhance his reputation for recklessness, particularly since the deaths of a 25-year-old amateur photographer and a 21-year-old track guard were regarded with the greatest suspicion by the local authorities. Gilles, it was said, showed scant compassion in the aftermath of this tragedy, but played along with his team's orders so as to avoid a diplomatic difficulty once he had recovered from his anger with himself for causing the accident. Lawyers, investigators, papers to be filled in, translations, problems and theories filled several days before he was permitted to travel. Some critics began to question Ferrari's judgement in gambling on Jacques' father in much the same way, a generation later, others wondered if Williams had taken a big risk on his son, but Ferrari stayed loyal.

The family dog, Princess, was given to uncle Jacques who was embarking on his own racing career. That meant little change of circumstance for her. Gilles and Joann had few luxury possessions to worry about and made sure that their move from one continent to another was as easy and painless as possible. Travelling light, carrying no extras, was their style, as it has become Jacques' style too. It is a trait he has accepted and it explains the lack of luxuries he indulges in; in his personal life, in his apartments and in his clothing. In many ways, this period showed some of the characteristics in the family which have made later observers nod and confirm that Jacques was a 'chip off the old block'.

They certainly acknowledged the similarities between the two up in Plascassier during the 1996 season, as Jacques Villeneuve began his pursuit of Damon Hill in the world drivers' championship. The village had a feeling of suspense about motor racing, as if it was tuned in to the races by remote control. It felt like a shrine, too, because of the close connections with the family and the memories of the place, once used for boules, but now a roundabout, where Gilles would park his huge motorhome between the Grands Prix.

The drive up to the village is by winding roads, dusty scratches on the landscape that twist back and forward as they climb above the valley. The switchbacks are not quite as violent as they are on the ascent to Villars in Switzerland, where Jacques was later to be sent to boarding school, but they are tight enough to require reasonable grip and tyres from a French hire car on the old broken road surfaces. There, on these winding strips of asphalt, it is easy to imagine Gilles, rushing and crazed by speed, making lurching handbrake turns on his way home to the plain, dusty, somehow desolate village with its friendly atmosphere and beautiful evening sunshine from the west. It is a place of spectacular natural qualities and said more, in its way, about the earthiness of Gilles and Jacques Villeneuve than any two sheets of their lap times.

The landscape here, in which Jacques Villeneuve grew up, is a slice of the unpretentious glory of the interior of the Côte d'Azur. Lucky Jacques! To someone brought up on the raw winds and icy winters of Quebec, it must have seemed a paradise. A most unlikely place to find a pair of gladiators, father and son, growing up together. Here Gilles parked his caravan and Jacques went to school. Here Joann entered the village community with the same serenity and elegance she did everything else. Here Melanie followed Jacques to the school by the green, up the steps through the gates in the village. A plain place, yes, but impressive; and a good place for a family life. It is an environment which adds to the puzzle of the enigmatic, modern Jacques Villeneuve when one realises that it was here, in this gentle place, among these good, ordinary village folk, that he grew up and had so many happy times. The headmaster of the school was Guglielmero and Jacques' class teacher was Madame Pascal. 'He was a very nice boy, *très gentil*,' said the head. 'Of course, everyone was fascinated by Gilles, but I am glad to say that both of his children were very well behaved and good pupils. They were *très bonnes élèves*. I remember that Gilles would sometimes come to the school with them, very occasionally by car in the same vehicle that Madame Villeneuve sometimes used. Or they would walk together. I recall, also, seeing a red Ferrari sometimes!

'They were always very kind and courteous. There was never

anything different about them from the others. One evening, for example, we had a film show at the school, to show what the children had been doing, and we assembled a lot of parents. We had to organise the chairs and Gilles was there and he made himself very busy helping to put them in place and to put them back again afterwards. That was typical of him. He was always helpful and correct. Jacques seemed to mix well with everyone and enjoyed the work. Of course, he was very young then, but we could see he was full of confidence and he was a happy child. He was never any trouble at all.'

According to Mariani, the Villeneuves' life in Plascassier was as simple and straightforward as those of any other family and as unmolested as the village could permit. 'They kept to themselves,' he said. 'We liked them, we liked them living here and we enjoyed it, but we wanted them to feel happy too. We did not bother them and they did not worry us. It was just normal life. But there was one thing, quite amusing actually, that made them different and that was Gilles' big caravan. Sometimes, they would eat in the auberge, but not often. Gilles, I know, liked ordinary food and he did not drink – not like us!

'It was more common for him to visit, just to say hello and to confirm it was alright for him to leave his big caravan parked outside on the ground where we played boules. It was a big American camper which he transported to Europe specially for the racing, for his family, but of course it was far too big to fit down the narrow road to his house. So, he was stuck. He had to leave it in the village. We did not mind. He was, you know, a Ferrari driver! Gilles offered to settle the costs, to pay for the parking, but we did not charge him anything. So, he came and gave us T-shirts, hats and mementos and told us about his racing and became my friend.'

Now they stand in the bar at the auberge, below the hanging pictures of Senna and Gilles, and they drink whisky and wine and pastis and remember the energy of Gilles and Jacques. Without the career of the father to follow, instead they trace their lives against the exploits of the son. A volley of questions about his racing, his learning of the Formula One lifestyle, his ability to adapt to new circuits is followed by mellow nostalgic tales of the past. Jacques' career, his successes, give them continuity to their broken camaraderie with Gilles. 'They were with us and part of our lives until the terrible end in 1982,' said Mariani. 'The whole village felt it. It was a big thing. A big shock. No one in our homes was not hurt by what happened when Gilles died and it changed everything, of course, for Jacques. Their lives were ended the way they were anyway when Gilles bought his house in Monaco and moved to live there. But it was not enough time and we always felt he was still one of us here.'

In the village now, on a September evening, you can hear music. A piano is played near the school. In the distance, all around it seems, bells ring. This is a place, on a quiet Tuesday evening, where a rhythm of life takes grip on all those who visit and are enchanted. It is the routine of the Mediterranean, like the near-invisible tides, the sunshine, the wonderful food; a light and easy attitude to life which infects everyone and renders it difficult to be earnest about too many things. From here, of course, the speed-crazed Gilles would set off on those extraordinary, legendary 'races' to Fiorano or Maranello in his Ferrari. That blood red car, which was a symbol of his vulnerability to simple joys and their perils. Life must have seemed so joyously easy and happy then for the Villeneuve family. They had this villa on the hillside, those wondrous views, the village behind and a life that many would envy.

Yet, despite all this, Jacques' father was not content. He was driven by the demons of speed and a lust for victories on the track. And this carried him into a state-of-mind and a recklessness which was to make him discount death as a possibility in his own mind, as he told Nigel Roebuck during a taped interview at Zolder, in Belgium, in 1978, four years before he was killed at the same circuit. 'I don't have any fear of a crash,' he said. Gilles told Roebuck another day, 'I cannot remember exactly when I got interested in racing. But I always loved speed. It is the earliest sensation I can recall. My father used to drive very fast and from being six years old I can remember telling him to go quicker, to pass the guy in front. He got a lot of tickets because of me, I guess! At about that age, I used to sit on his knee and steer. So, I just loved cars, but my first real touch with racing was a TransAm race at St Jovite, when I was about 17. They had Formula Fords there, as well, and I thought 80 per cent of the drivers were idiots – you know, guys with a lot of money, going very slowly. I'd been racing snow-mobiles a while by then, but I knew that day this was what I wanted for my life.'

In his biography of Gilles, Roebuck added: 'At times like this, when there was no particular hurry, Gilles relaxed the pace of his speech. Whenever he talked about his feelings for racing, it was with quiet and reflective emotion, almost as if speaking of the love of his life. Probably, he was. Once, I asked him what he might do when he had given up driving. From his expression, it had never crossed his mind. "I don't want to think about it," he replied. "Because I cannot imagine life without it." '

In all of this there are strong influences and similarities from father to son. They learned their trade the same way with the same sense of values and the same ardour. In this early period of their life in Europe, during the Plascassier days, Gilles raced at Dijon in the famous French Grand Prix when he duelled and beat René Arnoux, on the Gallic hero's home soil, his Ferrari edging clear of the rival Renault. It is a flickering image on video tape that has thrilled countless fans many times since, including the young Jacques who grew up on the stirring heroism of that drive by his father. Arnoux, a winner of races with Renault and Ferrari, said that race was the most memorable of his career, 'something I'll never forget, my greatest *souvenir* of racing. You can only race like that, you know, with someone you trust completely, and you don't meet many people like him. He beat me, yes, and in France, but it didn't worry me – I knew I'd been beaten by the best driver in the world . . . It was terrible when Gilles died. I cried that day. And the next one, too, even though I had to race. And I remember the feeling that we were all starting equal, from now on. Villeneuve was gone. We all knew he had a talent beyond our reach.'

Frank Williams, who later employed Jacques, regarded his father Gilles at this time as a man of fearful talent. After Jones, in a Williams, had won their great Montreal race (a contest which the Australian later admitted was possibly the best victory of his career), Williams admitted: 'I was very proud of Alan that day. We had the best car at the time, without a doubt, and the only driver on the track we feared was that little French-Canadian.'

Throughout this period, as he grew up at Plascassier, Jacques witnessed the massive blossom of praise which enshrouded his father. He was idolised for his talent and his attitude to the use of it and, as his fame and his wealth grew, so his resistance to all manner of temptations was reduced in proportion. His marriage became unsettled, he was away from home a lot and the idyllic life of Plascassier became just part of a blur of celebrity status events around the globe, coupled with the satisfaction in financial and material terms of all his needs and desires. 'Everything in Gilles' life moved at 200mph, whether it was driving, playing Monopoly, flying helicopters or spending!' said Tambay, one of his closest friends.

Yet, he stayed open with his friends, accessible to the media and beloved by his fans while his family, and in particular his wife Joann, found it more and more difficult to understand what was happening, as they saw less and less of him. For Jacques, particularly, this was the most difficult part of having a celebrity for a father. Gilles, who delighted in describing himself as no more than 'a hick from Berthierville' when he was photographed with Sean Connery after winning the 1981 Monaco Grand Prix, was actually becoming more and more the victim of the sophisticated world around him which he had, at first, despised and attempted to shun.

Gilles did not intend it to happen, but even in his role as father to Jacques and Melanie he began to find it more difficult to find the time he needed to maintain a close relationship. This was a trouble to him. His family had been always his favourite topic of conversation outside racing, particularly Jacques. When Jacques was six, Gilles was delighted to recount to the many journalists who covered every day of his life with Ferrari that 'already he knows how to hold a steering wheel. He sits on my knees, I press the accelerator and he drives. We are already up to 60 miles an hour.'

All this speed went down less well with some observers who were unenchanted by the Villeneuve family's craze, on and off the track, for what seemed to be a dangerous way of life. The many references, from father and son, to living on the edge, or finding the limit, were seen by some critics, including other drivers, as evidence of their threat as a hazard to other people. Ronnie Peterson, with whom Gilles had two collisions in three races in one brief spell, said of his illustrious rival: 'He came into me again from behind, just as he did in Japan. I really think that he has a pretty minimal judgement of the distance between things. The man is a public menace. He was going so fast that if he hadn't hit my Lotus, he would have driven straight off the circuit.'

But Gilles Villeneuve was a favourite, a crowd-pleaser and a celebrity sought by everyone. At Monaco, he was probably fêted more than anywhere else and he could ignore the nicknames he was given, often only in jest, including one created by the Ferrari mechanics who called him the 'Flyer' because they felt he took off in his car so often he was using it as an aircraft rather than a roadcraft. Despite it all, he knew they loved him and respected him for his lunacy, if such it was, and his talent. They also admired him for his independence, a quality that had encouraged him to ship the 36-foot-long Fifth Wheel Globestar motorhome to Europe after it was custom-made for him in Quebec. It was a fully equipped three-bedroom model including a kitchen, bathroom and wall-to-wall carpets and came to Europe together with the old Ford pickup which Gilles had used for towing in Atlantic racing. He used the old pickup to tug the motorhome around Europe, much to the indignation of some observers who thought that the family Villeneuve were lowering the tone of the paddocks with their strange living accommodation pulled along by a vehicle plastered in stickers for the Montreal Canadiens hockey team.

When Jacques and the family were in residence at a race, in their mobile home from home, any visitors were welcomed with a warning and a warm greeting. They were not allowed to smoke and all shoes had to be taken off indoors. Gilles regarded it as essential to travel with his wife and children around him, and he said, 'This way I can see my kids grow up . . . in fact, this is the only way to have a normal life in a moving career.' Many around Gilles did not understand him doing this because, for them, it was nothing more than a job to go racing. But, as his Ferrari team-mate Scheckter said: 'Motor racing was a romantic thing for him. We were close friends, doing the same job for the same team, but we had completely different attitudes to it.'

By 1981, it was becoming clear that life at Plascassier could not go on forever. The villa was owned by a Belgian who had bought it as a retirement home and he wished to occupy it at some time while Jacques' father wanted, also, to cut down some of the journey time from there to Fiorano in Italy. Joann suggested they move to Italy, to live nearer to the Ferrari base, but Gilles was very determined that his children should be brought up speaking French. They reached a compromise and chose to move to Monaco, the glamorous tax haven of many other drivers before and since. After much deliberation, and one failed study of the possibility of living in an apartment occupied previously by the late Ronnie Peterson, who had been killed at Monza in 1978, the Villeneuves finally found a villa they liked and purchased it.

It was called La Mascotte – as it still is – and stood in a small parcel of ground on a hill behind the Beach Plaza Hotel, on a twisting little road close to the main commercial thoroughfares of the rich Mediterranean principality. Joann still lived in the property in 1996. Before Jacques, Melanie and their parents moved in, it was owned by a jeweller's family whose heirs had been squabbling over its future ownership since his death seven years earlier. The roof leaked, much of the interior was in shoddy condition and the gardens appeared to be overgrown badly, but Gilles and Joann saw potential. Much work was done on the property, after it was bought for 750,000 dollars (with the blessing of Prince Rainier), including new utilities and the installation of a large garage, workshop, office and swimming pool. The domestic appliances – fridges, dishwashers and ovens – were imported from New York, as was Gilles' extraordinary red, yellow and orange Ford Bronco, a vehicle which Jacques' father felt he needed for forays into off-road endangerment. He also fell in love with flying helicopters and, after learning to fly them in record time, went out and bought one immediately. Jacques Villeneuve's father was not interested in taking life slowly on land, in the air, or on the sea. He also bought an Italian speedboat, adding two massive 700 horse power engines imported from Detroit to add power, and a chrome exhaust system from California to deal with its exhalations. This floating beast was banned from being started up in the port of Monaco and had to be pulled out to sea to be used.

Joann felt it was, literally, a pain for them all. 'The kids and I would be black and blue when we got out of that boat,' she told Donaldson. 'You couldn't sit in it, you stood hanging on. So, I had both kids in my arms, holding them so they wouldn't fly out. He was having a great time while I was trying desperately to stay in the boat with the kids. He would just bounce it through the waves to see how long it would take before the engines blew up or the boat broke. In the end, he was going out by himself because even the kids didn't want to go out in the boat any more.'

For Jacques, it was not an easy existence. The son of a famed Ferrari driver, a man who was obsessed by speed, he had also to accept that his father could be an overbearing, strict and demanding parent as well as a figure of such celebrated proportions that there was little room left to escape from his shadows. How could Jacques do what Gilles had done? How could he cope with the idea that his father was taking such massive risks all the time – not only with risking his life, but his reputation, every time he raced? Donaldson claimed that Jacques found it so tough that he had to leave the Monaco Grand Prix, on one occasion, because he developed a bad headache. 'His English nanny took him up the hill to the villa before the race was half over. John and Elizabeth

Lane were guests of Gilles and Joann that weekend, and Lane notes that, "When Gilles was racing, Jacques became almost a basket case. He would sit there and you could see him gritting his teeth with his jaw muscles working and eventually he would have to leave. Melanie was always screaming and cheering for her dad and she would stay to the end of the race. But not Jacques.'

'For several years,' Donaldson continued, 'Jacques had been experiencing nervous headaches and was having difficulty in school. Joann thinks it was because of the pressure his father put on him. "Gilles was very demanding with Jacques and not at all with Melanie. He spent more time with her and in his eyes she was perfect. He wanted his son to be more than perfect and accepted from his daughter all the little faults children have and thought they were nice and cute in her. But not in Jacques. I was the only one who really saw the difference in the way he treated the kids. I didn't have any problems with Jacques. He would sit calmly at the table and not drop his glass of milk. But when Gilles was there, he would drop the glass of milk. He would get very nervous just trying so hard to please his father. Towards the end, he was becoming a better father. He began to realise that he was too demanding and he had to treat them both more equally and fairly. But the kids sensed there was a lot of tension and friction between us. It made them unhappy and unsettled them." '

In the final months of his life, Jacques' father began tormenting his mother in the bickering, irritating ways that are common in marriages under stress. But they still put on a public face of smiles when it was needed, for example when invited to a diplomatic supper in Ottawa by the Prime Minister of Canada Pierre Trudeau, a great fan. With the advantage of hindsight, it is strange to analyse the comments Gilles made at this time. 'By the time I stop racing my son will be 17,' he said once. 'And, he will know so many girls in Monaco, there's no way we'll be allowed to leave here.'

By then, anyway, according to Donaldson's biography, Gilles Villeneuve was also getting to know the girls. He was not much of a playboy in the Formula One paddock, but, it was reported by

Donaldson, 'did have a flirtation or two with women in Italy, in company with Didier Pironi. Through an Italian fashion photographer, they met models and went out on the town with them in Milan. "Gilles could be naughty," says Jody Scheckter. "He didn't necessarily need to be led astray and could be motivated by things other than speed sometimes. That was one of the boy things Gilles and I talked about. There were a couple of people he took out, but it wasn't a girl in every port thing with him. I do know there was one he fancied in particular." '

This other woman, who entered Gilles' life and threatened Jacques' equilibrium even before his father was killed, was a Canadian who worked in a family insurance company. She became involved with him and was often flown, by secret arrangements, to races and hotels at Gilles' request. To his credit, Gilles struggled with his dilemma and fought hard to save his marriage even when Joann, aware their problems were deep-rooted and threatening, offered to give him a divorce. At one stage, Gilles agreed to examine the possibility but when papers were prepared, including a statement of how a settlement between them would be worked out, he rejected it. According to Donaldson, this was all enacted behind the pits at Long Beach during a race meeting.

'He read the statement. He re-read it, then asked for the copies each of them had, tore them up into tiny pieces, and threw them into the garbage.' Others said that Gilles knew he had reached the point where he recognised his problems created by his lifestyle but felt he still loved Joann, though he could not live with her.

In the end, this last sad chapter of their marriage was not resolved before Gilles' tragic accident at Zolder, and the effect the burgeoning difficulties had on Jacques are difficult to quantify. He rarely, virtually never, talks about his private life in public. He has hardly ever talked about his father or his mother or his feelings about them. He has said little or nothing about these childhood years that took him from Quebec to Plascassier and then to Monaco. Some people, particularly those who were admirers of his father, often find they know more about Gilles Villeneuve than his son is prepared to admit. They end up tracing out the anecdotes while he listens, as Adam Cooper found out when he interviewed Jacques for *Autosport* in 1992.

'When people come to talk to me, I'm quite shy,' said Jacques. 'I don't know what they think. Maybe, they think, "He doesn't want to talk about his father." It's strange when I'm racing myself and people come to talk to me and say to me "your father was blah, blah, blah . . ." But I like to hear people talk about him because I get to know more about him. Most of the people keep on saying he was crazy. Crazy in a good way! Most of what I know comes from the few videos I've seen. Like Dijon with Arnoux and stuff like that. It looked pretty good. You're always proud when someone talks about someone who's near to you, or your family. On that side, I'm proud and happy, but when they begin comparing, I think it's stupid.

'I won't get upset or anything, but I just think it's stupid . . . I don't really have any memories of when my father was racing. I was playing with my small cars when he was on the track, so I didn't care! The best memories I have of my father are probably when he gave me my Christmas presents! No, seriously, mostly I just remember being with him on the boat, going as crazy as he could. I would just keep on saying with my sister, "faster, faster!" and he went more crazy, while my mother was already scared as shit! Now that I think about it, it was really crazy, but at the time it was really nice.

'I can remember him working on his 4 × 4 in the garage. The best memories I have are of going with him in the 4 × 4. One time, while we were going up the mountain, the differential broke and we started rolling backwards. Then suddenly we went up on two wheels and we landed again. I just started laughing because I wanted some more of it!

'In any car, I would just say, "faster, faster!" We could have gone 250kph and I was still going, "faster, faster!" I wouldn't notice at all. But now, if somebody else is driving, I'll say, "slower, slower". Maybe I'm more realistic now.'

How he was in the last days, in Monaco, before Gilles' death, he did not say. For an answer, it was clearly most efficient to ask Joann herself. So a visit to the villa in Monaco was arranged and directions given to the Rue de Giroflees, where La Mascotte is still the home of Madame Joann Villeneuve more than a decade after the brutal loss of her husband. This house is five minutes' walk from the Place des Moulins (itself an extraordinary place, with its deep underground car park and old garages, a place filled with the atmosphere of vaults) and to march there by foot conjures up some feeling for the environment in which Jacques spent the second stage of his growing adventures in Europe. The walk takes you down a long and narrow street, busy with people on both sides, greengrocers, newsagents and jewellers, to a sharp reverse turn to the left. Up a hill towards the narrow, rising residential street where, on a corner, the road sweeps sharply again to the right in another hairpin, facing a banner-strewn German official residence, is the modest Villeneuve home.

The house has a garage off to the right at pavement level, where Gilles loved to tinker with his machines, and a garden lies above within a hedged perimeter which also houses a small outdoor swimming pool. All is visible from the road. The gates are drawn and closed, but there are no large dogs, no searchlights and no security systems. It is as plain and simple as Plascassier. Passers-by can easily incline their heads to see into the garden. Joann answers the door herself, together with her young daughter Jessica, just four and a half, in her arms, and a tiny yapping dog at her feet. Serene, soft and much prettier than some of the published news photographs of the past suggested, Joann stands and answers the questions with a dignity that becomes her. There is a hint of grey in her hair, but nothing more than that, and the atmosphere she brings with her is special.

After introducing myself and explaining my mission, she smiled her beautiful smile. 'And', she asked, 'does Jacques know about this?' I told her he did, but added with an almost overwhelming sense of honesty that he thoroughly disapproved and had told me so. She smiled again. And so I talked to her about the job to be done, the writing of the book, why it was I was there, standing on her threshold. Patiently, politely, she listened before confessing that she felt she could not do anything without Jacques' approval. An interview was out of the question. But as Joann spoke, her little girl, Jacques' half-sister, beckoned me to enter their house with a sweet smile and a laugh. I did not argue with Joann, or even attempt to present a case against her son's views on the freedom of speech. I knew it was fruitless. There was no reason to upset this serene woman, with her soft and engaging voice, with a debate revolving around a racing driver's life.

Chapter Five

After Gilles:
1982–1989

The Beau Soleil, College Alpin International, is high up among the Alpes Vaudoises in French-speaking Switzerland, at Villars-sur-Ollon, a pretty village close to Lac Leman. To reach the school, it is necessary to leave the motorway from Geneva and Lausanne and drive up a road that winds swiftly and dramatically from ground level to an altitude of 1,300 metres, at which height skiing is the obvious winter sport.

Here snow falls heavily in the season and the chalets, with their wooden balconies, their Subaru estates parked outside and the stacked chimneys and delightful colours provide a 'chocolate box' scene that would be described as unquestionably Swiss the world over. The college has its own natural setting, perched on a narrow plateau facing south, with perfect views back across the Rhône valley towards Mont Blanc, the Dents du Midi and the French Alps, its own facilities for sports and games, comfortable accommodation for living and working, and a reputation for kindliness and discipline among the children of the rich and famous who despatch their offspring there for education and board. Jacques Villeneuve was one such child and he lived in the community of Beau Soleil at Villars from the age of 12 to 17, or from 1983 to 1988, according to the records and recollections of Yula de Meyer, who owned and ran the place at the time. 'He was a very special boy, very bright and capable, but also very *contestatif*,' she said. 'He was exceedingly independent.' Her assessment has very few doubters.

For two generations, the school has been in the hands of the de Meyer family. They have been there since taking control in 1959 and use their own coat of arms on both the cover of their brochures and in the heart of the culture of the school. The motto of this coat of arms is 'fidei et virtuti', faith and courage, and it was awarded to Jules de Meyer by Pope Leon XIII in 1901 in honour of the members of the de Meyer family who had won fame and distinction serving with the pontifical troops in the past. The family believe and feel that it is reflected in the ethos of their school. 'The directors at Beau Soleil do their utmost not only to teach, but to educate the boys and girls who will be the leaders of tomorrow,' recited the welcome in their brochure, after a note which pointed out that this unique establishment had been in existence since 1920.

'Our main objective at Beau Soleil is to offer students a secure, family-orientated and challenging educational setting in which to work and mature,' it continued, adding that students from more than 30 countries come to study there. 'In this miniature world, they discover themselves, their colleagues, different habits and customs, thus acquiring a better understanding of the real world. Community life at this boarding school also instigates a strong sense of responsibility, respect, discipline and an acceptance of social obligations.'

The school includes a French Lycée, in which students are prepared for the Baccalauréat, but by the time Jacques Villeneuve had passed towards the final stages of his education his mind was no longer fixed on such academic goals – in fact, it never had been – but on quite different career ambitions in other areas. He wanted to become a racing driver, like his father. It was a desire which grew in strength throughout his years at Beau Soleil where, when he first arrived, he was still recovering from the shock of losing his father following his death at Zolder in 1982. His boarding school, recommended to Joann by Patrick Tambay who lived close by in

Switzerland and knew it well, was filled with sporting attractions (and distractions), including skiing in which Jacques grew to excel, partly due to the advantage of having skiied as a boy in Canada. It was chosen for its proximity to Geneva, its reputation, its family tradition and its atmosphere. It was seen to be a fine place in which Jacques could grow up and blossom in his life after Gilles.

The death of his father had a profound effect on Jacques, turning him from an outgoing and boisterous boy into a far more introspective and moody child, his powers of deep concentration becoming more and more difficult to understand and fathom. What had been a near-idyllic life, aside from the tension between his parents, which he could hardly have been aware of, was shattered. Jacques was, from then on, faced with the recurring question: why? And, as it is for all bereaved relatives left behind after such a tragedy, he could find no adequate answer. Joann had been baking biscuits in her kitchen when she was told the news by Jody Scheckter. 'A friend of mine called me from Zolder and said "Gilles has had an accident, a big one, and it doesn't look good at all",' he told Donaldson. 'So I phoned Joann and shot up to her place very quickly. From then on, it was chaos and disaster. You don't even want to think back on it.'

According to Donaldson, Joann went into shock and Scheckter gave her some tranquillisers he had been given following a hernia operation. 'He couldn't travel, so his wife Pam went with me to Belgium,' she recalled. 'The doctors took me into an office and told me there was nothing more they could do. They'd been on the phone with several specialists, in Montreal and elsewhere. I wanted them to try and operate, to do something, anything. They told me I had to make the decision to cut the life-support machines off. I told them they were crazy. Eventually, Gilles died. From then on, everything is blurred for me. A lot of people helped. Jody was very, very good. Very strong.'

The stunning and tragic news left many people in shock, but both Jacques and his sister Melanie, then aged only ten and eight, found a way of soldiering through together. Family friend John

Lane recalled, in Donaldson's book, that they 'seemed to be doing much better than I expected. That first night, they both went upstairs to bed and later, when I went up to check on them, they were asleep. When I saw Melanie I started crying. She had a picture of her dad with her. She was holding it in her arms.'

Jacques withdrew into himself, but coped in his own way as all around him arrangements were made for his father's funeral and friends, relatives, associates and acquaintances ensured his mother was kept company, looked after and prevented from being left alone for too long. Scheckter, Lane and Ray Wardell, Gilles' former mechanic who also flew to Europe from America, organised themselves in a rota system while the Canadian government organised an armed forces 707 jet to fly to Brussels and then carry the coffin back to Montreal. Six Canadian soldiers carried the burial-chest, draped in a maple leaf flag, on board for the seven-hour flight. Joann flew with the children, Jacques and Melanie, assisted by Linda Marso, the musical girlfriend of Bruno Giacomelli, and the others. Observers said she was 'suffering terribly with grief' and reported also that 'the children spent the flight drawing and writing poems about their father, and Jacques drew pictures of racing cars'.

The entire episode was almost unbearable for all those who had been close to Gilles. His body lay in state in Berthierville, in the town cultural centre, for two days during which an estimated 5,500 people filed silently past the open bronze casket. Donaldson wrote that 'Gilles lay dressed in a white cardigan with a single red rose on his chest. At his feet were his pock-marked red-and-blue helmet and his orange driving gloves. Nearby lay a model of a Ferrari made of red flowers with a card reading 'Papa et Mama' . . . All the church bells in Berthier pealed.'

After the funeral, the next race was in Monaco. Never could the sound of Formula One cars echoing through those streets have sounded so unwanted and strange as then for those in the principality who were friends, followers and admirers of the little French-Canadian who had died. In the programme for that 40th Monaco Grand Prix, one of Gilles' old adversaries, Clay

Regazzoni – who had been paralysed for life after crashing at Long Beach in 1980 – wrote one of the most eloquent tributes to the father of Jacques Villeneuve. 'So long, Gilles,' he wrote. 'You were young, loyal, daring, simple and you loved to express yourself in our sport like no one has done in recent years. You had just attained the heights of glory and, like a lightning bolt, destiny cruelly stole your life. You leave an immense void. Your talents were fantastic exhibitions which the many fans you loved and for whom you always gave your best will miss. They never will forget what you did and you will leave unperishable memories for automotive sport aficionados. Joann, Melanie and Jacques, like us, will always be proud of you. Adieu, Gilles.'

There is no doubt this period of Jacques' life must have been sad and deeply traumatic. Joann admitted that she devoted herself to her children after Gilles' death and found them to be a source of strength in a very difficult period. After the funeral, she had brought Gilles' ashes back with her to the villa in Monaco, where she worked at adjusting to her new life without him. She concentrated on comforting her children and putting on a brave face for them, and both Jacques and Melanie emerged from it all as strong, resilient and courageous people, single-minded and determined. Both of them were enrolled to go to Villars, where, according to Yula de Meyer, they arrived the following year after spending some time living with a family in the Haut-Savoie in France.

Jacques did not like school, nor did he hate it. For him, it was a 'passing through' experience. 'At Villars,' he said, 'I acquired the taste of independence.' At least he found snow again. The winters must have been the source of some rekindled memories, but they also gave him a chance to revel in skiing, a fast-moving sport in which he was not only blessed with talent, but also found excitement and satisfaction. He was also pitched in among some happy, attractive and rich contemporaries, some of them from famous families, though it seems Jacques himself was little bothered by his colleagues or their antecedents. Indeed, according to his school reports – certainly one published in November 1988 at Villars – he could be *pénible* (tiresome) and he had an attitude which was *arrogante* (arrogant). But the report allowed him a 'green light' to take time off to begin his weekend trips to Italy to start his training for motor racing. These journeys, intended to be recreational escapes from his academic work, soon overtook all else in his life and led, ultimately, to his failure to study and his decision to reject an opportunity to complete his work for the Baccalauréat and leave. 'What's the best thing that ever happened to you?', he was asked in a magazine article. The answer was simple: 'Being kicked out of my school, Beau Soleil, in Switzerland, because I started racing.'

It was a cool answer, but did not fully reflect his scholastic career in the family atmosphere fostered by Pierre and Yula de Meyer, the husband and wife team who ran the international Alpine college during Jacques' years at the school. Their son Jerome is now the director and, to their regret as well as amusement, has made the place rather more commercial than familial, probably changing it quite considerably from the place that was selected by Patrick Tambay and recommended to Joann when he was helping her through her hardest times. 'We were good friends and when Gilles passed away, Joann was taking it hard,' explained Tambay. 'I was living at Villars and we suggested to her that she put the kids into a boarding college near us. She couldn't handle them, they were on their own and she wasn't sleeping that much. We suggested the college in Villars. I knew we would be close to them for any needs they may have and from a short distance we could oversee their well-being. We also knew the people at the college so it was a good arrangement for everyone.'

Tambay recognised that Jacques was determined and head-strong, qualities that were to shine through in his schooldays in Switzerland. His desire to be a racing driver was not strongly apparent to begin with, but emerged gradually, as he grew older. 'He was always very quiet and very poised and probably very determined about it,' he said. 'But he wasn't shouting out every day that it was what he wanted to do. He was not, and is not, like his father. He is very calm. He calculates a lot. He is not as outspoken and generous and outgoing as Gilles was. But I think he is a calculator.'

In the school, there were all sorts of conflicting views about the young Villeneuve. While he showed great ability on skis, he demonstrated little interest in the academic side of life in the classroom and, in many ways, failed to utilise his obvious intelligence and ability.

'He was a good boy, but he had a very strong character,' said Yula de Meyer. 'He had a character that could change. But he was a powerful little person. He was *contestataire*, I don't know how you say it in English. It means that if we say "you have to get up at seven o'clock and to go to bed at nine," he does it because it is the rule. Then, he will always say: "Why seven o'clock – if I can get up at half past seven?" It is not the same as the nice boys who would always say, okay, if that is the rule then that is it. But he was not really a rebel. He did everything, but he contested everything. He was very independent. He obeyed things, but he had different feelings in his head.

'He left us when he was 17. He came here when he was about 12, after his father had died. When his father died, Madame Villeneuve put the children in Haut Savoie with a French family. We saw them in a video that a Canadian television crew showed us. It was Patrick Tambay who organised this, I think. He was a close friend of the family and with Jacques. He fixed up his studies and his school. The Canadian man of the video told us all this when he came here. He said: "Did you know, before Gilles Villeneuve died, that the relations between Madame and Monsieur were bad? Well, they were nearly finished." We did not know that. When he died, Madame Villeneuve was very busy travelling and other things, I don't know exactly what. And she put the children in Savoie, in this family. They were very small and they went to the village school and everything was okay.

'But when Jacques was 11 or 12, the village school was too low academically and Patrick Tambay came here and asked if we wanted to take the two children at Beau Soleil and we said "Yes, sure." Patrick had a chalet here in Villars before and some weekends the children came from that family and came with Patrick Tambay and Madame Villeneuve to Beau Soleil.'

At Beau Soleil at that time, Charlotte Gainsbourg was among the students of famous families and Paul Stewart, son of Jackie, was registered and studying at another school in the village. Martin Elford, the photographer son of Vic Elford the racing driver, was one of many other people from well-known families who passed through in a similar era.

'We had all kinds of children,' said Yula. 'My husband spent 45 years and I spent 33 years working here. We were father and mother to the children who lived in the school. During the period Jacques spent here, it was very family orientated. Jacques was very good at everything. A very clever boy.

'In the class, everybody spent two hours studying something, for example, but for Jacques just half an hour would be enough, if he was interested in it. If not, nothing. If he did not want to study, because it was not interesting to him, then he would not study. He was always between the top of the class and the middle. One day, Patrick Tambay told Jacques he had to work differently. He said: "Jacques, listen. If, after the next two weeks, you are the first in the class, I will get you a computer. A Commodore." Well, he spent two weeks studying and he was first . . . just to get the Commodore. He was about 15 or 16, but this was typical of Jacques and I am sure this is what has helped him to succeed.

'He is a very good thinker and he did what he wanted. He was clever, but he was strong with his mind and his will. And, of course, he was a wonderful sportsman, particularly in skiing. You know, in the winter we have a ski-resort here and everybody goes to ski three or four times a week, but Jacques was excellent. He was before he came here and he was always very good here too.

'Craig Pollock, who is his manager now, was our sports teacher, the head of the sports department, and a very good skier. He and Jacques became friends on the snow because we always prepared a team for the Concours. But also, at this time, I remember, it was the beginning of jumping and all the students made by themselves a trampoline jump. It was very interesting. All the time we saw this, we noticed that all the other boys came rushing down and they just jumped and went. But not Jacques. He would come down and look before at the ski-jump and he would say, "no, it's not good, it's badly prepared, the slope is wrong." He did not like risks. He would see if it was good and well-made and safe, and then he would jump, but if it wasn't, then he would not jump at all.'

This calculating aspect of Jacques' character first emerged at Villars, even though it may have been spotted earlier by Tambay, but it developed later into a mind that was respected for its intensity and depth. 'In skiing, he excelled and he won races,' said Madame de Meyer. 'He accepted the risks, but he studied them first. He calculated, but he never jumped without knowing what lay ahead. He was not crazy. Not Jacques. He was a good downhill skier and he was good at slalom and he nearly always finished. He rarely fell down because he knew what he was doing.

'He was capable of all this reasoning when he was quite young. He could calculate risk and avoid making big mistakes. He could be the Formula One world champion this year, but you know he could be the world ski champion too. He could be champion of anything he wanted in sport. He is good at everything. He loved them all. I remember once he was here for a weekend training with the Swiss junior ski team. At that time, on Friday morning, waking up at half past five to go with the bus, it was easy for him. He could do it without any problems. Always for sports! No trouble. That was Jacques all over.'

Jacques' special ability on skis came not only from his frequent practice sessions in Switzerland, but also from an enthusiasm sparked by his father's friendship with the downhill champions Steve Podborski and Ken Reid, known as the 'Crazy Canucks'. He also preferred to be alone in sport, rather than to take part in team games. He seemed happier to be a solo competitor. 'I would challenge my friends at school to anything and everything,' he said. 'Even if I hadn't got a clue what I was doing! I wouldn't be happy unless I was performing in some way or another. Most of the time it was on skis, trying to go faster, wilder and crazier than the next guy.' Asked by *Arena* magazine in 1996 if he had been serious about skiing as a career, he dismissed the idea. 'I didn't train hard enough. I got into downhill, some slalom and some giant slalom, but really, I liked getting into the rocks, jumping as high as possible – just going nuts really. Besides, I always knew I would end up racing cars.'

At Villars, Jacques was regarded by Pierre de Meyer as a bright student with the intelligence and talent to have passed all his exams and to have enjoyed a solid, prosperous and professional career in almost any discipline he chose. But in the year when he was in a class known as Première, a year before Baccalauréat, his academic work began to take a back seat. Madame de Meyer explained: 'He was supposed to be ready for the examinations in June, or he should have been, but that year, in October, when he came back to school with Madame Villeneuve, they asked us some questions. "Listen, Jacques is very happy to come back," she said. "But we want you to give him permission to leave the school, maybe every weekend, or maybe just one or two in the month, to go to Milan to practise racing with a team."

'We said "Yes, sure" to Madame Villeneuve because Jacques could do both – study and work on *les voitures* – if he wanted, but we made it clear that if Jacques had good records for study only then could he go every weekend for racing. And we made this deal with Madame Villeneuve – and, at the beginning, it was nice. But he was supposed to come back on Sunday night and it became Monday morning. He had to leave on Friday, and it became Thursday. And, you know, the studies were not so good. So, at Christmas, we called Madame Villeneuve and we said: "Listen, do you want Jacques to be a pilot or do you want Jacques to have the Baccalauréat? We ask, because we cannot go on with this." This was in 1988.

'For us it was very important because every year people ask us how many per cent of our students succeed. Jacques said: "No, I want both." So, we tried again, but at Easter we let him go. We knew we could not present him for his exams. It would have been useless – and at that time anyway he said, "I prefer to leave my studies and to go to Milan." He was just 17. He left all his studies behind and he left Beau Soleil. I know my husband feels strongly it was a shame that Jacques never finished his education here. But, he has come back here every year since because, I think, he likes Villars very much and because we have kept a good contact with him. So he comes here and, sometimes, I say to him: What do you think about your Baccalauréat? Do you regret this or not? And he said "Yes", but he never did do it! Not yet, anyway.'

Madame de Meyer said that there were about 12 or 14 pupils on average in the same class as Jacques. Boys and girls. He had good friendships and he had some very good friends. It seemed, in Villars at least, that he found it easier to form relationships with girls than boys, she suggested.

'One was Celine Datwyler. She is 23 now and she lives in Villars, but he was friends with lots of others and, also, he was friends with some of the men, too. Look at Craig Pollock, for example. He was his teacher, his sports teacher, and now he is his manager! And there was Miguel Ernand and Fausto Martinelli, who had been at Beau Soleil since 1954. He was the gymnastics teacher. And there is a story about him and Jacques which is interesting and very nice.

'It began when Jacques was young and he never liked to do any gym work at all and Fausto told him one day that if he ever became a driver in Formula One then, that day, he said, "I will jump with a parachute." So, when Jacques won the Indy 500, he sent a picture to Fausto and he wrote on it and the message said, "I am the champion now, when are you going to jump?" '

Madame de Meyer continued to talk about Jacques with the pleasure of a woman warming to one of her favourite subjects. She almost revelled in the tales of his obstinance and individuality, his easy talent for sport, his selective laziness when it came to academic work. And she could recall details about the young scholastic Formula One star of the future which left her husband quite amazed.

'There was no one particularly famous in his class,' she recounted. 'Charlotte Gainsbourg was younger, not older. Jacques was not a particularly popular boy in the class. His father, Gilles, was not famous among the boys of that age. Maybe, later on, when older, they would have known of him better. He was always drawing cars, engines and anything to do with Formula One. It interested him very deeply even as a young boy.

'In regard to his father, I don't know what to say. But one thing I can say. He was very against his mother. For example, the last time I saw Jacques was at Christmas when he came here for three weeks for his holidays. I asked him what is happening with Melanie, what is she doing and he told me she was in New York, studying to be a singer. "And what about your mother?", I asked. I liked her very much because she was always with us when we discussed Jacques' studies and she did not, like many other parents, look for an excuse for him. She would say, "Is that right?" and then speak to Jacques and say, "Okay, you stay here for the weekend." Well, when I asked about his mother on this occasion, he said in French "Huh" in a certain way and then, in French, he referred to his half-sister Jessica, his little sister, and said she was conceived with "a mec", a very bad expression for a guy, very pejorative. I said, "You cannot say that – she is still your mother" but I think he was in one of his certain moods!

'It's good that he comes back to Villars, but I don't think he comes back just to see us. He likes it here. He comes very often. Every year. And he says hello to Beau Soleil. The first year he came back after he had raced in Japan, my husband noticed he was wearing jeans which are not allowed here and he had very long hair. He said it was because he was in his university year and that is why he behaved like that. He had long hair and lots of fun!'

According to Madame de Meyer, when Jacques went to Japan, some fans in Italy, who knew him from his time in Italy, said that they felt that after one year Jacques had left them because they did not believe he had the ability to become a champion. 'So, after that, he went to Japan and it was there that he met Craig Pollock again, who I think had helped him to decide to go there. Craig had left the school to take a very good position at Honda selling old sports items and he went to Japan for a training course. Craig came back often to Villars and so he saw Jacques and they made the arrangement for him to go to Japan.

For the young Jacques, the years from his 12th birthday to his 17th were filled with strong, sometimes conflicting, emotions. He was growing up. He was finding his own way in the world – and through the Swiss Alps – and developing traits of a personality that reminded many of his father. 'Yes, it is true. He was a boy with a very strong head who showed little real emotion demonstratively,' recalled Yula. 'Gilles was certainly an excellent driver, but with a head of unpredictable thoughts. I think Jacques inherited from his father all the qualities of his driving, but in a more refreshing and intelligent style. He is better educated with a better sense of self-preservation and more self-control. But there is the same big force inside him. But Jacques was always a very introverted boy. He did not talk very much. But he was, I think, a boy who missed his father very much. He was very jealous of his mother because, if he could choose, he would rather have had his father staying and not his mother, if you know what I mean. Sometimes, here, he would speak normally and be like all the other boys. But, at other times, he would be very closed completely. Just like that. I could see him like this and then I knew it was much better not even to speak to him.'

Pierre de Meyer sat and nodded his head sagely as his wife Yula talked her way through her own feelings and thoughts on Jacques' childhood in Switzerland, but when he heard this he was quick to speak himself.

'What my wife has said is a very feminine and intuitive judgement of the boy,' he explained. 'For myself, I have a very different impression – that of a man, like a father, in a different way. It was never easy for me, with Jacques, to give him any discipline or to steer him in any way. He was very strong-willed and independent, as we have said, and it made him a problem sometimes. But he was so hard and so strong. It was his best way to deal with everything. Headstrong. The story with Fausto and how he did it is typical of Jacques. Absolutely typical. He could be so cold and hard.

'Certainly, he was immature in an emotional and psychological way, not really developed. Obviously, he had some problems and difficulties. He never showed any outward signs of special affection for his father, or the memory of him, while he was here in Villars, but I am sure that inside him, he was filled with admiration for his father. But he wants to be recognised for himself in the same way that the son of Alain Delon also wishes to be known as something other than "Alain Delon's son".'

According to the two retired teachers, Jacques' favourite subject at school was mathematics and his favourite recreation, apart from skiing, was anything else to do with sport or speed. In his school report of November, 1988, Yula wrote: 'Penible, attitude arrogant et desuivolte, provoque, saus depasse les limites. Malgré un bulletin vert . . .' In translation this meant he was distressing, arrogant and always pushing everyone to the limits . . .

On re-hearing the words, Madame de Meyer was animated again. 'Exactly,' she said. 'Find the limits. Gilles always went beyond the limits. But Jacques went to the limit, not beyond.'

She talked with delight. She went out of her way to find reports, photographs, recall anecdotes and ideas of the past with Jacques Villeneuve and as she did so, her husband Pierre found a copy of a Swiss magazine, *L'Illustré*, published in Lausanne, which had run a long feature on 'Les années Suisses de Jacques Villeneuve'. In it, his school report was reproduced, together with a photograph of a cherubic-looking Jacques smiling out of a passport-sized photograph. Her delight, however, was cut short by the memory, more recent, of how Craig Pollock had reacted on Jacques' behalf to the publication of the old report. 'Craig Pollock came here and I did not see him, but he did see the secretary and he said to her: "Tell Madame de Meyer that Jacques was very unhappy that she gave this report to the newspapers. Very unhappy." ' Madame de Meyer's feelings on the subject are best left absent from this passage, but suffice to say that she retains a strong belief in freedom of speech and a less enchanted view of other things and people.

She continued: 'He was always polite, never vulgar or indisciplined, and he was very faithful. He had the same girlfriend here at Beau Soleil through nearly all his years here. Her name was

Laura Cases. Many boys changed their girlfriends every month or every three months, not Jacques. He chose her and he was very faithful. The last three years they were together, but she is married now to someone else. This is normal! She was a Spanish girl. At the end of his last year, he was very keen on our own daughter Sophie. He telephoned her often. They were the same age and in the same class. But Sophie said no. At one time, she would have liked to be the girlfriend of Jacques, when they were here together, but at that time he preferred Laura and later when he called Sophie, she said "No, it is too late."

'Jacques was very changeable. Very open and nice, if he wanted to be. But then he could be the other way and it would be better to forget it. He has some problems. It seems with his mother, to some degree. She seemed to be a natural woman, someone who always knew how things were and she was very comfortable and at home with herself. But Jacques, he finds this difficult.'

Monsieur de Meyer agreed. 'Jacques Villeneuve,' he boomed, 'he likes to have something to fight against. If he is left without obstacles, he can be lost. He regrets, I am sure, not taking the Baccalauréat. He could have been a doctor, an engineer or an architect.'

By now, both were deeply involved in discussing the inner workings of their complex former student. 'I think he has no family, Jacques, but he regrets it very much,' said Madame de Meyer. 'I don't know, but he seems a boy who prefers to be alone. He seems to find a lot of things with people difficult. He is too young for all that has happened to him. He does not care for things outside his own head. He has a near-fatalist attitude. I think he is very simple about everything. Too simple, but it is his life.'

Chapter Six

Preparing to Race:
1985–1988

When Jacques left Beau Soleil, not through expulsion as has sometimes been suggested, but rather by mutual consent between his mother and the De Meyers, he embarked on the first chapter of his life as a young racing driver. Few at the school in Villars, where he had been happy enough if not wholly satisfied, were not sad to see him go. The great feeling was that he had under-achieved, a sense of frustration pervading many of the comments of those who had taught him. 'He was so hard and strong, but gifted too,' said Fausto Martinelli. 'He was so good at all sports, but especially at skiing and skating. But he hated to exercise and do fitness work to maintain his muscles and his condition. I worked very hard to encourage him, but he was never easy. I think Craig Pollock found him a good student and they were friends. But for me, he was impossible!'

The headstrong Jacques managed to retain a cordial, friendly relationship with most people around him, regardless of his antics and his attitudes. He could turn on the charm when needed to get what he wanted – or he could be as surly and cold as required to ensure he maintained the privacy and solitude in which he would wrap himself from time to time. Deep and strange, difficult to understand, he was as inscrutable as they come. Yet in March 1989, he returned and he has gone back regularly ever since to visit friends in the village and at the school. One of these friends was Celine Datwyler, 23 in 1996, a fresh-faced outdoor girl from the village who was a keen and accomplished skier and a member of the national team. The daughter of Jean-Daniel Datwyler, Celine was a former pupil at Beau Soleil and had skied with Jacques for much of her life, since they were very small.

'He liked to go fast and straight, he was not keen on jumping,' she smiled. 'When I call him on the telephone, he asks my news and he encourages me. I am doing courses in television. When I asked him about the impressions he has while he is driving a Formula One car, he said it was like a game of Nintendo!'

Jacques himself, in an interview in the same magazine, *L'Illustré*, to which Celine had talked, said Villars had a great significance in his life. Asked to look back and explain what the years he spent there meant to him, he said: 'An enormous smile, lots of memories. This place represents for me the advantages of a holiday place. I grew there and I put down some roots. I can recall the picnics, the walks. We were a group of children with our own society, like a miniature world.'

He said he gained his taste for independence there, 'confirmation of my personality and, with the discovery of my friends, a new kind of family'. In Villars, on return visits, he found 'tranquillity, when I look for it. But if I want to find some dens for fun, I can also find these places. I revisit when I can. Each time, I find I have some very nice times.'

The reporter for *L'Illustré*, Mark David, asked Villeneuve if he had returned the previous Christmas (1995). He replied: 'With my friends, with Mika Salo, we had a lot of real life. As much so because I was no longer a student in the village with the right to have only one hour's rest each day. I could go where I wanted.' 'And did the view of the villagers towards you change?', he was asked. 'Those who were kind towards me were exactly the same. With the others, there were some who suddenly adored me – so I was on my guard. At Villars I rediscovered a lot of people who I had never seen or met before!'

Jacques told David that he had never hesitated in his decision to give up school and skiing and to switch to racing. 'Never,' he said. 'Skiing is a passion. Driving is a devotion, a career, a way of life. But I need to ski. It gives me a total sense of freedom . . . It is true [that I do not take crazy risks and do myself injury on skis], I cannot remember ever having injured myself. At six years of age, I sprained my thumb . . . But I do not do ill-natured things . . . I am always at the limit, trying to do my best with the challenge of a corniche or to descend a *piste de bosses* and I like the idea of competition, the possibility of beating the other person.'

'Have you never gone beyond your own limit?' asked David. 'It has happened. I have paid for it,' answered Jacques. 'Why did Williams allow you to continue to ski?' 'I also do it like a physical training exercise. I find it is a good exercise for concentration, for visualisation. It is good for my eyes and for my cardio-vascular system.'

In the village, Miguel Ernand, 42, a friend of the family, and his son Fred, were happy to talk about Jacques. So too were Thomas Christen and Anthony Mean, two of his colleagues at Beau Soleil. Younger than Jacques, they were in the same class as his sister Melanie. But their overriding recollection of Jacques – one which adds to the contradictions about his attitudes to danger and risks on skis in particular – was of a 'kamikaze on skis. He could do things and fall, and he never got injured. In a car, he would swallow up the Ollon–Villars road like a lunatic.' Thomas recalled also that Jacques was 'a little in the clouds', but added that he could make easy contact with everyone at school where everyone knew him and where everyone still followed his career. They did not say so, in so many words, but these young men were confirming the impression that Jacques, a rich, perhaps spoilt young man, was known by reputation for his name and his 'switch-on and switch-off' charm as for anything else. 'We saw him last Christmas, when he came back, and he had not changed at all,' they added. 'Always simple and nice.'

The contradictions grow. 'He was the smallest in his class, but he was also the one with the most character,' said Craig Pollock, who was asked by Jacques in 1990 to be his manager. After hesitating, Craig finally accepted. They formed a close bond as driver and manager in those years, but it was nurtured and started when they shared some crazy, fun-filled days on skis in the Alpes Vaudoises. 'Jacques, I think, could also have been a champion on skis,' said Pollock, talking to *L'Illustré* in 1996. 'Today, in Formula One he is still making mistakes, but never the same one twice. But he likes to have fun. In life, he has his limits, but he tries to pass them.'

Pollock, who has continued to struggle with finding a true understanding of the sometimes melancholic, introspective, cheerful, kaleidoscopic and curious personality of his client throughout their working relationship, emerged from the years at Villars and through the period when he prepared to race (during the runaway weekends from school, with the Jim Russell School in Canada during a holiday, karting in Imola, and then with the Salerno Corse Italian Touring Car Team and the PreMa Formula Three team in Italy) as probably the most influential figure on Jacques' career, apart from the legacy of his father's talent and reputation.

Pollock remembered Jacques at school, reported Richard Huet for *Edition Special*, published in Montreal at the time of the 1996 Canadian Grand Prix, that 'he was determined, he had lots of concentration and was most energetic. Even better, he had the killer instinct. He did not compete for fun, but to win. Furthermore, physically he did not have the body of an athlete. For anybody else, it would have been a serious handicap. But Jacques turned it into an advantage by working harder than the others. During this period, his individualism – which is now his trademark – was already most noticeable.'

The former sports teacher also supported the theory that Jacques enjoyed skiing far more than the prospect of being a racing driver during his schooldays. 'He was a daredevil on skis, always trying things never attempted before,' said Pollock. 'He was, of course, enormously popular with everybody at his college. Nobody knows if he was just trying to find his own limits, but he was daring and already had personality, style and panache.' For Madame Villeneuve this was good and bad news as she had always hoped that by sending Jacques to school in Switzerland she might persuade him that skiing was more interesting, and more fascinating, than motor racing. Unfortunately, skiing was no more than a prelude, an introduction to the thrills of speed.

'We all believed it for a long time,' Joann was quoted as saying in *Edition Special*. 'Because he had a real talent for it. Should he have decided to become a professional skier, I am sure he would have been as successful as he is now as a racing driver. Jacques, who has always refused to compromise, always gives 300 per cent in everything he does.'

'He was the smallest kid in his class, but he was also cheekier and more intelligent than any of the others,' added Pollock, a Scot with a Swiss wife, who lives close to Villars. 'He did not try to be leader of the pack. He just was . . . If there was trouble, he was in the middle of it. But he never seemed to get caught, or if he did, he got away with it because he had the most incredibly nice smile.' Pollock added that 'it was pretty evident to us at the school that Jacques was destined to do something with his speed. Even the way he skied he was exceptionally fast and talented.'

Jacques delighted in any form of high velocity. In one episode he went out and attempted to conquer the Swiss Alps on a motocross bike, a venture which did nothing to dampen his spirits or reduce his innate desire to become a *pilote*. In the summer of 1986, when he was 15 years old, his annual trip back to Quebec with his mother and sister (a pilgrimage that became a tradition after the death of his father) included a visit to the Mont Tremblant circuit where he enrolled on a three-day course at the Jim Russell driving school. It was literally a case of the son following in his father's footsteps, or wheel-marks. Gilles had done exactly the same, although he was 23, not 15, at the time. Jacques loved it, passed the course with flying colours and, when he returned to Europe, found himself obsessed by the idea that, as a matter of natural course, he would be racing in the future. The following year, 1987, when he returned to Canada, he attended the Spenard-David Racing School in Shannonville, Ontario, where he also succeeded. At Mont Tremblant, he drove a Formula Ford 1600,

Melanie and Jacques enjoy a moment of togetherness with father Gilles, whose fame as a Ferrari driver made him a hero.

How Gilles will be remembered by his fans: at the wheel of a red Ferrari number 27.

Mother and son. Joann Villeneuve with Jacques, in his Camel yellow shirt, at the start of his racing career.

Jacques, in his first season in Formula Three, found it tough going at Monaco.

Growing up in the East. Jacques, with hair growing long, is pictured at the 1991 Macau Formula Three Grand Prix.

The student racer. Jacques said his year with TOM's Toyota was like a university year.

Brilliant pit work and astute tactics played a major part in Jacques'
Indianapolis 500 success.

On the way to a famous victory in the 1995 Indianapolis 500 with his
Player's Team Green Reynard.

Jacques during pre-season testing at Estoril in February 1997, with Frank Williams the man who brought him into Formula One. (above)

The 1997 Luxembourg Grand Prix at the Nurburgring, Germany.

Jacques just ahead of title rival Michael Schumacher during practice.

Jacques celebrates with Alesi and his team mate Frentzen on the podium.

On his way to victory.

Jacques and Schumacher before the start of the crucial 1997 European Grand Prix at Jerez in Spain.

Jacques is hoisted high by his Williams team mates in their 'Villeneuve wigs', having secured the 1997 World Drivers' Championship.

On the podium at Jerez.

but at Shannonville, he drove a Formula Ford 2000. Each proved to be part of a classic education for the track, if not for the classroom, but his racing career proper was to begin in a most unclassical fashion – through entering the Italian Touring Car Championship, driving an Alfa Romeo. Jacques' mother Joann had paid for him to go through the two racing schools and his uncle Jacques had played a prominent part also in arranging things. 'She very reluctantly decided that if he was going to pursue this career in the sport in which his father was killed, she didn't approve of it necessarily, but decided that she would give him all the help that she could,' said Donaldson. 'And she called on Patrick Tambay and some of Gilles' racing friends to advise her. They gave him help to get him off to a good start.'

Jacques himself was delighted and could not wait to prove himself. He had been karting in Canada with his uncle Jacques and had been given an opportunity to go karting in Italy, at the invitation of Paolo Moruzzi, who worked for SAGIS, the company which managed the Autodromo Enzo e Dino Ferrari at Imola, near Bologna. He had raced in karts several times in Canada. His first run in karts at Imola took place in early September 1985, when he was 14, and he was assisted by Luigi Buratti and his son Massimo, two Bologna-based karting and racing enthusiasts who worked with many youngsters attempting to break into Italian racing. They were also great fans of Gilles and were delighted to have the chance to supply the karts that would give their late hero's son his entry to motor sport.

'I always thought I would do it one day,' Jacques admitted later in an interview with Adam Cooper. 'Even when he was racing. Since I can remember, I wanted to do it myself . . . My mother and family were not happy at all. My mother would have preferred me as a mechanical or aerodynamic engineer or something. But she kind of helped me by letting me do what I wanted to do. It just seemed normal that I was doing it.

'I did one racing school, Jim Russell in St Jovite, when I was 15. Then I worked as a mechanic in the Spenard-David Racing School in Ontario for three months in the summer when I was 16. I made a few laps in the cars by working as a mechanic. The cars were Formula Ford 2000s with street radial tyres, not slicks.'

Later, talking about the same subject – his learning period – Jacques told Richard Williams, in an interview for *GQ* magazine, that his mother had really not wanted him to race at all. 'She was hoping I'd do something else. I don't know why, really. I don't think it was because she was scared that I'd get injured or anything. After all, for her it was a normal world. I think it's more that she was afraid I wouldn't succeed and that the pressure would be too much.'

It was during this period of his teenage life, on his regular summer trips to Canada, that Jacques – ostensibly a bespectacled Monaco-based European schoolboy – allowed his own lust for speed to enjoy some freedom for the first time by tearing off into the forests of Quebec on a motocross bike, usually alone and at very high speeds, according to Donaldson. This speed craze, however, had been there all the time, but it only rose to the surface from time to time as Joann, his mother, hinted.

Apparently, according to *Edition Special*'s focus magazine on Jacques, published in Montreal in 1996, the young driver knew exactly what he wanted to do from a very early age. When he was only three years old, every time he was asked what he would like to be in later life, he replied: 'A racing driver – just like my dad.' This comment was sourced to Joann who, it was reported, added that: 'Jacques and Gilles have always been very close. Gilles would bring toy cars to his son, who would then play with them for three, five, eight hours non-stop. In fact, they were the only toys he was really interested in.'

The same magazine continued to report on Jacques' school life immediately before he began his racing career and said he had two sons of presidents, those of Mobutu and Houphouet-Boigny, as companions, in addition to the French film actress Charlotte Gainsbourg. 'But he challenged discipline and authority,' it noted. 'And he did not always win these challenges and very often had to be disciplined.'

In this period of his life, from 14 in 1985 to 17 in 1988, young

Jacques' life was a mixture of terms at school in Switzerland, summer holidays in Canada, other vacations in Monaco or elsewhere and long reveries about racing, combined with excursions on any form of machine at speed that he could lay his hands on. Although he did not finish at the top of his class at school during this period, he was not one of the lowest achievers either. He was above average in French, mathematics and biology, but not bothered enough to work in many other subjects. One thing, however, above all else attracted his attention: computers.

'It is a fascinating world,' he said. 'And I like to take refuge in it as often as I can. As a mental exercise, I can easily spend 10 or 12 hours in front of my computer without getting tired.' In the mind of Jacques, it seems, computers and skiing are just parts of a modern-world method of preparation for racing, the taste for which was aroused in Jacques most noticeably on his trip to stay with his paternal grandparents in Canada in 1985. That summer, he went karting and racing at Sanais.

'He enjoyed this experience,' said Gabriel Gelinas, of the Jim Russell Racing School. 'And shortly afterwards, he came to our school. He said he wanted to see our cars. He was obviously interested by them and we told him to come back when he was a bit older. Well, of course, come back he did!'

When he returned, in 1986, Gelinas said: 'It was somehow the continuation of a tradition. Before him, his father Gilles and his uncle Jacques were taught at our school. I remember that Joann asked us to be very discreet. She did not want her son to be bothered by journalists. I do not really know how the *Journal de Montreal* got to know about it, but several days after Jacques left, his picture, driving a racing car, made the front page.'

For Jacques, it was a significant summer, but it was not one he passed through with ease. Not only did he have to master the tricky art of racing cars, but he also had to contend with a frustration that was to remain with him for the rest of his life – his diminutive size. When he first reached the Jim Russell School, he was found to be so short – at the age of 15 – that he could not reach the pedals. 'We had to bolt several blocks on top of the pedals and mould the seat so he could sit nearer the steering wheel,' said Gelinas. 'In spite of all this, he did show some promise. He handled his car very well and all his instructors thought he was naturally talented. He was not quite like the other students. In particular, I was very impressed when, on the third day, he had to drive on a wet track. He drove brilliantly. That is the least I can say.'

It was probably the driving sessions at the Jim Russell School that helped to convince Jacques that he had inherited his father's talents and that he had the ability, if he used it well, to become a serious racing driver. Gelinas agreed this was likely, but declined to compare the talents and abilities of father and son, a sensible decision when their eras are generations and decades apart. 'The driving style of the 1970s and the one prevailing today have nothing in common,' he said. 'It is as ridiculous as trying to compare Wayne Gretzky and Mario Lemieux with Maurice Richard. However, a good racing driver will always be a good racing driver. Jacques does not drive to be in his father's footsteps or to revive the family fortune. After his initial triumphs, we should all agree that his approach to racing is sound and reassuring.'

If any one figure played a major part in ensuring that Jacques made a sound transition from schoolboy karter to qualified racer, it was his uncle Jacques who set up the sessions at the Jim Russell School. 'He called us one day in 1986 and said he wanted to put his nephew through the school,' said Vince Laughran. 'I said it would be a fantastic idea and we agreed that we would keep the whole thing quiet and not put any pressure on him. There were no fanfares. He struck me as quiet and reserved, just like any other 15-year-old fellow. He did not give any impression of being a youngster who was aggressive and eager to go racing. He just took it all in, like a very attentive student. And that was the most impressive thing of all. You know, to try and get a 15-year-old to do anything for an hour and a half is very hard. But he was able to concentrate and we were just amazed at that. Maybe he had picked it up with his karting. He was in good shape and he had plenty of endurance.'

It was clear to all those at Mont Tremblant, once the home of the Canadian Grand Prix, that the young Jacques Villeneuve had the talent required to succeed. He applied it well, too. Sitting behind the wheel of a Formula Ford 1600 from Van Diemen, he ran through the full three-day programme without a hitch on the 2.65-mile track broken up by 11 corners which was used at the finish of the course. For most of the three days, the young students – including Jacques – worked on a shorter club circuit.

His performance left everyone impressed, including Laughran who said: 'Jacques can sit down and work through problems. He is a great test driver, he can work with engineers and he can work with just about everybody.'

Jacques and his uncle stayed at a local hotel while the course, which cost about 1,200 Canadian dollars, was taking place. Uncle Jacques took on the role of a caring father, but tried not to interfere, while his grandparents Seville and Georgette took serious interest too. 'I did what I could for him when he started out,' said uncle Jacques, modestly. 'But I did not have a lot to do with his early formative years. I only knew him when he was around 12 to 14 years old, just after his father died. I guess he saw me as a surrogate dad.

'He came from a family of racing. I took him to tracks here and there. I knew that he was going to be good, but even from an early age, he did not have a lot of interest in the mechanical side of cars. His father and I had always been tinkering with machines, but that did not interest Jacques. You knew that he had racing spirit in his blood, but he was not mechanically minded.

'Obviously, his mother was hoping that he would do something else, but we are all proud of what he has done and what he has achieved. Racing is something he can do and he is very good on his own. He has been that way since the age of 10 or 12, but he is doing very well.'

Given his chance to open up and speak on a subject close to his heart, uncle Jacques went on to touch on subjects which related to his nephew's career, his decision to move to Formula One and his all-round performances as man and driver. In a telephone interview, he said: 'My personal opinion of Formula One is that it is not as good racing as in Indycars. It is all about the car, rather than the driver, and it does not have the spectacle of Indycars. If you put Damon Hill or Jacques into an Arrows, they too would be at the back of the grid. When my brother was racing, the right car was not the most important thing. He won two Grands Prix because he was Gilles Villeneuve and that made it something important and special.

'My nephew sees racing as a business. It is not as deep in his blood as it was with his father or with myself. We two would drive anything and everything as hard and as fast as we could, 24 hours a day, seven days a week, but to Jacques, it is just a business. He may win one world championship and then go back to Indycars, but it will not be because he loves the sport. It will be because they will pay to have him back in the country. I would be surprised if he was still racing by the time he was 30 years old, because he does not race for the love of it.

'He started racing because of his dad. We all did. We all wanted to go fast and always have our foot on the floor. But, with Jacques, he lets his girlfriend drive to the races because he likes to relax. That is not a problem. It is what he likes to do, but it is not the way his father and I used to live.

'He got into Formula Three and he has made a name for himself in racing. But most of his success is because of the name of his father. He did not bring with him a lot of money to Italy, but because of the Villeneuves' name and legend, doors opened up for him that wouldn't have done otherwise. If he had had another name, there is no way he would have got where he is today. But that is not to put him down as a driver. He has a lot of skill and a lot of talent. But what I am saying is that he got his breaks because of his name.

'The Americans were interested in him as a marketing deal. Gilles would drive anything he could get his hands on. So will I. Jacques can push his car over the limit, when he wants to, but he will not do it too much. Schumacher will try in whatever car he has. He is a hell of a good driver. In my opinion, there were only three great drivers and, unfortunately, only one of them is still alive. Senna was killed two years ago and my brother was the third one. I think that if you could have put them together there would have been some wild racing. Jacques would not be able to keep up. He would be behind them, hoping that one of them would break down.

'Jacques will only fight to get into the points and then he will stop. He was not always like that – as I said, he can push a car a long way. But he did not like doing it. His opinion is that if he finishes 20th or something, there is nothing in that. But if he finishes sixth, he will get some points which will go towards the title and a lot of money. That is what is important, not the actual racing itself, to Jacques.

'Jacques did not do many races in karting. Gilles was always a hard pusher, but Jacques is quite different. When I was young, Gilles and I would go out in our Mustangs with no power, no brakes and so on. Now they have power steering, brakes . . . and cops. There is no fun any more.

'But Jacques was never a wild person outside the car either. I got him into street cars and put him on my lap when he was young and I was out in the car with him. I was not a hunter or a fisher, so that never happened either, but I did try to teach him about cars. He would always want to watch a video or television. He was not into girls at that age – he simply was not a girl-chaser.

'He was travelling a lot so he did not have too many friends who he saw a lot of, so he watched TV and he played games. You cannot force anyone to be different from that. That is what he wanted to do. He has always done what he wanted to do. Formula One was the right thing to do, with the right team at the right time. Maybe if he had left it another two years, he would not have been desirable in that category, but he did it at the right time.

'I follow his races on the television as much as I can, but I spoke to him around a month before the Canadian Grand Prix and I did not hear from him afterwards. I cannot understand that because I am a family man. He lives in Monaco, but not with his mother.

I have no idea how he got to be like that because we were always very close as a family and it saddens me a bit. But, that is what he wants to do. I cannot change him.'

Uncle Jacques' comments may reveal a sense of bitterness at the distance that has built up between him and his nephew since the early days when he put both Jacques and Melanie into karts on their long summer holidays with him and the family back in Quebec. They may also show a lack of knowledge, in depth, of the modern and rapidly developing Jacques Villeneuve who challenged so powerfully and drove so splendidly in his maiden Formula One season in 1996. Not interested in girls? This was manifestly not true, as many of Jacques' excursions into the night during that year (and several previous seasons, particularly when he was living in Tokyo and playing around with Mika Salo and Eddie Irvine) revealed.

But uncle Jacques was close to both Gilles and Jacques at different times and saw him through his learning phase as a driver. He was also the recipient of sums of 'sponsorship' from Jacques' father during the days when he was struggling to put together his racing programme while Gilles was thrilling Europe with his speed-crazed antics at Grands Prix.

'Nobody was supposed to know about the money that he gave me for my racing,' said uncle Jacques. 'I did not tell anyone, so he must have done. It was not a big deal compared to what he was earning. He was a sort of sponsor in the deal. If I needed $100,000 but I only had $95,000, then he would help me out with the last little bit. But it was not easy to get money out of him. I nearly had to break his arm off to get it!'

And then returning to Jacques, in a further outburst of his robust opinions, he added: 'To him, he does what he wants to do. He spends what he earns and he has a life. Why not? But he never had racing in mind. He just said that to please people. People say he was a zealous kid, that he had a steering wheel in his hands when he was born, but that is not the case. We brought him to it. He was still a natural, but he did not love the sport. When Gilles was 13 or 14, he had his head almost permanently buried in a book on Formula One, but not Jacques. Jacques only started to like it once he was pushed.

'Why did I push him into it? Why not? I am a racing person and I wanted everyone around me to be like that too. I had to work at him a little bit to get him interested. I got him a 5-horse power kart as a youngster and he and his sister would go off and race together. Actually, she was better than he was at the time, but that was not a problem for him as they were always close. She was a bit of a tomboy at that time and she was better behind the wheel. She took tidier lines through the corners than Jacques, who was then a little bit wild.

'It was not in his mind to race at all. That all came later. He was not even pleading to go racing after the first few times we took him. We would just say "Let's go racing" and he would say "Okay" and we would go. The competition with his sister was healthy. But they were always close and they looked after each other.'

Looking back, uncle Jacques could call upon a reservoir of memories. He recalled easily the musical interests which Jacques and Melanie inherited too. 'We had a piano,' he said. 'As you know, my father was a piano-tuner. They used to play on it together. It was not any specific tune or anything like that, they just played around. She was never super-good, but then you don't notice these things until they are 15 years old. They were only eight and ten then.

'Jacques was always very involved in things and he would always be trying to get into things. If he wanted to play on a computer, there was nothing that was going to distract him. I believe he has taken up the guitar this year, so no doubt that will keep him amused for hours on end. When we introduced him to karts, he had his mind set on motocross, so I suppose that was the reason he did not get too interested in karting until later. But he never came up to me and said "I want to drive cars." That was not what he wanted to do.'

Notwithstanding his remarks, uncle Jacques, it should be noted, was at the circuit when his nephew Jacques showed his true ability the first time in the wet on the third day of his Jim Russell course. Apparently, he walked around the track with a video camera as Jacques proved his speed by finishing up nearly six seconds quicker than all his fellow students. The chief instructor at the school was Gilbert Pednault, who said: 'He has natural car control. Taking into account that he's only just turned 15, and he has hardly ever seen a street car, I would say he's the best student I have ever seen. One doesn't want to get carried away by the Villeneuve name, but it's mind-boggling. It must be the genetics.'

At the end of this extraordinary three-day introduction to motor racing in Canada, Jacques was presented with his diploma by Pednault and, almost simultaneously, found himself the target of autograph hunters for the first time in his life. The other drivers on the course were the ones seeking his signature as his family closed in to congratulate him. He had taken the first step and he had found that his name, as much as anything he did, was to guarantee him much attention.

In the following year, 1987, he returned again to Canada, but instead of spending the summer with his family he went to Shannonville, Ontario, to the Spenard-David Racing School, set up by former Jim Russell man Richard Spenard. It was situated about 90 minutes' drive from Toronto. 'Jacques came for the summer and we had a mechanics' training programme, a kind of trade-off between manual work and racing where, in return for the work a pupil did in the garage, he was learning to drive and doing a series of tests and courses, and practice,' said Spenard. 'I have to admit Jacques didn't work much!'

Shortly after this summer trip to Ontario, the *Autosprint* magazine in Italy published a feature in which Jacques admitted 'I have contracted the family virus.' He blamed the infection on his uncle Jacques for showing him some cars in 1985, the year he also started to enjoy some serious kart racing, and he also revealed that he had impressed Spenard by driving uncle Jacques' Lamborghini Countach, adding 'I hope the Canadian police never find out!' This kind of risky, tongue-in-cheek humour, centred on his own audaciousness, was to remain his trademark for the decade that followed during which he would pull off stunts, including racing New York taxi-cabs for the David Letterman show on television, crashing road cars, being stopped for speeding and generally behaving with the abandon of someone with little or no respect for authority.

'People might think all I had to do was go to my mother to get the money,' wrote Jacques for *Autosprint*. 'But it wasn't like that at all. She opposed it and said it was much more important to continue my studies. An application form for the school arrived at home. She said nothing and threw it away, hoping it was only a summer infatuation of mine. I'd guessed the form might finish like that, so I'd asked for a copy to be sent to the college. By Christmas, and after a thousand complications, I obtained permission, but not the money. Fortunately, the owner of the school took me on as a mechanic and working at that paid for my driving lessons.'

Spenard reported to Christopher Hilton, for his book on Jacques Villeneuve called *In His Own Right*, that the young Canadian who came over from Europe that summer was 'playful, quiet, a little lazy and didn't like to get his hands dirty. As a matter of fact,' he added, 'there's a funny story. Most of the kids were working on the race cars, but because he didn't like to get his hands dirty, we ended up having him paint the garage. The guys realised that the garage was painted by Jacques Villeneuve so they're going to keep it that way for a long time.'

The school owner was amused also, as someone who knew Gilles Villeneuve well and who had in the past been a baby-sitter to Jacques, by the new boy's spoilt nature. 'Well, he had been raised in Monaco,' he explained. 'Obviously, he didn't have to worry too much about anything in his life, whereas his father had had a very different upbringing; but otherwise you could see he had some natural talent. Not polished – he was a spur of the moment kind of driver.'

And so he remained. Whatever advice he sought, or received, he did it his own way. Not for Jacques Villeneuve the comfort of a complete education behind him from Beau Soleil, but a fragmented incomplete schooling which included transatlantic forays into race schools as a prelude to his first serious competition in Italy.

'I spoke with Tambay a little bit, before I started racing,' Jacques admitted, when asked by Williams for *GQ* about his early days. 'But I don't think you can really learn from the others, because everybody's situation is different. The only way you can learn is by your own experience and making your own mistakes. Someone can tell you something, but once you're in the car, how can you transfer what you've been told? Everything happens so quickly. You have to be able to understand your own mistakes, to feel what you can do to correct them. That's the only way to progress to the next level . . . Anyway, I hardly ever do what I'm told just because I'm told.'

Chapter Seven

Italy, The Young Apprentice:
1988–1991

'I think I have been in good schools. Racing in Italy, in Formula Three, and then in Japan, and then in north America, you see different places, you work with different mentalities and racing is so different. You learn to work your way up and to work really strongly. It's so important to just commit yourself 100 per cent. Even if you have problems, just let it drop. Work hard. Work hard until it gets better.'

This was Jacques Villeneuve speaking on the record to Toni Toomey for the *Eurosport* Indy Car magazine. His old teachers and schoolfriends at Beau Soleil in Villars would have fainted. The notion, to them, of seeing Jacques work hard until something got better may have been difficult to believe; to them, he was the boy who always seemed to want to contest the inevitable, fight for extra time in bed and dodge the worst jobs of the rota!

But it was true, Jacques Villeneuve did pass through some very good schools of motoring on his way from kart-racing enthusiast in Quebec, while still a chubby-cheeked schoolboy, to the highest echelons of single-seater circuit racing. But probably his most bizarre experience – and certainly the most extraordinary item to be found on a detailed study of his curriculum vitae – was to begin racing in the Italian Touring Car Championship of 1988. In that year, while still studying at the College in the Alps, he took part in three races in an Alfa Romeo 33 for the Salerno Corse team. His results, for a boy of just 17 making his competitive debut in the final races of a competitive series, were unremarkable, but not disgraceful. He finished 10th on his debut at Pergusa, failed to finish after an accident at Monza two weeks later on October 9, and then ended up 14th at Imola in the final round. It was a fair effort for a boy who only a short while before had been learning his way round with Spenard-David.

Italy, of course, was always going to fling open every door and almost every bank for another Villeneuve. They loved him, the name, the legend and the emotion which came flooding back. Every Italian could remember Gilles Villeneuve in a Ferrari and each one of them would weep, if moved to, at their own recollections of his wildest and most extraordinary stunts in the famous scarlet cars. From the start, it was clear to Jacques and his family, friends and followers that attracting sponsors was never going to be a serious problem. The really serious problem was going to be choosing the right ones and, even more fundamentally, obtaining a driving licence.

In 1988, at the tender age of 17, he was a full year away from the minimum age requirements of the Italian and Canadian authorities for qualification for an international competition licence. Typically, however, Jacques showed resourcefulness under pressure and chose to apply through Andorra, though it reportedly required the intervention of, and assistance from, the Canadian Automobile Federation to ensure he could take part in his first outing for his team, Salerno Corse, at Pergusa.

The fact that, by this age, the young Villeneuve had developed in stature enough to be regarded as an identikit version of his father did nothing to diminish the pressure on him. He was, quite simply, similar enough to encourage all this balderdash, as if it mattered, even though their backgrounds and approaches were not only different, but separated by generations. Physically, when Jacques began to race, he shared the same kind of short, muscular physique as his father, showed the same kind of direct, honest approach which suffered no fools and took no hostages and, notably, showed no signs of fear or intimidation in any circumstances. He drove with his head more than his right foot, but that was his only appreciable alteration from his father's example.

He had learned well from his early karting outings in Canada and in Italy, he had taken on board the lessons of the Jim Russell school and Spenard-David and he was intent on doing his best in his first real contests in late 1988. His approach, while not as spectacular to watch as his father's (he did not go in for the same sliding, the destruction of cars), proved to be no slower and he made a reputation quickly for being rapid and sensible. At least those who watched him carefully realised this even if the media, in some quarters, chose to highlight his mistakes, the first normal mistakes made by any young driver. Jacques, however, despite all the pressure on him because of his name, never made the same mistake twice and also seemed to flourish under the extra pressure of being a Villeneuve. Indeed, it could be that he actually found that additional stress may have accelerated his progress as a driver when he moved into the highly competitive Formula Three series in Italy for three seasons from 1989.

His initial experiences driving that Group N Alfa 33 were not among those he has wished to preserve and recall on a regular basis later in his career. 'I did three races, but I don't call that racing,' he told Adam Cooper for *Autosport*. 'It was just touring around. It was the most shitty car I ever drove. I finished the first race, but just by taking the kerbs, the car was all smashed in. I prefer to forget about it.'

He was inexperienced and burdened with a reputation, a name, which was not of his making and the pressure was a big factor for him. But he loved driving cars fast and this, above all, burned in him and pushed him on. He felt a bigger buzz, a stronger adrenaline charge, than he did when he was skiing. For Jacques, this was it, the real thing. He had, of course, gained his Canadian driving licence the previous year, but had to wait a full 12 months and more to gain his European qualifications. It was frustrating, but it helps to explain why he entered the Italian

Touring Car championship more than a year after his visit to work with Spenard-David.

The delay (for that is how it must have seemed to Jacques) was a nuisance, but not something that could not be overcome with a little imagination and, according to a feature in *Arena* magazine in 1996, some stealthy runs through the streets of Monte Carlo in borrowed cars. 'Pinching the keys to his mother's Fiat Uno, he would career around the streets of the little principality, following the circuit he had seen his father Gilles take in the Grands Prix,' the magazine reported. 'Like many boy racers before him, the romance of Monaco, with its world-famous straights and corners, eclipsed any sense of responsibility. Flooring it around Tabac and Casino Square, screaming along Portier and the tunnel section, he would push the dinky 1000cc hatchback to the limit.'

Jacques had an explanation for his enthusiasm, of course. 'I didn't see any reason why I shouldn't,' he said. 'When you are that age, a car is there to be driven and the road is a race track. Everything is a big game.' Apparently, Joann was not too hard on him when he was caught finally and she later even helped him to buy a muscle-bound Chevrolet Camaro as an upgrade from the Fiat, *Arena* reported.

Stories about Jacques and his cars, his accidents and his escapades were legion in Italy around this time as he began to grow and take to the roads. According to several sources within PreMa and the RJ Reynolds' Camel organisation that was to back his Formula Three breakthrough, he was learning to drive and survive at the same time on the Italian roads, but with a sometimes scary, and exciting, record of successes and narrow misses.

One source said of Jacques' Italian adventures: 'At first, Jacques used to travel by train. As he started racing in 1988, even before he had come of age, he could not obtain an Italian driving licence. He was allowed to race in the Touring Car championship thanks to the existence of a Canadian licence (it has been said that the Canadians only supported him because his original event was a race involving foreigners, rather than a true international-class event). His first European road car, in 1989, was a Fiat Uno turbo, which he first drove to a race event on April 2, at Vallelunga (his first Italian Formula Three event) and that was to last only until Sunday evening, when he crashed it on the way home to Monte Carlo. This was followed by a Peugeot 205 GTI, which had a not-much-longer and more troubled life. Finally, the glorious Chevy Camaro . . . Jacques was extremely proud of it and sometimes he would fool around with it in a garage. Eventually, unfortunately, the Camaro ended up banana-shaped as Jacques had taken up the dangerous habit of driving round a roundabout as fast as he could and clearly, one day, he went over the limit as he hit the inner wall.'

According to the Italians, all this was just a normal part of the Jacques Villeneuve development pattern, just as his tampering with his helmet design was also to be an attractive topic of gossip among the frenzied observers following his career as he made his first tentative steps into motor racing. 'Jacques started his racing career flying his father's colours on his helmet,' said one. 'Then, together with the Fiat Uno turbo came the new colour scheme, the one with the "acid" stripes.' It was quickly dubbed 'tropical' by his experienced team-mate Antonio Tamburini, while other people at the famous Vallelunga event wondered – many of them aloud – if he had taken the helmet from a drug addict. He has retained more or less the same helmet scheme ever since.

For Jacques, at this early time in his racing career, there were many facets of the business to learn and understand, not least money and sponsorship and coping with the demands of his curious army of fans. His first contact with car racing, in the Touring Car Championship, came courtesy of *Autosprint* magazine in Italy, which sponsored his programme in the Alfa 33. 'Needless to say,' said one of the Italian reporters around at the time, 'Jacques could not make very good use of the machinery. In particular, he is remembered for using bumpers instead of brakes!'

Jacques himself said at the time of his deal with *Autosprint* and Salerno Corse that he wanted to be treated as normally as possible. 'This year, I'll enter the racing world seriously in the Alfa 33 and next year I'd like to do single seaters. I don't know if I'll compete in Formula Three or Formula Opel Lotus. I hope to be able to establish good relationships with the other drivers, especially the young ones, because although my name is Villeneuve, I'm just a boy like them who, when going to sleep, thinks of nothing but cars and races. I must also keep the promise I made to my mother to continue studying until I graduate.' He was, sadly, unable to do as he wanted on either point. He left school early, before completing his education, and he left Italy behind him in 1991 with a tiredness in his voice as he told Angelo Rosin, of PreMa, his Formula Three team: 'I must leave Italy behind me. Wherever I go, people used to remind me of my father. They always want to make comparisons.'

The foray into the Italian Touring Car championship coincided with his last full term at Beau Soleil, but it did nothing for his reputation as either a driver or as a student. Talking about Jacques' career in Italy, at this time, the journalist Julian Thomas wrote: '*Autosprint* organised a competition for young drivers in Alfa Romeos and Jacques was given the opportunity to do the last three races. Absolute disaster. He smashed the car up virtually every time he drove it and it had to go back to the bodyshop.'

Once the disastrous opening gambit of Touring Cars was behind him, the still very young Jacques moved on to Formula Three with the PreMa team, for 1989, and the sponsorship came from an unlikely source, but one that both the team and the young Villeneuve were pleased to accept. 'At the end of that first year, it was time to step into Formula Three,' recalled one Italian reporter. 'Marlboro was not eager to take up the initiative because the people in Lausanne feared that it would have looked like an over-exploitation of the Villeneuve name. Camel, on the contrary, was ready to take the risk. Villeneuve was accompanied by his mother and his first manager when he met the Reynolds–Camel people in Rome, in the office of CSAI's general-secretary Mr Erasmo Saliti. Negotiations resulted in a three-year deal with PreMa.'

The same source recalled, in detail, another morsel of interest to those who followed Jacques' 1996 Formula One scrap with Damon Hill for the Formula One world drivers' championship.

'When he failed to qualify at the 1991 Formula Three race in Monaco, the Italian daily *Corriere della Sera* wrote "This is the result of Camel's policy of supporting a driver with an illustrious name and no talent at all". In the same race, Damon Hill was another dnq [did not qualify]'.

And so, Jacques Villeneuve, with the help of a manager who was apparently, according to Patrick Tambay, 'a guy in Monte Carlo, who I think was a lawyer', went into Formula Three. The director of his team, PreMa, was Giorgio Piccolo. He said: 'The first time we met was in 1989. I remember one time I was standing outside the Monte Carlo circuit, with him and Antonio Tamburini, who was the team's other driver, at my side. At the time, Jacques had already expressed his will to be a racing driver.

'In fact, I knew he had attended the Jim Russell school in Canada and supported himself doing menial jobs and so on to get by. But what struck me most about him was that he seemed unable to recognise the cars as they zoomed by. Yes, he could say that the red one over there was a Ferrari, because you cannot ignore that, and maybe also because it had been his father's car, but apart from this, he was an absolute zero! Tamburini and I were laughing at him. "Now you say you want to be a racing driver and you cannot tell one F1 car from the other?" But it was just the way he was at the time.

'We took him to Fiorano, the Ferrari test track, for a first evaluation test. And I quickly realised that he had absolutely not a clue how you drive a Formula Three car around a track. We had to start from scratch, from the basics. He would just try to steer the thing in by sheer force, with no idea whatsoever about ideal lines and this sort of stuff. As a result, obviously, he was slow. But later on, when I could have a look at the sort of system we used at the time, and that in a way could be called telemetry, we saw that despite all this he managed to be really quick through the fast corners.

'That's where I saw he had a talent that could be taken out of him. Otherwise, it would have been useless.'

Angelo Rosin, the technical director of the PreMa team at the time, said he was surprised that Villeneuve even attempted to go straight into Formula Three, pointing out that it is not the 'usual route' to begin a career in Formula Three. 'All he'd done was a little karting, but he was not at any professional level. Quite suddenly, he came to Formula Three because there were people around him who believed that that name and that boy could be good for them in a promotional sense.'

Rosin endorsed some of the many impressions among Italians that Jacques was out of his depth in Formula Three and that he was attempting to learn, on a steep curve, as he went along. He said that Camel paid for the budget for most of the season and that this was the chief reason why PreMa signed the young Villeneuve. 'Anyway, we got a driver who knew almost nothing. It was difficult and it was all a question I kept asking myself. But it was a big challenge to try and take this complete novice and make something of him. He was so young! When he first tested, in December 1988, he didn't even know how to use the gears!'

To help build up his knowledge, confidence and ability, Jacques spent some time at the Magione Driving School with Henry Morrogh. Morrogh found the experience an enlightening and, at times, entertaining one. He said, 'At that time, we had Jacques at our track just to teach him the basics of our job. Well, he was absolutely incredible. He would insist on braking so late that he missed the braking point by four or five metres. And then the car, it was the PreMa Formula Three, developed understeer as he tried to turn in and the lap times showed it. As for settings, he would go the same way. So, we tried to explain to him that driving was not only a last-second braking affair, but that by braking earlier he could have steered through a fine line and therefore be quicker on coming out of the corner.

'He would listen to all the explanations, but Lord, he was a stubborn kind of fellow, wasn't he? It took us a long time just to persuade him that what he was doing was wrong. We also took Tamburini's lap times and driving style as a reference and we told Jacques, "Look, he is doing this and he is doing that and he is quicker than you – and he is the experienced guy. So, why don't you try to do the same?" Well, we needed patience. So, we started by anticipating the braking point by just a little bit and then more and more, and in the end the lap times would just come as if by a miracle. And then Jacques was persuaded too. But despite being so nice with all of us, he wasn't the sort of guy that you can quickly talk into doing something different.'

Learning the ways of Formula Three was to be a trying and tiring process for Jacques. He stayed three years in the Italian Formula Three championship before flying to Japan to take on another year of the same, having escaped from the pressure-cooker atmosphere which he felt followed everywhere he went in Italy, simply because of his name. It was to be in Japan that things really changed fast for him, where he learned about playing around on the streets at night in Tokyo and where he learned, as he put it, to behave like a student. But all this came later, after he had graduated without flying colours from Giorgio Piccolo's team.

'When he came to Italy, for racing,' said Piccolo, 'he had not grown his hair long into that ponytail which he was to have later on, in Japan. I remember, however, that even at that time, he was afraid of balding – I have been told that his father was the same. So we at the team would sometimes make a fool of him by joking about this. When he came to the track, for example, after a certain period of time, we looked at him and said: "Hey, Jacques, what about this? You seem to have become a little thinner here at the top . . ." and this would just set him into a sort of panic.

'He would dress more or less as he does now. I mean the "grunge" type of appearance. At that time, he hardly had a dollar in his pockets when he came to see us. He was living with his mother, who as far as I know was not very happy in those early days about him becoming a racing driver. Instead, she would have preferred him to become a doctor or something, to finish his school in Switzerland, which Jacques didn't do. But he just quit school because of his passion, while getting by pretty well in such matters as literature and so on. He's a clever guy. He always has been! Anyway, Joann would give him just enough money for the train fare, lest he would squander all the money he had on buying

CDs and that sort of thing. He was an avid music fan, just as he is now. All kinds of music.

'Once he had taken on the basics of racing, he developed his skill to the full extent. His best race with us was at Monza, when he was leading and about to win before being rammed by Niko Palhares at the second chicane, Roggia. Niko simply didn't brake. He was just trying to go for it, but he hit the rear of Jacques' car and sent him into a spin. Palhares' car was a write-off, but Jacques managed to recover and he finished third. Right after he had crossed the finish line, he came out of the car and started staring at me, leaning against a gate.

'I came around with a bottle of water. He looked at me and he said: "Now, he's a real arsehole." It was the only comment he made. He never had rows with the other drivers. Only once, I remember, he went over to see a guy who had held him off during practice, sort of cruising around in a very dangerous way. He went to him and he shouted something at him in French, which the poor guy probably did not understand.

'In general, though, he had the utmost respect for the other drivers. The point is, he was convinced he was being very slow at the time. So, whenever he saw another car coming in his mirrors, he just pulled off the track and onto the grass for fear of hampering the other guy. We tried to explain to him that it wasn't the way to do it. We said, "Fine, you must bear respect for the others, but don't let them abuse you or you won't be given any respect in return." Then he would reply, "Listen, I don't want all the guys around here to think that I can bloody well do what I want simply because my name is Villeneuve." Again, I had to explain to him that if he kept his line and stuck to the rules, it was okay. No one would think such things about him and his name.

'Later on, I must say, he seemed to develop a much clearer vision of the race and he seemed to know his rivals pretty well. I remember a race in Vallelunga, back in 1990. He was starting from the second row of the grid with Zanardi in front of him. Our other driver, Roberto Colciago, was way back on the grid, in 16th place. But Roberto had a chance to win the championship. So, we briefed

Jacques like this: we told him: "You must get ahead of the other two guys at the start and keep holding them off (actually, we said, literally, "bitch them") in order to make them lose time to allow Roberto to come through." He obeyed the orders to the letter, pulled away at the start and in the first 15 of the 38 laps, he steadily broke the lap record, while Colciago was charging from the back of the grid.

'Eventually, Jacques got a one-minute penalty, but up to then he had done exactly what we wanted him to do, showing that he could understand tactics. He may have had a reputation as a shunt-maker, but with us he never had a big one except once in Vallelunga when he really destroyed the car and another occasion, in Pergusa, when he went straight through a chicane. But, in general, he had a certain respect for the mechanical stuff and, in due course, he developed a good understanding of the machinery.

'In fact, I can recall one of the few times when I saw him really pissed off. It was at Fuji and at the time he had Mimmo Schiattarella as a team-mate. I noticed that he was in a bad mood and I took him away with me to eat something. I asked him what the trouble was all about and, finally, he burst out and said, "It's the race engineer . . . I mean, I have been working with him now for three years and he won't listen to me. He won't bother about the way I want the car to be set up and he insists on making me drive Schiattarella's car." '

This sort of complaint came about because Jacques, as he was to later in Formula One, often wanted his cars set up in a particular way that was special to him and paid scant heed to other drivers' or engineers' views. Piccolo went on: 'About his ideal settings for the car, when he was with us, he wanted a car that was stiff enough and quick, in that it could slide across the track, without being "glued" onto the tarmac surface. What he required was a front end that he could turn in easily and he was happy. He used to say, "If the back slides all over the place, no problem. I can master that. But I've got to put my wheels exactly where I want them."

'I often get asked about Jacques' behaviour with his team-mates. All I can say is that I think he doesn't give a damn about that [his relationship with his team-mates]. If the guy's quick, fine. Otherwise, it's the same thing. He had several team-mates when he was driving with us and no one ever seemed to trouble him. He went his way and that's it.

'And he also dismissed all the rumours about team orders, the different equipment and so on. When we had Alessandro Zampedri, he was always complaining that the team was too supportive to Jacques and he was not getting equal treatment, which, obviously, was not true. Jacques was different.

'He would say, "I think you're giving me the best material that is available and I will try to make the best of it, irrespective of who my team-mate is or how quickly he goes." Well, I don't think it was a calculated attitude. It's just his nature. He doesn't care. Hence, stories have been created about him psychologically destroying his team-mates – but I believe it is just Jacques' character.

'He may be naive, in a way, but he will just say what he thinks. And I think he has carried the same attitude right through his career, all the way to Formula One with the Williams team and with Damon Hill. When he says something like "I hope Damon will mess up his start tomorrow", he is not testing his nerves. He's simply expressing his wishes.'

It was in the hard school of these races in Formula Three in Italy that Jacques also began to learn more of the world. Despite the fact that he was well-travelled and had been exposed to many different places and cultures, he remained as unrefined in many respects as his father had been before him when he was first racing in Europe, with Ferrari.

Piccolo explained: 'When he first came to Italy, Jacques impressed us with his manners. He really was very kind to everyone, although he was a little on the shy side too. Also, we thought, living abroad had taught him how to behave. He was a man of the world. In a way. But, like many drivers, he liked to be pampered and to live cosily.

'At first, he spent some time at my house and I well remember the first time he took a shower. There was water splashing all over the place. It was out of control. His room was always a total mess, too. And when he undressed, at his place or in the team's transporter, he would always toss all of his clothes around. He once had a team-mate, who I won't name, who was very particular. Every time his turn came to climb into the truck to put his overalls on, he was horrified to find that Jacques' underwear was hanging there, or just thrown away in some strange place.

'Jacques also had some habits with food which needed to be corrected at once. He ate the American way. He seemed to be particularly fond of junk food smothered in heavy sauces. But once he had realised the importance of proper nutrition, he took to stuff like pasta with enthusiasm. He was never difficult about his meals anyway.

'As a person, he liked to read books, especially the historical sort . . . particularly those with plots set in the Middle Ages and so on. But he hardly ever commented on such matters as politics or religion. He also hardly ever referred to his father, except when we talked about other drivers and the respect question. But once I recall having spotted him wearing a badge – just a piece of some black tape – on his nose before he donned his balaclava for a race. It was not the sort of breathing aid that is used today, but just a regular bandage. I asked him why he did it and he replied: "My father used to do the same." He didn't give any further explanation and as far as I recall it was the only time he referred directly to something that Gilles had done.'

In his first year with PreMa, the results were unworthy of record (they appear at the back of this book), but the time was spent helping Jacques learn about motor racing. 'He was not an aggressive driver,' said Rosin, team manager and technical director at PreMa. 'But if there was a fight on the track, he would not be the first to brake. In fact, if there was fighting to be done, he would get involved. But he wasn't the kind of driver who pushed others off or anything like that. His first year was just a learning year. It was his first opportunity to drive a racing car. He needed that year just to understand it all. He had to learn about the car and the tracks. The second year, he was able to fight with his team-mate without any problems. Remember, he was competing in a championship with 50 cars in it. It was very competitive and he did very well.'

Standards and, indeed, finances were high in Italy at this time and Jacques had to contend with drivers like Alessandro Zanardi (who made such a good job of switching from Formula One to Indycar racing in 1996) while he struggled with the basics like starting well – he often slipped the clutch and stalled – and coping with the unfair media pressure heaped on him because of his family name.

'He was a clever driver. He still is,' said Rosin. 'He was really clever on choice and what he is showing now and has done for the last two or three years is what he learned in Italy with us in Formula Three. He is getting better and better.

'I always thought he was different to his father in that he did not drive only with his heart. He was always talking with the engineers, trying to find solutions to the problems of the car and, when there was a problem, he would be there until late at night to find the right solution. It was important for him to show that he was not like his father.

'Gilles was faster. Jacques was not faster than his father, but he was fast in his own way. For him, the adoration of the public for his father was not a problem. Jacques is just another person. He was pretty quiet. He stayed with me sometimes and it was easy to see that the name Villeneuve opened doors for him.

'I think he was fast in his second year and unlucky in his third year. In one or two races, he was pushed off by other drivers when he could have scored some good results. In 1990, there was Zanardi, Angelleli and some other really good drivers and he had their respect. They had some good races together. They all respected each other.

'None of those guys had any problems with his name. But then he never considered it as a major issue for himself, not in the way the public did. He just wanted to drive and if the others had a problem with him being a Villeneuve then that was their problem not his problem. I think, sometimes, there were a few other drivers who did not treat him fairly, but Jacques had to put up with that.'

So, from a boisterously supported début at Vallelunga with the Venice-based PreMa team, when he was part of what the Italians called the 'yellow table' because of the Camel cigarette company's backing, Jacques graduated through three seasons of hard-learning lessons. Accidents and incidents were par for the course for him, as one of the few well-backed drivers in the category, in his opening season in his Reynard-Alfa Romeo. During this time he failed to qualify five times and did not finish three out of 11 races, including the Monaco race. His other results were 19th at Misano, 16th at Imola and 10th at Pergusa.

For Piccolo, it was a frustrating experience but at least a rewarding one financially, thanks to Camel. And Jacques had the consolation of learning and progressing. But the results were there to be seen in the following season when Piccolo, who had the habit of buying delicious fresh pastries and cakes after good results by his cars, was finally sent to the bakers'! Jacques gained his first points at Pergusa and then, at Binetto in July, he went within a whisker of victory. He ended up second, his natural talent overcoming his relative inexperience with the aid of all his newly-acquired knowledge, much of it being the sort of knowledge that other drivers gain on their way through at much lower levels of the sport.

In the 1990 season, his second, he scored ten points and finished up 14th in the drivers' championship, having qualified for all 12 races over the length and breadth of the Italian peninsula, and often when up against difficulties which would have been a serious problem for lesser men. His best results were second at Binetto on July 8, fifth at Imola in June and that long-awaited sixth place at Pergusa in April, just six days after his 19th birthday. He may have turned 18 in the previous season, but it was in 1990 that Jacques came of age on the track by qualifying for every race and failing to finish only four of them.

As a result, he was mentioned among the pre-season favourites for the title in 1991. This, however, was a false dawn as the team, catastrophically, stayed with the Reynard chassis that had taken Roberto Colciago to the title in the previous year (thanks, of course, in no small part to Jacques' efforts at Vallelunga in October, where he had finished first on the road). After three disappointing outings, which saw Jacques fail to finish twice and then come home eighth, the Reynard was replaced by a Ralt, but it was too late to save the title. For Jacques, however, even though he did not win, the switch offered an opportunity to demonstrate his burgeoning, if still inconsistent, talent and panache, particularly on the full-sized classical circuits, like Monza and Imola, where he took pole position, the first of his career, in a most impressive fashion on June 1. It reaped impressive rewards – three podium finishes, including his 'lost' victory at Monza in September, where Palhares' lunge wrecked his hopes of a maiden victory. He finished sixth overall with 20 points, but the harvest of the year was again mostly in encouraging hints rather than in hard results. At Imola, for example, Jacques learned how vital it is to make a good start and to exploit that advantage and ended up finishing fourth behind the victorious Luca Badoer, another young driver on his way towards a brief career in Formula One.

Badoer had begun his Formula Three career alongside Jacques in 1989 and admitted, during an interview at Hockenheim in 1996, that 'he didn't make much of an impression on me.' He explained, 'In Italy, at that time, it was very hard for a driver in Formula Three because there was 50 cars and 20 of these were driven by experienced men. It was difficult. The same for me as for Jacques, but he stayed with the same team, PreMa Racing, for three years, while I kept changing!

'We were quite good friends. We would talk, mostly about cars and stuff. His Italian was not at all perfect at the beginning! But he soon picked it up and it got better very quickly. My memory of him then is of a nice guy, very *simpatico*, very simple and easy to know, but also a little bit crazy in a good kind of way. I liked him.

'That victory at Vallelunga is still a beautiful memory for me, if not for Jacques, because I was in a new car. I felt wonderful. I did think about him sometimes. There was always a crowd of journalists around him, asking all the time about his father. I think that was not nice for him. His father was my hero when I was young, too. I don't think he liked to talk about his father at that time, but the Italian press creates a lot of pressure on drivers, even in Formula Three. I can understand why he went to Japan . . . He was a strong character, but you could always have a joke with him. We spent most of our time together at the circuit and we did not go to the discos much at all. He did not seem that kind of guy to me. He had no special friends or girlfriends then, not that I can remember anyway. He was just a guy doing his job.'

In 1991, his season consisted of 15 races and only one failure to qualify marred the record. That came at Varano, while he also failed to finish three times, one of those occasions was the Monaco F3 event, where he impressed in qualifying (all the practice runs in his mother's car may have helped!) and led the times for much of an exciting session, which took place on the tenth anniversary of his father Gilles' famous victory.

Unfortunately, his race at Monte Carlo ended after only five laps when an impatient young Frenchman, Laurent Daumet, made an impulsive and ill-judged dive to pass at the chicane and ruined both their races. At the end of the season, however, he made up for this in some way by flying east, to Macau and Fuji, for the two traditional end-of-year Formula Three events, where he was to finish eighth each time.

Jacques' own assessment of his Italian years was given to Adam Cooper in *Autosport* in 1992. 'I was lucky because PreMa is one of the best teams,' he explained. 'The first year was really good for experience. I was one second off the pace for most of the year and was not qualifying with that. That was really good for learning. To be a second off the pace – and still to have to push hard to qualify on the last row!

'The second year, everything went much easier. I was qualifying on the third row at most races. I don't know why, but I was a second faster without pushing harder. After one year, everything came better in my head, I guess! Everything was easier and maybe I was more relaxed. I got my first point in Pergusa, which was the second race of the season, and then in Bari (Binetto), I finished second to my team-mate Bugatti.

'But in 1991, we just couldn't understand the car. We switched to the Ralt for the fourth race. We received the car one week before the race and didn't have any testing and it didn't go well. Then we had Monaco the week after. There it went better. My team was really surprised because we qualified third. And then, in the race, some idiot French driver ran into me and we both finished our races at the chicane . . .'

Jacques also revealed his passion and his feelings at the second Monza race where he led for so long before being thwarted so violently. Cooper said he had been 'taken out after leading all the way' and Jacques said, 'I got out of the sandtrap and still managed to finish third. I was so pissed off when I crossed the finish line that I banged the steering wheel and broke my hand.'

After this, he went on to discover that in Macau and Fuji he was under less pressure and had a better opportunity to forge his career. It was on this trip that he performed with more control than previously, showing hints of the ability that would shine in the future, and it was there that he met a pack of his young contemporaries from around the world, whose paths were to cross his (including the triumphant Macau winner David Coulthard, driving for Paul Stewart Racing, whose seat at Williams was to be taken by Jacques in 1996).

'For 1992,' said Jacques, 'We were supposed to do F3000 for PreMa. But the money was lacking. We also thought about doing another F3 season, but I had a good offer from TOM's Toyota when I was in Macau. I thought about it in Fuji and after I got back to Europe I decided to go to Japan for two reasons. One, because it was TOM's Toyota, which might be good for the future, and also because the F3 championship is nearly as good as the Italian one. It's better than the English, French and German. And I was tired of being in Europe.

'If I wanted to go up in Europe, I would have had to bring money for F3000, which is not racing professionally. You're never sure to find it anyway. And only if you're in one of the few top teams can you win . . . '

It was understandable that after this first flight east he decided to leave Italy and to move on, in 1992, to race in Japan. It was a chance to start anew and to enjoy the growing-up experiences which the Italian spotlight had made such a tortuous undertaking for him. For Jacques, it was like going away to college.

Chapter Eight

Japan, College Days and a Few Crazy Nights: 1992

Tokyo. Bright night lights and flashing filters, speed, noise and people everywhere. It is the kind of city that young men get lost in, especially in the Roppongi district, but in which some can find themselves. Jacques Villeneuve was one who went there and did this, the opportunity to race in a series which attracted him, and in a country which would give him some respite from his surname and the attendant publicity it always attracted, persuading him to sign to race for the TOM's Toyota team. It was a decision which had a major influence on his life.

His racing was to produce improved results, his social life became his own with a new group of friends away from the claustrophobia of the European media and the Monaco 'set' and he found a new way to enjoy life. He found freedom. And, during the course of the season, he discovered not only the growing up, independent experiences – which young men and women have done for generations – but also the benefits of having a reliable and helpful manager in Craig Pollock, the former head of sport at Beau Soleil in Villars. The former teacher had, by 1992, moved into commercial and promotional work around motor sport (Madame de Meyer suggested his first job was with Honda) and he was in Japan, where he met Jacques again in the paddock at Suzuka.

By now, an easy-going, free-wheeling, but still sometimes diffident Jacques, who had shed his mother's protective influence and transformed himself at the same time into a scruffy student-like kid of the future, was wearing baggy clothes, granny spectacles and had hair long enough to reach his shoulders. He was also committed to becoming a racing driver and sharing his time in Tokyo and around the circuits with contemporaries like Mika Salo, Tom Kristensen, Eddie Irvine and Rickard Rydell, all of whom returned to Europe to establish their reputations and careers more firmly after being in Japan.

When Jacques bumped into Pollock in Japan, they reportedly agreed to go for a meal and they talked over old times, their skiing adventures in Switzerland, where Pollock lived and ran his business. Two weeks later, Pollock was surprised when, after returning to Europe, Jacques appeared in his office. 'He tried to convince me that he was going to be a great driver and that I should become his manager on the spot,' Pollock recalled, according to the *Daily Mail*. 'I told Jacques no, but he proceeded to come back three times to insist that I did what he wanted. He said: "Listen, I want you to manage me. I'm lucky and if you manage me some of that luck will rub off on you too." '

Eventually, however, the stubborn and persistent young Ville-neuve talked him round. 'As it turned out, it hasn't all been luck,' said Pollock. 'He's worked very hard for his success. He is very sure of his capacities and he is extremely strong-willed. That is probably the strongest characteristic that people don't see. He is highly competitive in anything he does, whether it is skiing, computer games, basketball, tennis or racing. He just hates being second.' In fact, it is likely that Jacques' first approaches to Pollock were made the previous year at the 1991 Monaco Grand Prix.

Pollock was to be an influence, of course, but it was the Japanese experience itself which helped shape Jacques and which gave Jacques the chance to shape his own life. He raced in the All Japan Formula Three series and this gave him vital new lessons in driving. But, more importantly, in the overall scheme of his life, he lived alone in an apartment in Tokyo, increased his levels of self-discovery and self-sufficiency and learned how to become comfortable with himself and his life. He began to read avidly, particularly science fiction and escapist fantasies, listen to music and collect a wide range of compact discs of his favourite rock music and to play both the piano and the trumpet. According to one source, a feature article in *F1 News*, written by Gerald Donaldson, he also linked his computer in Tokyo to a keyboard and wrote his own music to accompany the lyrics based on his personal thoughts and experiences. These were inklings that the intense intelligence that had been left unchallenged in an academic sense since Villars was to guide him, in the future, in all sorts of unexpected new directions. As *Arena* magazine put it, in its report in 1996, 'Villeneuve was different, a first-generation, fast-lane Nintendo kid. He was a charger like his dad, but instead of a brain, he had a 64-bit nervous system of fibre-optic tagliatelle between his ears.' No wonder *Wired* magazine called him 'the ultimate man–machine interface'.

It is difficult to know why Jacques turned out as he did. A combination of talent, intelligence and interest seems the most likely reason, but some observers have speculated that Jacques' strong sense of individualism and his rather exotic range of interests, his dress sense and his insularity, all come from the allegedly troubled relationship he had with his father, however brief it was. It has been reported frequently that the adult Gilles put great pressure on his young son Jacques and that the boy could barely function when they were together. Jacques, however, told Richard Williams for *GQ* in 1996 that he did not remember any of that.

'I know it because my mother told me,' he admitted. 'But personally, I don't remember. Maybe it's a blockage. Or maybe it's something that I just forgot.' He told Williams that he remembered little about their relationship. 'Not much. There wasn't much of a relationship,' he explained. 'I looked up to him because he was my father, but the few times I was seeing him it was holidays or in the mountains for Christmas. Stuff like that.

And at Christmas, when you're a kid, you have presents and that's all that matters. A few things that I did with him, when we went out on his boat or in a four-by-four or on skis, it was a lot of fun. Always out over the edge. I remember that side and that's all I remember.'

Asked further about his father, Jacques agreed that maybe he had spent some time after his death learning to know him and more about him. 'Yeah, probably true. My father died when I was twelve [sic],' Williams reported him saying. 'What do you know at that age? All you see is Father Christmas. The rest of it is very important, but you just don't pay attention to it – unless it's really terrible, of course, and I can't say much on that. I know more now because I've been told so much. It's as if people talk three or four times more about a person after he's dead. But I honestly don't know my father.'

In the year 1992, apart from going to Tokyo and racing in Japan, Jacques did other things which opened up his future and linked him ever more closely with the image of his father. One was to return to Canada in August when he raced at Trois Rivières, in a Formula Atlantic event, driving a Ralt-Toyota. This, for the local people and, of course, for Player's, the cigarette company and sponsors, was an emotional experience, such was the high esteem in which Gilles Villeneuve had been held. It was, also, a test of Jacques' ability to withstand the emotional pressure on him on the other side of the Atlantic.

A glance at Jacques' results in 1993, compared to the previous years, shows that he was better prepared for anything. He was technically more adept, had greater knowledge and was happier, in terms of knowing what he wanted from life and how to obtain it. Jacques had taken advice from Patrick Tambay again on what next to do with his life and his career, he had chosen Japan and it was working out. Another friend who reportedly helped him was Mauro Martini, then driving in Japan in Formula 3000. He said: 'His father was a legend in Italy, a God. But, in Japan, he was just a driver who'd died in Formula One. Of course, Gilles was famous, but it was completely different. I think that helped Jacques because he grew up quicker.'

In his rented apartment, surrounded by his newly acquired possessions – Martini said Villeneuve went out and spent around $10,000 on all the domestic and electronic equipment he required in one day – the newcomer to Tokyo began his new life, learning about life itself from his new racing driver friends. 'It was pretty funny because we could tell him whatever we wanted,' said Martini. 'He would believe it! He was a very, very nice guy.'

Two of Jacques' other contemporaries were Rickard Rydell and Tom Kristensen, a Swede and a Dane, both of whom also drove for Toyota, though only Villeneuve received the works' support from TOM's. Kristensen, in an interview at Silverstone in August 1996, was wearing palladium shoes, a trend which was developed in Japan. His first pair was bought for him by Jacques, he said. 'He bought me green, dark green – and they were the ugliest!' he said. 'But the next year, green was a good colour, so I had got the best colour. This is my second pair. That first pair, I gave Jacques 5,000 yen for, but he bought them.'

Kristensen said he had first met Jacques 'at a Macau Formula Three race – but I didn't speak with him at the time. At that time everybody said he was quick, but quick off the circuit. But that impression changed during our time in Japan where he did a good job and he also developed his personality. He is a nice kid and I would say he is very down to earth. He says what he thinks and has no problem with all the fuss around him. We ran for different Toyota teams, but all the deals were done with TOM's and the different drivers, but we ran for different teams.'

They grew to know each other reasonably well, but were not, as Kristensen put it, close enough for him to be his best friend. From talking to many of those people who were with Jacques at this time, it seemed that several of them found the same – he was a good friend, but difficult to be close to. 'I remember sending a fax,' he said. 'I don't know if he ever saw it. It was when he was second at Indy in his first year there. I was very impressed. I speak to him sometimes, but only at the circuits.'

Kristensen supported the common notion that Jacques' year in Japan was his university time. 'Yes, definitely,' he said. 'It was a very good life. There was good food, you go out in Tokyo and he had a flat in Tokyo, I think for the whole year. I stayed there sometimes when I crashed over for the night, not so often! He bought this huge fridge, an American fridge, and the only thing in it was the milk for the cornflakes and a few cans of Coke, but he was good. And, he had no curtains – when he stayed there for the whole year!

'He bought the latest karaoke stereo. The CDs he had were not stacked up, but spread all around the floor. I remember the first time I went there to sleep he didn't really have anything to sleep on. He just had a blanket and a sheet, but no mattress. He pulled something from either his karaoke system or his television, the plastic bubbly packing, and he had a long strip of that and I slept on that with no sheet over me. And the sun comes up early in Japan so the sun is straight in on me because he has no curtains. In the karaoke bars, I think Jacques thought he was the best. He had that impression, but he was the worst, definitely the worst. Rickard and I were not good either, but the Japanese are very polite and it was good fun. When Jacques bought that karaoke machine I was there that day, but my wallet stayed firmly in my back pocket!'

According to Kristensen, Jacques had no problems with money and was able to enjoy every moment of his sojourn in a city that is buzzing with life. 'No, Jacques had no problem with that. But I'm not used to that. I'm not from a rich family at all, so I was a bit more careful with my money, but Jacques was living for the moment. Tokyo is very trendy, but it's a very different world to come into – culture-wise, everything. Jacques had no problem mixing with people. Sometimes, he needed a slight introduction to people, but after that he got on well. He was enjoying that. He wanted to stay in Tokyo, whereas Rickard and I didn't. It was so cramped. Jacques was easy-going with all the foreign drivers. He went out with a different one occasionally, but with Mika Salo having a flat in Tokyo, they met more than we did. We met at the track and went out in the small cities, not in Tokyo. It was the small places where we were racing. The night after qualifying, it was a pretty different world.

'You see, here [Silverstone], when we have had qualifying, everyone goes. But there you had to stay and say "you got in my way" and it is a completely different thing. You learn to have a good time together and for sure I have learned a lot like that. I am sure Jacques did.' He added that Craig Pollock arrived on the scene at this time and had a good effect on his young charge. 'He was very good with Jacques and for Jacques. It was very good to have him, very important. So, I think it is a package.'

Pollock may have been a calming influence. In Tokyo, there are many temptations and this group of drivers, including Jacques and other Formula One men, Salo and Eddie Irvine, enjoyed their lives. They were also given the chance to party a little when they were out of the capital city at the provincial city circuits where, Kristensen said, 'for sure, we tried a few kamikazes!' This meant, in normal terms, that these young men went out and tried to join in the fun of the local night scene, sometimes consuming drinks which may have had a strong effect on their behaviour. 'We don't know what it was,' said Kristensen. 'But it definitely made us funny. In Japan, you see other Japanese drivers and they are smoking and drinking sake at night, these experienced drivers, so the whole thing – when you are there as a young driver – is that you see it is possible to live a life outside. Going out is possible.'

Asked if it was easy for Jacques to shut himself off, away from the madding crowd during his racing, he went on: 'Yes, it was very easy for him, but it wasn't so easy for me. I don't know, because it's difficult. We were there for different situations. I was Japanese Formula 3000 champion, thinking about my career, so it was important that I did well and things like this. I think I am a bit more relaxed now. At that time, you brought your world back home and that meant back to the hotel, but Jacques was a good guy to be around. He was thinking about everything else.

'I don't know how many CDs he suggested I bought, but it was a lot. I don't think I've heard them all, but that year was my CD-buying year, but I got nowhere near him. I felt I could come out of a shop with ten, he would have twenty – every time. I think he got into his computer games later. I also know that he did music himself. I know he bought a very good DAT machine, a huge Walkman. He always had it on and he always looked like he was in a studio with it. But the sound was very good and he always brought that along because you spent a lot of time travelling because Japan is so big. Rickard and I had a Toyota each, but Jacques had no car, so we went on the train. He lived in Tokyo and he went by underground.'

Towards the end of the year, Kristensen said, they were asked to drive a 'youth car', shared with Eddie Irvine, in the final Group C sportscar round of the Japanese championship at Mine. It was an invitation they were pleased to accept, but which led to a strange adventure during which the young Dane and the young Canadian ended up sharing a bed in a provincial Japanese hotel room. 'Irvine was driving in Group C anyway,' he said. 'He did all the year with a turbo car, so he was one driver and Jacques and I were the other two drivers. We had a Formula Three test at Suzuka and were supposed to have our first Group C test down in Mine, in the very south of Japan, the day after. We were supposed to take the *shinkansen* down. After the test, we were talking and after we swapped trains, we were still talking and talking and, in Japan, when trains leave, they leave exactly on time. We had to change and we just walked in to the other train and it was two minutes early. We just got to sleep and we realised it was stopping everywhere and we asked what time we would be there. They told us the final stop was Hiroshima, which was about 300 kilometres away from where we had to be and we would arrive there at midnight. So, we were in big trouble!

'Jacques was in his palladiums, his T-shirt and shorts – his usual stuff – and his long hair and we were both dirty from the test. We called them. "Listen, guys, we are in Hiroshima and we need to be there at eight o'clock to do our belts." The only thing to do was to take a taxi or an early train. We were left looking for hotels in Hiroshima. Well, they have golden week there, some weeks where everything is full, and they go "no" and they look at us like we are aliens or we are gays or whatever! I don't know. But there were no rooms.

'Finally, we got to one which was a bit nicer and we try to approach him in a different way, saying we are racing drivers. He called another hotel, so they didn't see us actually, before he said okay. He had a suite room. It was all he had. We said we needed it because it was one o'clock and we knew we had to catch the train at 4.30 or 5 in the morning, and we stayed in the suite in this huge double bed for four or five hours. It was just funny.'

This kind of escapade exemplified the fun Jacques was able to experience in Japan. Kristensen explained that he was aware always of the pressure Jacques was under because of his surname, but pointed out that he never played to it. He said that they both had girls chasing after them, female fans who were keen for autographs, or an opportunity to be close to or to touch their heroes, but that this 'sometimes was too much because we are all human beings after all. I once had a girl who, wherever I went in Japan, she was there. She took pictures and gave me presents and I am sure Jacques had the same thing happen to him.'

Among Jacques' favourite diversions at this time was ten-pin bowling. 'We bowled a lot actually,' said Kristensen. 'But I was the safe guy who went down the middle with a small speed and just rolled it straight. Jacques – he wanted to destroy it! I've seen him almost be in the middle of the lane that he fell into, he was swinging so hard that he was lying on the line, in the oil, and he was really dirty. I remember that he had a massive swing and he was lucky that he didn't end up in another lane altogether sometimes. He was very mad. We played a bit of tennis as well.'

Asked about the young Villeneuve's ability to succeed, Kristensen added: 'You only have to look at why he went from Indycars to Formula One. I think it helped him there for sure. It's not just the name, but it helps him. He was running with a very good team.'

Kristensen said he had heard that Jacques telephoned Salo regularly and treated him like an older brother, often calling him every day for advice on many of the challenging aspects of life as a single young man. 'Sometimes, he was always straight out and he was asking things – and that is what I mean, like a kid.

Rickard and I were a bit older so sometimes he was asking funny questions. One time, I remember, we were sitting in a small Italian restaurant and he was saying, "Maybe Indy will be good. I think I'll do Indy." And we were thinking "Oh, he is crazy!" And two years later, he was there running in it.'

It seems, however, that there was always method in all the madness. Kristensen said he found that underneath the sometimes zany antics, there was a solid plan taking shape for Jacques. He believed this was due to the influence of Pollock. 'I think they got along very well together,' he said, before hinting that they knew there were aspects of their business which were to be kept private at times. 'Sometimes they would speak French together and I didn't know what they were going on about. But Jacques is straight. In 1992, we were together and since then I am a friend.'

Asked about girls – and about the arrival of Jacques' steady girlfriend of later times, Sandrine Gros d'Aillon – he said he recalled she was not 'on the scene' in Japan, but linked up with him during his time in Formula Atlantic in 1993. 'I don't know if he knew her before,' said Kristensen, who added that Jacques did not have a steady girlfriend in 1992. 'No,' he said. 'There were lots of different girls. A university year! Everybody had the impression that he was just a wild kid, but he didn't do a lot of damage!'

Kristensen confirmed one other incident of Jacques' wildness which occurred at the TI Circuit, Aida, in June. 'After the race, we were staying one more night before we got the flight back and we were having a good time,' he said. 'There was a Danish restaurant there. We got to know it well. All of us in the team went down to the city and Jacques was running over the top of cars and he made a huge dent in the roof of Rickard's car!'

Jacques' behaviour certainly left its mark. Not only during his year in Japan, but previously, in Italy, he had surprised Massimiliano Angelleli, another of his contemporaries in the Formula Three series. He said he raced against Jacques for three of his four years in Formula Three. 'I only spent time with him during the weekend and also during winter testing,' he said. 'He surprised the hell out of me when he was racing in Italy and afterwards when he was racing in Japan.

'At Macau, at the end of the year, he surprised me a lot because when he was racing in Italy he was just driving the car. If it was possible to win the race, then he would do so. But otherwise he was not interested in racing. It did not look as though he was interested in driving a racing car and that was not only my opinion, but that of others also.

'Then, when he went to Japan, he said to me and to Roberto Colciago, who he knows very well, "Okay, I go to Japan to earn lots of money and to go out in Tokyo. I will race in Formula Three one year maybe, just for fun." Then me and Roberto, we met him at Macau at the end of the year and it was a completely different thing. He was changing a lot, he was really a racing guy and that was after Japan, not before. He came back a quick driver, a clever driver. Not strong in the qualifying, but winning the race. He was not making those big mistakes and he was better. Very quick on the lap time and so on. It was a big surprise for me and for Roberto.

'In Formula Three, in Italy, he was unbelievable. He was having accidents, big accidents and big mistakes all over the place. I can understand it because in Italy there was a lot of pressure on him and a lot of other people were pushing a lot. It was because of his name. If he had started in Britain, or Germany, or somewhere like that then I think he would have been okay. I think Italy was difficult for him.

'He was relaxed before Japan – and after Japan also! Jacques was human. Just like you or me. He chased the women, drank the wine and had a great time and he was very good at it. I hope for him that Formula One has not changed him at all. I do not think that it will. It is difficult because I raced against 90 per cent of the Formula One drivers. I raced against Schumacher, Irvine, Barrichello and so on and they have all changed. After one year of Formula One, it was all completely different. There was no chance to speak to them. I went to the Monaco Formula Three race and I was not allowed in to speak to them. I hope for his sake that he will be the same. I think that he will be because he is very strong. You cannot win Indycar and then go on to Formula One without being very strong inside.

'He is strong, I think, because he is alone. His mother is a long way away and so he is stronger than another driver with a family and a good wife. He was always alone. In Italy, we have people who travel all over the world and they sleep "without house", just on the grass with newspapers for a roof. We call them *zingaro* and we said that Jacques was a *zingaro*. He changed country without any problem, no hassle. For the Italian people, it is impossible. We like to race in Italy, win in Italy, have a Formula One world championship in Italy. For us, he was unbelievable.

'I was not that close to him away from the tracks because he was always with his team and was still very young as a driver. He was 18, I think, but then he had got older and got more experience when we met at Macau. We meet each other in the restaurants and in the discos and so on. It was automatic. He did not say to me or I did not say to him that we would meet anywhere. We would just bump into each other and have a fantastic evening. It was a good life.

'But in Italy, it was very straight. When you become a professional racing driver, you take the mentality of a professional and so you have the fun outside the car. Jacques was a case in point. As soon as he spent that time in Japan, he came back to have different fun.'

Learning to have a good time was not a problem to Jacques. But he had more difficulties dealing with the constant media pressure and in 1992, of course, there was enhanced interest in him in Japan because it was ten years after the death of his father Gilles. Rickard Rydell, another of his Toyota contemporaries, recalled: 'For sure, in Japan, Villeneuve was a very big name and I think he thought it was quite hard with all the interviews and things like that. Especially in 1992, because it was ten years since his father died. I remember that all the journalists wanted to talk to him about that and he was not keen to do interviews about it. He wanted to drive for himself and he wanted to be recognized as Jacques Villeneuve and not Gilles Villeneuve's son.'

Asked for his first impressions of Jacques as a driver and as a person in Japan, Rydell said: 'He was quite young then. He had long hair and he was very laid-back, very relaxed. At first, when I met him, I thought he was a bit arrogant, but I think that was only because he was quite young and immature. After a little while, when I got to know him a bit better, we became really good friends and we had a really good relationship I would say.

'I thought he was quite good, but nothing special really. We were obviously quite close, but he always finished. He was not brilliantly quick, but he always finished and he always got quite good results. He was third and fourth in a number of races and never broke down, so that's why he finished quite well in the championship. A calculating driver, I guess.

'We got on really well. I lived near Fuji and sometimes I went to stay with him in Tokyo when I could. He was relaxed like any other normal person, we didn't talk about racing when we were away from the race tracks. Most of the time, after tests and races, there was a lot of time to spend in Japan and, of course, we didn't have our girlfriends or our families there so most of the foreign drivers in Japan got on really, really well.

'It was the same every year I was in Japan. The foreign drivers got on really well, much better than when we were racing in Europe. I think it is because you are so far away and there are only Japanese people around.'

Rydell confirmed Kristensen's view that Jacques enjoyed his new sense of freedom and the social scene of Tokyo, but was still capable of what they described as crazy behaviour. He said they often went out to a karaoke bar, 'had a couple of beers and sang karaoke in the evenings'. He added too that he felt 'he grew up a bit living in Japan, on his own in a flat in Tokyo. You learn to take care of yourself and do what you want to do, so for sure he grew up a lot.'

Rydell added that he was amused by some of the things that Jacques did, like travelling first-class when Rydell felt it was not necessary and was a waste of money. 'I asked him why he didn't go second-class and put the money in the bank instead of just spending it, but he didn't really care about spending money. I guess he always knew that. He wasn't that well off then, but he was paid to drive and he was a professional driver and I guess he always knew he had a chance to continue and to do other things. He was always very sure of himself and that he would have a drive the next year. He was certain he would continue in racing, whereas some of us were never sure what we would be doing the next year and we always had to take one year at a time. The reason for this confidence was Craig Pollock. He was a really good guy and I think that helped him a lot. Without Craig, I don't think he would have been so sure of himself.

'Craig didn't come to Japan that often and Jacques had to take care of himself. I really like Jacques and Craig and they are really great fun to be with. In Macau, we went out together after the race, they had a really great relationship and they knew each other really well from school days. So, to have someone like that who could help him and push him, it wasn't like a manager he had just taken on to go racing. It was someone he had known for a long time.'

During the course of that season, Rydell said he often out-qualified Jacques. 'I am sure he was learning then. He was too young,' he explained. 'I had done a lot more Formula Three than he had done. I am sure he is a lot better driver now than he was then. He is learning so much. I think he is really good if he sees something and if he has made a mistake, because he learns from it and he just builds on experience. He is a very good driver now.'

Rydell said Jacques was not known as a particularly aggressive driver while he was in Japan, but was someone who was 'just exploiting the limits'. Asked why he felt Jacques had made it to Formula One while he, Rydell, had gone only as far as the British Touring Car Championship, he said: 'I am sure it is because of his name. Without his manager and the Villeneuve name, he wouldn't have done it. It would have been as hard for him as it would have been for a number of drivers, but with all respects he is one of the few very good drivers. There are less than ten paid drivers in Formula One and he could probably have done it if he had worked hard with sponsors, but he has never really done that and he has had it all laid out for him really. But, I would do the same if I was him.'

The first time Rydell visited Jacques at his apartment in Tokyo, he was surprised to see how many CDs he had. 'I remember he had four or five hundred of them,' he said. 'He was really collecting them. And a month earlier, he had just bought a nice CD player, with radio and cassette player. A week later we went out shopping and saw the same one, but you could do karaoke with it with the right discs. So, he bought that one instead and it was twice as expensive and I bought the old one for half the price. He always wanted to have the latest in CDs and films and he played computer games and things. He liked all that.'

From a racing perspective too, Jacques was well regarded, but seen also as a young man who was in the learning process. Kuomi of TOM's Toyota, said he 'only spent one year with us, and that was not a long time unfortunately. We enjoyed having him as a driver as he had a lot of character. He was taken away from home, away from Italy, his mother and his sister to live in Japan. It was different for him. In Italy, I think he was treated like his father Gilles and he was therefore spoiled. He was not mature enough to take his racing seriously.

'We obviously taught him how to drive and how to balance and set up the car. He was not so adamant that he was right all the time. He had his opinion, obviously, but he knew that he had to listen to a more experienced engineer. We treated him like a professional driver. His treatment in Italy was not so professional. We gave him a lot of pressure because Toyota wanted him. We paid him. Politically and money-wise, it made sense for us to train him. We paid him money as a professional driver and we wanted him to drive with us in a higher category. We gave him a lot of pressure to deal with. He did not act like a kindergarten kid any more, once he found that that was not acceptable. He scored points in every race he took part in, with no retirements and no crashes. He was very consistent.

'We wanted to have him for higher categories, including

Japanese F3000, and we were trying to get sponsorship. But I am afraid that we failed due to the Japanese recession which started at exactly the same time. We could not take that chance, as much as I would have liked to. He had a choice anyway to do F3000 in Europe or to race in Indycars. He was a very enjoyable guy. But he was like a kid when he arrived. He was not behaving himself. Normally, he was immature, but sometimes he was completely different. As time went by, he began to show his mature face and he was obviously growing all the time.'

Like many others, Kuomi commented on Jacques' liking for oversized clothes and a 'grunge' appearance. 'All the time, he had people laughing around him. Everyone liked him. He was not childish. But he was very stubborn. Even when he was not racing, he had his own ideas, such as on food and so on.'

All this independence did nothing to dampen Jacques' concentration on his driving or his consistency in the car. In Japan, he learned about results and about finishing races and he broadened his experience with the Group C race at Mine, with the outing to Trois Rivières, which added an emotional dimension to his conviction that he would become a serious professional racing driver, and with the end-of-season races at Macau and Fuji.

It was a successful year. It began at Suzuka, where the TOM's car was said to be less competitive (because of revised weight distribution problems caused by new regulations) than its predecessor of 1991, but where Jacques finished sixth on his debut in a race won by Anthony Reid, a journeyman English racing driver. That was on March 8. Three weeks later, at the Tsukuba circuit near Tokyo, Reid won again, and Jacques took fourth place when his friend Kristensen was disqualified for swerving back onto the track from the pit-lane entry road.

On May 3, at Fuji, Reid won again and Jacques, once again profiting from the disqualifications of others (this time Kristensen and Rydell, for being underweight, while Eugenio Visco of Italy was docked one minute for start-jumping), was placed third. This put him third in the standings.

Reid scored his fourth consecutive win at Suzuka on May 24

where Jacques moved up from sixth on the grid to finish third in his TOM's Toyota 032F, following that result with a dash home to Europe for the Monaco Formula Three classic in which he qualified sixth, for PreMa, and finished ninth after an accident at Mirabeau, where he was in a collision with Roberto Colciago. At Nishi-Sendai, after flying back to Japan, he scored his first Formula Three victory on June 14 in the fifth round of the Japanese series, in the process ending Reid's hot streak of four wins in succession. Four years later, another Englishman, Damon Hill, was to have his hot streak of four successive F1 wins ended by Jacques too.

Jacques' victory at Nishi-Sendai lifted him up to second in the championship with five points-scoring races in succession behind him. He was second on the grid alongside pole-man Rydell and made the better start to take command. Kristensen, in a TOM's-backed Ralt, was third, according to Adam Cooper's report in *Autosport*. This first significant victory of Villeneuve's career gave him the confidence and the platform he needed to build on and at the TI Circuit at Aida, on June 28, he maintained his solid start to the year with a good third place after Kristensen was disqualified again for running with an irregular airbox.

The seventh round of the series took Jacques and his friends down to Mine on July 12 when he won for the second time and closed the gap on Reid on a day when the English driver could have wrapped up the championship. It was a comfortable victory, after working up through the field, and it left Jacques with an afterglow that he took with him to Canada for his appearance at Trois Rivières, in the Formula Atlantic race, on August 16 (there was to be no further race in Japan until September).

For the locals at Trois Rivières, Jacques' appearance was a 'very moving experience', said Leon Methot, the president of the Player's Grand Prix. Not only did it coincide with the tenth anniversary of the death of Gilles, but it also offered the intriguing prospect of Jacques racing against his uncle Jacques, who was the defending champion and a three-times winner of the event. To help promote the race, it was arranged that Jacques would make a personal broadcast appearance, reported *Hors Series Sports*. 'From his family living room, he says he is very excited at the prospect of Trois Rivières and the media do the rest,' said the magazine.

A crowd of 70,000 was reported at Trois Rivières on the day and Jacques, aware of the hype and expectation surrounding his appearance, did his best to avoid being taken in by the public game of comparing him to his father. On arrival, reported the *Hors Series* magazine, Jacques said that the people of Quebec showed him courtesy and 'do not harass me as in Italy'. In a brief summary of his expectations, he told Serge L'Heureux, a journalist at *Nouvelliste*, that 'it is not very realistic to think that I can win this race . . . Everything is new to me: the car, the track, the team. I come here to do my best and to learn.'

Asked about the presence of his uncle, who was apparently struggling to find sponsors for his budget, he said: 'It is certain that I would like him to be here. He would give me sound advice.' Local reporters noted that Jacques was a young man, like many of his age, with a 'long ponytail and French glasses with a fine frame' and that he charmed everyone he met. 'He celebrated his return with two hot dogs and a *poutine* and the following day with a meal at Saint-Hubert,' it was reported. 'Then, when Claude Bourbonnais, his new team-mate, arrived with some corn on the cob, he smiled approvingly. But he did not come back to Canada to eat *poutine* and barbecued chicken.'

Four days before the race, he began his preparations by going with the Swift DB4, lent to him by the ComPred team, to Saint-Eustache to test. Little more than half an hour into the test, his car stopped in a cloud of dust, giving everyone a fright. Those watching, according to *Hors Series Sports*, included his mother Joann and sister Melanie. The ailment was a failed rear suspension, which required four hours' repairs. Eventually, he returned to the track and improved the track record – an achievement which pleased his team and their sponsors.

For the race itself, Jacques qualified 12th to ensure he lined up alongside his uncle, who had raised the funds he required to race.

Uncle Jacques, in fact, emerged as the star of the show. He climbed up to second behind eventual winner Chris Smith, but retired with a blown engine following a virtuoso performance during which he broke the track record three times and revived memories of the Villeneuve legend established by his brother. Jacques, junior, by contrast, worked his way through methodically to finish third behind Smith and David Empringham. 'Great show from the uncle, but the nephew gets the result,' was the headline of the *Journal de Montreal* the next day.

Jacques received a glowing press for his cool driving and demeanour and, in that weekend, the seeds of his next career move were sown. He was to receive offers to stay in Japan and race in the Japanese Group C championship, but admitted during his time in Canada that he was attracted by the possibility of staying in Quebec. By December 15, he had hardened up those feelings and Player's announced that he had decided to return again in 1993 to race in the Formula Atlantic series. The tug of his roots – and the *poutine* – had won, but his debut in north American racing that August weekend had played an influential part in this.

After Trois Rivières, Jacques went back to Canada and raced at Sugo where Reid claimed his fifth win of the year and, with it, the title. Reid took pole ahead of Villeneuve, who struggled to resist Akira Ishikawa at the start. Jacques had complained about his engine, changed following the warm-up, and ended up fourth. At Suzuka, on September 27, he took pole, but finished second behind Rydell. He improved on that result on November 15, by claiming his third win of the year from pole position with a dominant performance, including a fightback after allowing Kristensen to beat him to the first corner. It was his tenth successive points finish and left him second in the final standings behind Reid.

In between those final rounds, of course, he also raced at Mine in the sportscar with Irvine and Kristensen, acquitting himself well in a car which finished fourth, Jacques learning much as he went along. And, at Suzuka on October 25, in a non-championship race, he endured his first retirement of the year after an incident involving Rydell and Tetsuya Tanaka before setting his Formula Three sights on Macau and Fuji.

On the flight from Tokyo, Rydell pinched Villeneuve's allotted window seat, an act of determination and humour which was to be a prelude to his victory on the streets in the classic race which, in 1992, included such future Formula One stars as Pedro Lamy, Rubens Barrichello and David Coulthard among the entry list. Jacques qualified fifth and finished second in both heats, a solid showing. At Fuji, on November 29, one week later, he qualified second for the first heat, finished seventh, but secured a place in the final which proved to be a non-event since he suffered a gearbox failure before the start with his TOM's Toyota 32F. It was a downbeat end to an upbeat year, but it did not bother Jacques. He had made up his mind to go to America to contest the 1993 Formula Atlantic series with the Forsythe-Green team and, at that time, he had no thoughts of Formula One.

Indeed, he seemed negative about the very idea that he might, one day, follow his father into the top international category of motor racing. 'What's important to me is to race professionally in a good championship for many years,' he told Adam Cooper, for *Autosport*. 'Now, if you look at F1, there's not much interesting about it, is there? Of course, I would like to go to F1, like any driver, if there's a good opportunity at a good level, with security to race for a few years. I might even go to the States. The Indy 500 sounds really interesting, so perhaps I'd like to go there . . .'

Chapter Nine

Racing in the States:
1993–1995

Back home in Canada, the family were happy that Jacques was coming to race. Uncle Jacques, who had raced in snow-mobiles, Can-Am sportscars and Formula Atlantic, knew what it meant. He was pleased. But he could never have guessed at what was going to happen. He could never have known or imagined that his bespectacled and long-haired nephew would grow so rapidly into the most talked-about winner of the Indianapolis 500 within three years of his arrival.

Jacques signed to race for Forsythe-Green, a team backed by the business acumen of Gerald Forsythe and the racing know-how of Barry Green, an Australian. It was a good combination. His team-mate was Claude Bourbonnais. The team had backing, too, from Player's who had supported Jacques' return to race at Trois Rivières the year before and who were keen to support the return of a Villeneuve to the forefront of north American motor sport. The deal for Jacques' return was set up by Player's and, after a meeting involving Barry Green and Craig Pollock, it was done and a three-year plan was agreed. Green, seeking supplementary financial support in addition to that supplied by Player's, approached Forsythe late in 1992 to ensure he had the right kind of package set up.

Jacques was ready for it. He impressed his uncle, he impressed everyone. Gilles, of course, had raced with great success in Formula Atlantic and this gave him a record to try and emulate in his first season of 15 races. That he did so, with seven pole positions and five victories, was a wonderful endorsement of his talent and helped to carry him into third place in the championship overall and sent him onwards to Indycars with his confidence intact. His most memorable victory of 1993, indisputably, was the one he achieved in Montreal on the Circuit Gilles Villeneuve, where his father had claimed his first Formula One win back in 1978. When Jacques appeared on the podium at that race, he was given one of the most emotional ovations seen at the track and the crowd included his mother Joann and his sister Melanie, both reportedly in tears.

All this helped carry him onwards and upwards, into 1994 and the Indycar series in which he managed to win a race in his debut season (an extraordinary achievement for a rookie, but one which helped him earn the rookie-of-the-year award) and to finish a close second in the Indianapolis 500. That result, on top of his family name, made him an overnight star in America and set him up for 1995 when he completed three meteoric years by becoming the youngest winner of the Indycar drivers' championship and winner of the Indianapolis 500. In August that year, of course, he signed for Williams in Formula One.

The three years in America, therefore, were the important final stepping-stones to the top for the man his uncle revealed is known only as 'junior' or 'the kid' in the family. 'We also have a family nickname for him in French,' added Uncle Jacques, in an interview with Gerald Donaldson for *F1 Racing*. 'Ti-Cu. Which means "little ass". Jacques isn't very big. But neither am I and Gilles was the same.'

Uncle Jacques added: 'The kid's very good at setting up a car. He gives his team good feedback and is very smart about race tactics. He's not like his dad, or myself, wanting to be quickest on every lap. The kid's not as spectacular and always seems to be able to control himself and the situation around him to make it work to his advantage. Jacques also knows how to give the team and sponsors good results. He is very intelligent and cool, like a block of ice. The fact that he is good-looking and speaks well in public means he's got the right appearance for sponsors. What's more, he learns fast from experience. Besides, Jacques has always had a good entourage around him for advice.'

All this was, indeed, good for Jacques. And the Player's-sponsored Toyota Atlantic series of 1993 was the perfect choice of stepping-stone towards the top for him at that time. A series of 15 races, nine in the United States and six in Canada, it mixed street circuits with ovals and with purpose-built tracks in an effort to provide a proving ground for the Indycar drivers of the future. And Jacques, true to his character, added something extra with an appearance at Macau scheduled in again for November 21, at the end of the season. It was to be another learning year, in readiness for a breakthrough to Indycars in 1994.

Green and Forsythe had been partners before, running a short-lived but highly successful Indycar operation which split up in 1985. After this, however, they had gone their separate ways: Green to work with Michael Andretti, then with Maury Kraines' team, and Forsythe to look after his growing business interests. But in their original operation, they had run another rookie Indycar driver named Teo Fabi, an Italian fresh out of Can-Am racing, in 1983. He had stunned American racing by winning six poles, including the Indianapolis 500, and winning four races on his way to second place behind Al Unser in the championship. It was a breathtakingly successful debut season, but two years later on Forsythe Racing, as it was known, closed its doors.

Forsythe walked away and never expected to come back to racing, unless it was to be with Green. 'Primarily, my reason was business,' Forsythe told *On Track* in May 1994. 'When I got into Indycar racing in 1981, it was more from the sponsorship side to help a young upcoming driver and his father to get into racing . . . After that, it didn't take me long to want to do it on a different scale. I was told by so many people in the industry that there is no way you can go out there and beat a Roger Penske or a Pat Patrick.

That was the interest that sparked me because when somebody tells me you cannot do it, I want to prove them wrong.'

It was to be partly due to the influence of Robin Herd, of March, that Forsythe met Green towards the end of 1982 and together forged the partnership that not only turned the following years into successful ones, but also brought both men great satisfaction and joy. Green had previously been with John Surtees in England and Paul Newman in America. Their partnership gelled well and Fabi's success brought them some fame and repute, but, in 1984, the balding Italian left to go racing in Formula One. It was to be another decade before Forsythe was lured back to racing by Green – as the other man in the operation he was putting together for Player's and Villeneuve junior.

Forsythe said he was attracted back to racing because he could see his two companies were both doing well and also because he respected Green, a 'hands-on guy'. He said: "He has a lot of experience in Indycar racing now. I'm working with him on the financial side and all the other decisions are discussed between the two of us. I respect his opinions and, most of the time, go along with his suggestions.'

He added that Green had 'approached me in 1992, early on, and explained to me he was looking for other opportunities and would like some day to be an owner of a team. I asked him why he wanted to be an owner because it is very difficult to make any money in this type of sport. He had worked for a lot of different owners and felt he would like a different venue. I said, "Fine, if we can put together the right sponsor, the right financial leads, I'd love to do it with you." ' And they did.

Forsythe recalled the way the deal to bring Jacques to America was done. 'He [Green] called me up and asked if I would come to Nazareth and meet the people from Imperial Tobacco Co,' he told *On Track*. 'I met the sports marketing group and Jacques' manager and spent the day with them. Then, at the race in Laguna Seca, they asked if I would come and meet with some of the senior executives of Imperial. Although they weren't prepared to make a commitment, the vice-president shook my hand and said he couldn't sign a contract at the time, but he wanted to do a deal with us. Based on that handshake, I went ahead and ordered all the necessary equipment to put the deal together. It was four or five months after that when we signed a contract. I think reputation had a lot to do with it.'

According to Forsythe, Green handpicked his team, selecting people who could offer both individual experience and the capacity to work cohesively as a unit. Among them was Tony Cicale, a man described by Green as 'the best race engineer in the business'. He worked with Jacques, forming not only a close and successful racing partnership, but also a close human bond. Cicale became, many people said, almost a surrogate father to Jacques, giving him support and advice at every level. In the plan, created by Pollock, Forsythe, Green and Player's, Jacques was to build up progressively towards Indycars and Cicale was the man who helped him do it.

Looking back later, from the advantage of a 1994 perspective, Green said: 'I think it was a tremendous advantage. The plan was to cater for the fact that Jacques was not experienced enough to run Indycars in 1993, so let's do Formula Atlantic. I liked Formula Atlantic cars and really liked that category.

'Halfway through the year, the plan was to buy an older Indycar and start testing and we did that. In August, we were out testing and ran an older Indycar. We ran in one of the CART open tests in Mid-Ohio. All that was tremendous experience for Jacques.'

Green had first met Jacques at a test for Formula Atlantic in late 1992. 'He wasn't the kind of person you get really close to straight away and it took us a while to understand each other,' he said. 'But, after a while, we came to the conclusion that he was a good guy. He fitted in really well with the whole team and he was a pleasure to have on board. He was a good guy to go out to dinner with and he was a good guy just to be with. When you worked with him, you got to understand that, because he was so focused on what he wanted to do, he really knew what he wanted.'

According to Green, it was during his time in America that Jacques learned how to work with computers both in a working sense and also in a recreational way. 'There was an awful lot of that. He worked closely with Tony Cicale and they picked their way through computers for hours on end. They would go through everything. I think Jacques became very computer literate out here and if he thought he could find an improvement, he would stay until he found it.

'Every race, he improved and we were very impressed. If you complained about anything, he would take on board and then forget about it. If you told him something, you would only need to tell it to him once. If he was going too fast in the pit-lane and you told him, then he would never do it again. He was a very good student and his greatest point was that he would always give 100 per cent to his racing.'

Cicale played a major part in Villeneuve's development from sapling to tree, bringing into their relationship all the experience he had gleaned in his years with several well-known drivers before, including such stars as Mario Andretti, and a desire to help the young and relatively inexperienced newcomer learn his way around all the subtleties of motor racing at the highest level. They developed a rapport, built on trust, and as the three years went by it became a firm foundation. Clearly, they liked and respected each other enormously.

Cicale, for his part, was most impressed by Jacques' intelligence, his ability to learn new things very quickly and to absorb information and data swiftly without any complaints. He was impressed too by his coolness under pressure, a trait that was to surface with dramatic effect from time to time, and his ability to pull away from the job of being a racing driver and revert back into his other interests. 'He had many different interests,' he explained. 'And he wasn't one of those people who talk about and think about motor racing the whole time.' Cicale also noted that Jacques could appear to be cold towards people at times, particularly when he was concentrating on something or trying to put something out of his mind.

Some observers felt that the closeness between Cicale and Jacques caused problems within the team and that it alienated

Bourbonnais. It was also said that Jacques disliked his team-mate and that, at times, he did little to disguise these feelings. Bourbonnais has said since that he did not have the use of an engineer during sessions, but was permitted access to Cicale between sessions, an arrangement which hardly assisted harmony. Cicale, however, has responded to that by saying that the team did have an engineer for Bourbonnais in Scott Graves, who was inexperienced, he admitted. But, he said, he was available and he was very bright and that it was Bourbonnais who made the situation a negative one. Green was adamant, also, that the situation was even between Jacques and Bourbonnais, a former Canadian kart champion, and he has gone on record denying any claims or suggestions that there was a hidden agenda which favoured Jacques, designed to accelerate the young Villeneuve's progress towards the top. In other words, even if Bourbonnais felt it, he was not an accessory in a team built around his partner.

By now, on the eve of the season which was to open in Phoenix, Arizona, on April 4, it was clear that the Player's-backed team were going to be serious about their racing and that Jacques was, if he learned quickly enough from Cicale, going to be a fast driver. Accidents, however, were to be expected – and, predictably, they came. In Phoenix, Jacques crashed twice, prompting memories of his father's desire to find the limits. His second accident caused serious damage to his car in the morning warm-up when he hit the wall and, as a result, he had to start the race from the back of the grid. Predictably, he was a non-finisher. At Long Beach, California, a fortnight later, he took pole position, made a disappointing start, fought his way back into contention and then collided with a back-marker. He finished second with a damaged wing. These two early races marked him out as fast, committed and uncompromising, not to mention courageous, and it was clear that a first victory may not be long coming.

It was not. It came on May 9 at Road Atlanta, Georgia, a circuit on which his father had twice been victorious. Again Jacques took pole position, but it was Bourbonnais who led, following an early mêlée, before spinning off and leaving his team-mate with the opportunity to claim his first win in the series. For Villeneuve, it was a coming of age; a triumph on American soil in a series in which his father had made his name. After this, there was no turning back. 'Winning your first race in any series is always very important,' he said. 'Until you have that first win, you never know if it is really possible.'

From then on, his season stretched ahead across north America with signs of happy encouragement and he continued to deliver the sort of results to be expected from a young Villeneuve: accidents, fast laps, more accidents and victories. At Milwaukee, on June 6, he became entangled with a Texan driver called Greg Ray and both went out. At Montreal, on June 12, an impressive performance brought a victory of which his father would certainly have been proud, and, the same weekend, it was confirmed that Jacques and the team were to move into Indycars in 1994, but that Bourbonnais was not going with them. In the race, Jacques diced successfully with David Empringham throughout the 26 laps and managed to grab the initiative in the closing stages from the eventual championship winner. It was a thrill for both his mother and his grandmother to see him winning on the track named after his father, though Jacques himself continued to eschew all such connections when speaking in public.

Eight days later, at Mosport, Bourbonnais delivered a performance filled with vim and, no doubt, motivated by a desire to prove himself. He took pole position and won convincingly, Jacques finishing second and Empringham third. The result left Empringham with a small lead in the championship and the two Player's drivers together only seven points behind. The next race was not until July 11, at Halifax, and it was to be a memorable meeting with Jacques again producing a performance that reminded many spectators of his father. Bourbonnais had crashed three times before the race and did not start, but Jacques, who had survived two accidents, at least made the grid, ran third in the later stages when it seemed he could make some inroads on the points, but did not finish because of a differential failure. Another week later, in Toronto, the fierce three-way battle for the championship led to another dramatic episode, with Bourbonnais, despite suffering burns in his cockpit from a fuel leak, winning supremely and Jacques finishing third behind Empringham.

At New Hampshire, in early August, Jacques took pole and the early lead, but was passed by Bourbonnais who then drove to victory, leaving his team-mate to come home second. This was a significant defeat for him, one that taught him that Bourbonnais, with his superior experience in the series and greater determination, was out-racing him despite not being able to beat him for lap speed in qualifying. According to Green, it was this factor more than anything which encouraged Jacques to dig into himself and raise his performance level.

August was not a good month for Jacques. After New Hampshire's lesson in commitment and poise, he went to Trois Rivières and Vancouver and failed to finish in both races. Trois Rivières was, of course, the event at which Jacques had made his initial 'homecoming' the previous year and in which his uncle Jacques took part. It was, to all intents and purposes, seen as the Villeneuve family fortress, in motor racing terms. In the heated atmosphere, it was no surprise that all the three main championship contenders were committed to proving something and all three promptly went off at the first corner. Jacques recovered, but clashed with Bourbonnais on lap 17, at the final corner, and had to retire, leaving his uncle to finish second behind Empringham. The accident brought the in-team rivalry between Jacques and Bourbonnais to a head, but it was dealt with firmly by Green and Cicale, two experienced campaigners, who quite simply refused to allow any nonsense to interfere with the running of their team. In Vancouver, it did not: Jacques, simply, retired with mechanical problems while running fifth.

All this left him with little hope of winning the title over the last four races, but it was then, almost against the odds, that he began to show what potential he really had. He took pole and won three of the final four events, starting in Mid-Ohio on September 11 when, as *Autosport* put it, he won the race in 'the style of Formula Atlantic double-champion father Gilles'. He took pole position convincingly, lost out to Bourbonnais again at the start, but stormed back to seize the initiative and victory. A week later, at Nazareth, Bourbonnais retaliated by taking pole and winning comfortably while Jacques crashed, pitted and then chased in vain, breaking the circuit lap record along the way.

The season thus went down to the final two races, on successive days, at Laguna Seca on October 2 and 3. Needing victory in both to have any hope of claiming the title, Jacques not only took pole position twice, but followed it with stunning wins. In the first race he held off Bourbonnais and Empringham, a model of consistency, finished third. This left Bourbonnais with a good chance of taking the title if he could finish close to Empringham, but an engine failure put him out of the race. Jacques won easily, Empringham finished fourth and was champion. Cicale, so delighted at the progress made by his protégé, declared after this race that 'he will win the Indy 500, he will win the Indy car championship and he will become Formula One world champion.' He also decided that he had enjoyed it all so much he would carry on in motor racing with him.

At the end of the season, on November 21, Jacques raced in Macau with Alan Docking, taking with him a Ralt-Toyota sponsored by Player's. He did not finish and it was a sorry weekend. A week later, in Fuji, he was involved in a ten-car accident and failed to qualify. Looking back, in August 1996, Docking recalled: 'He had definite ideas about things. Right or wrong. We did a little bit of work in England, a couple of days at Snetterton, using Warren Hughes, and went off to Macau. Jacques and Warren drove the car. Andrew Fitton was Warren's manager and boss of March and he was very keen on Villeneuve as he drove what was called a Ralt in the States. Jacques came to Macau and got to know the Ralt. The car was a poor car, no doubt about it, and he had a very sure idea of how he was going to fix it. We did that during the course of the weekend, but we never got the car up to any speed at all. It had too much drag from its underbody and that made it a slow car.

'Jacques tipped it into the wall a few times, just about every time he went out. He is a hell of a trier and he really gave it one! He is quite strong-headed about how he wants to run a car. He was quite adamant about that. He had this way, that if you made the car stiff, you made it faster. He was applying that theory of life to the Ralt, but it wasn't going to respond as it was a piece of shit anyway! They were middle field, middle to the back, and they were never going to make any headway. Jacques hit walls and Warren didn't. That was the difference. Jacques was trying hard and making mistakes. He was overdriving the car and he should have kept it within the limits. But he is a lovely little bloke who got on well with the team.

'Probably now, as I have heard since from sources in Williams, he has very strong views on how the car should be. This is not helping his cause. But any successful person is very positive about what they want and he is like that. It is not that he is blindly going down a dreamer's path on set-up. He believes it and he is very positive about that and there is no harm in that at all. But he has got to learn that not every car will react to it like that. He will get there. Obviously, he drove a car once that fitted into that style of driving, setting a bit of a trend into his thinking about how to set up a racing car.'

Docking added again that he felt Jacques was 'a lovely little bloke. And I have had Mika Salo with me too. He and Jacques got on very well. Mika enjoys life to the full and has a good head on him. He might experiment with life with the best of them, but he is not an idiot so he can spot a fool and he gets on very well with Jacques. They are good mates. That suggests that the Jacques we met and worked with through the weekend is a true little fellow, but you cannot make a judgement over a weekend.

'He was into the team and he wanted a result like a team wanted it and he was willing to work at that. There is probably a bit of Schumacher in there. Schumacher is demonstrating leadership qualities all the time. Schumacher, Lauda and so on were very successful at motor racing because of their organisational skills and that is the area which will make Jacques very strong too. I didn't know his father. They said that he drove with his heart and was great to watch. I wouldn't put Jacques into the Einstein class, but he is doing a good job. He lives and eats it, there is no doubt about that.

'I would have loved to have had him in the team for a season. There is no doubt about it, the kid has a lot of talent and what he has done up to now is all his own doing with no pressure from his family. He decided he was going to do it. He decided it. I think that if there had been any money in the family coffers, he would not have put it on the line. He has been very fortunate because of his name. He has been given the breaks because of his name, but he has lived up to the breaks he has been given and he has done a good job.'

Hughes, whose career followed a flat plateau since that race in Macau compared to Jacques' near-vertical learning curve, had his own recollections. 'Jacques was very fussy. He had seven or eight attempts at a seat fitting and sent the mechanics up the wall,' he said. 'That was even before we got to Macau. That was at Snetterton, when we were testing the car. He was always left-foot braking. I did not think that was necessary in a Formula Three car, but he felt comfortable doing it so he carried on. I did not try to change him, and he did not try to change me. We were setting identical times. This was a new car so we were just getting used to it. It was the Ralt 93, which was built to try and break the Dallara stranglehold on the series. He was a decent driver and I think we were evenly matched.'

Hughes said the car was nervous and jumpy. 'Show the car a bump and it would jump out of its skin,' he said. 'Macau was a nightmare. Jacques had been there before and so he knew the circuit a little bit. He had finished there with the TOM's team in third place, but the year I raced with him he qualified 21st, I think, and I qualified 24th. But he was alright about it. There was no prima donna attitude or anything. He was there to get the job done.'

Hughes remembered Jacques attempting several bizarre alterations to the set-up. 'We were both concentrating on our own thing and were not afraid to try anything too radical. Jacques, for example, decided that we had far too much down-force and needed to lose even more than we were. So, he took the rear wing off! It looked like a rudder, because you have to have something of the back wing on, but he took out the horizontal plane. It looked very funny and didn't work, but he was not afraid to try it. The car got too unstable under braking, surprisingly enough! But he did have the speed down the straight.

'In the end, we measured the size of the diffuser on the Dallara and cut ours to the same size. We changed the shocks and springs and made the whole thing a lot softer and suddenly we were better. Jacques was doing okay in his heat, but he hit Pedro de la Rosa. We had a Benetton-style nose on the car and that pierced the tub on de la Rosa's car and there was a bit of a furore over the legality of our noses, but it blew over. But it did mean that I never had the chance of racing against Jacques.'

Hughes said he found Jacques at this time to be agreeable and easy company. 'We had dinner a few times over a two- to three-week period outside the racing track,' he said. 'He was very laid-back and relaxed. I did not know what to expect. His father had made motor racing exciting and I was nervous about meeting his son. But that soon went away because I liked the guy. I soon forgot who he was and accepted him as himself. He was not mega-serious, but was interested in music, as I was. He had asked me to get him a Rebel MC song, 'Street Tough', I think. But I never got it for him, as I have not seen or heard from him since then.'

Towards the end of that year, 1993, Jacques gave an interview to James Allen, for *Autosport* magazine, and looked forward to the challenge of racing against such celebrated stars as Mario Andretti, Nigel Mansell and Emerson Fittipaldi in 1994. 'It will be a big challenge,' he told them. 'They've got a lot of experience and they are really quick. I'm going to learn a lot. There's always something to be learned from watching the experienced. But once you're in the car, you don't think "Wow, that's Nigel Mansell!"

'I'm looking forward to the Indy 500 very much. It's great speed and it really gets your heart pumping. At 200mph, you've got to remember which corner you're in. Not turn in and then realise "God, this isn't the flat one." '

Asked what he thought was the secret of going well on ovals, he said: 'There is no secret to it. I would even say it's easier to drive than a normal road track because you don't have to brake or downshift. It's like a boomerang, you just get quicker and quicker. But the set-up of the car is critical because you cannot afford to fight with it on an oval.'

At the end of the Formula Atlantic season, Jacques took part in an Indycar test at Phoenix. It was his first oval outing in one of the bigger and more powerful machines and he denied the view put forward that he might be under pressure to make an impact. 'That's not the way I approach racing,' he said. 'If you start thinking like that and you go off, you hurt yourself more than if you take time to learn, and then maybe go quick, maybe not. We wanted to get used to the car and start adapting to it and working on it. That's always been my approach – take my time. Having said that, it's not been a difficult transition for me.

'The Formula Atlantic car I've raced this year is a great little machine – quite light and quite powerful. It has big tyres and ground-effect, so there's plenty of grip. We pull 3g on some ovals. The slightest change in the car makes a huge difference on oval so you learn a lot and it's interesting to work on. I'm a technical driver. We spend hours after every session analysing the car and getting it right. Attention to detail is very important.

'On a street course, you can drive a car even if it has flaws. But, say you are fighting to go three-tenths of a second quicker during the race, if you can work hard analysing the car before you start and find those three-tenths in the car, then it's better on the tyres and it's better on you physically. In a race, I fight just as hard as I can. I react quickly to the car sliding and I catch it early, so although it may not look as if I'm pushing as hard as the guy who's really sliding spectacularly, maybe he's just got slower reactions.'

According to Allen, Jacques' reactions were honed on the ski-slopes of his youth when he was instructed not only by Craig Pollock, in Switzerland, but also by the Canadian World Cup downhill racers Ken Reid and Steve Podborski. Both, he said, were amazed at the young Canadian's sensitivity to any sliding movement of the skis. Comparisons to Frenchman Alain Prost seemed more relevant than to his father in this context.

Asked to sum up his own style at this time, Jacques said: 'Smooth. I'm aggressive underneath, but not stupidly aggressive. You have to think all the time. If you have the championship at stake, you must work for that. If you have to fight the car to run fourth, then don't try to finish first.'

Inevitably, the subject of his father, his relationship with him and his feelings towards him, cropped up in the interview. 'I never think about my father during a race weekend,' said Jacques. 'I'm totally dedicated to my job and I don't think about anything else. Maybe he has helped me, maybe not. When he died, we went to boarding school. We were away from the house and the souvenirs, so that helped me to become an individual.'

The 1994 Indycar World Series opened at Surfers' Paradise, on the Australian 'gold coast', in Queensland, on March 20. The strong field, including defending champion Nigel Mansell, Mario Andretti, Paul Tracy, Al Unser junior and the rest, were all experienced men ready for a scrap on one of the toughest street race circuits. It was hot and the Forsythe-Green team knew that it was going to be demanding and difficult for their young rookie. It was, after all, Jacques' first race at this level.

Jacques had been as well prepared as was possible for this big challenge, but even that was not enough. Green admitted that at their last test he had written out three pages of notes for Jacques to absorb and, over dinner one evening, he had gone over them with him like a teacher and a pupil. 'It was like an exam,' he said. 'He was asking me questions and I asked him questions. We had prepared him. It was all part of our plan.' In Surfers', in that debut Indycar appearance, Jacques qualified on the fourth row of the grid and looked sensible, consistent and strong. He did well in the race too and was in fifth position when he was forced to retire after a collision with Stefan Johansson's Bettenhausen-Penske. Three weeks later, in Phoenix, he was in action on the oval circuit that is dubbed 'the world's fastest one-mile oval', the Phoenix International Raceway, an amphitheatre amid the cacti and a place which had upset Mansell in 1993 on his oval debut, causing him to crash and watch the race from his hospital bed after damaging his lower back. No one, least of all Jacques, wanted that to happen again, but he never once allowed any sign of fear or trepidation to creep into his thinking. He qualified on the front row, celebrating his 23rd birthday on that Saturday with a lap-time that broke the track record, thanks at least in part to the expertise of Tony Cicale and the fine set-up of his Reynard-Cosworth car. His time was 20.442 and it was enough, it seemed, for pole until Tracy delivered an even more impressive effort in 20.424 to sneak ahead.

The race was to be a traumatic one for everyone who was there, as it featured a near catastrophic accident, in which Jacques played a full part. Everyone, that is, except for Jacques himself who, according to close observers, was able not only to survive and walk away from the carnage but did so as if he had been out for a Sunday stroll – instead of a massive accident in which he carved another driver's vehicle in half.

In *Autosport*, Gordon Kirby, the magazine's regular contributor on Indycar racing, reported that a 'wild multi-car accident' took place. He went on to say it was triggered by Hiro Matsuhita in a Simon-Lola clipping wheels with Teo Fabi's Hall-Reynard in turn three as Fabi tried to lap the Japanese driver. 'The leaders were running directly behind this pair,' he wrote. 'And as Fabi and Matsuhita's car spun into the retaining wall, Tracy (in a Penske) found himself with nowhere to go. He was taken into the wall by Matsuhita's car, which was then hit amidships by Villeneuve. The young Canadian rookie's Reynard t-boned Matsuhita's car, and was then in turn hit by Dobson. It was remarkable that Villeneuve escaped uninjured from his wrecked Reynard which ended up partway down the pitlane.'

It was a colossal accident and a near miracle that Villeneuve and Matsuhita were not killed. Jacques, according to several observers, appeared not to notice any need to slow despite the fact that the yellow warning flags were waved and Mario Andretti was slowing ahead of him. They said he ploughed into the accident and only braked a few feet before the impact. Matsuhita's car was smashed apart, but the driver escaped with only a dislocated shoulder. Jacques said he was not driving in a crazy way at all and insisted he had braked, but could not avoid the accident. It meant his first two Indycar outings had ended in accidents and his reputation, unfairly it seemed, was being tarnished.

Cicale sprang to his driver's defence. When people began to talk about Villeneuve as a wild man, he hit back and, in the *Eurosport* Indycar magazine, delivered a virile riposte to the critics. 'At the Phoenix race, I think he drove really spectacularly. He was very decisive, very aggressive in his passing. In general, people do respect his ability. I think people do see he has massive ability. If you're aggressive, this is going to happen sometimes. But having said that, obviously he has a lot to learn about when to push, when to be aggressive, when not to be aggressive. I'm just afraid that because of some things that people have said, that he is continually going to have to prove himself that he's not wild.

'He is not a wild driver, by any stretch of the imagination. He drives well within his limits and the car's limits. He always drives in control. In some ways, I think he's gotten a bad rap on some of these accidents. And unfortunately, I think part of that reputation's perhaps that they remembered his dad – there was a perfect example of a driver who tended to seem to overdrive every car that he was in. He was always sideways. He was always flat on the throttle. And that was his trademark.

'But keep in mind that back then it was a lot of people's trademark. You didn't set up cars back then. You gave a car to a driver and if it wasn't good he drove it beyond the car's limits. And to a certain degree his uncle had that type of thing too. He was always a fairly aggressive driver and perhaps overdrove the car more than he should have done. So part of that reputation has followed Jacques and unjustifiably so because I don't see that in Jacques.'

Cicale then analysed the two accidents which had opened

Jacques' Indycar career and caused his problem. Referring to Australia, he said: 'The first lap, they black-flagged him for fuel spillage. We told them what the problem was, that it would clear up, and they said "he has to come in anyway because we think it's oil". So, we brought him in and he went to dead last. He fought his way back to sixth. My view of that was that he tried an outside pass on Johansson and Johansson never gave him a chance to see if he could do it or not. In my view, Johansson turned right into him and knocked him off the track.

'Now whether Jacques would have been able to make that corner on his own, I cannot say. Maybe that was an aggressive move. I'm not saying he's not aggressive. But he's not wild. Michael Andretti drives aggressively, he's not wild. Mansell drives aggressively, he doesn't drive wildly. But, because he's a rookie, he's labelled wild.'

And then, talking about the big accident in Phoenix, Cicale admitted 'certainly what happened in Phoenix was a mistake on his part in not seeing the yellow, but wasn't a mistake in over-driving the car. It was a totally different type of accident. And it was a totally different kind of reason why he got involved. Obviously, you can't say it was right. He has to recognise when a yellow happens early enough and realise what he has to do, but that's a question of learning what to do in a yellow situation. It's not a question at all of being a wild driver.'

Cicale's faith in his driver stood firm throughout Jacques' three years with the team in American racing. The old engineer, with a dozen years of experience of the highest levels of competition behind him, never once let him down. But the two early incidents set the tone for a spell and it needed something sensational – in the form of his brilliant second place at the Indianapolis 500 – to turn the tide.

That, however, did not come until the fourth event of the season on May 29, a full six weeks after the third round at Long Beach on April 17. There, where Bourbonnais made his Indycar debut for Performance Lola, Jacques qualified on the seventh row, battled with Marco Greco's Lola and later spun off into the tyre barrier.

He was classified 15th, five laps down on the victorious Unser. These three early results did nothing to inspire thoughts that Jacques was a potential Indianapolis 500 winner, but he listened to his lessons from Cicale and Green and the team, concentrated on fuel and pits strategy, and worked as hard as he could at improving his all-round game in readiness for the event which had captured his imagination at that time more than any other.

In 1994, the month-long build-up for the 500 began early in May, just days after the tragedy at the San Marino Grand Prix at Imola in Italy where accidents on successive days had claimed the lives of Roland Ratzenberger and Ayrton Senna. This black news from Europe cast a long and macabre shadow across 'the brickyard', created a frenzy of soul-searching in Formula One and an unexpected vacancy in the Williams team which, at the end of 1995, was to be filled by Jacques himself in succession to David Coulthard. Back in 1994, however, none of this was known; nor could it be foreseen.

Typically, according to Cicale and Green, Jacques took his first Indianapolis appearance in his stride. He prepared thoroughly, he learned about obeying instructions, keeping to prescribed plans and speeds and fuel levels, and he delivered. He passed all the requisite tests for rookies, he built up his speed and when it came to the qualifying day, the first Saturday 'pole day', he was ready to impress with a series of laps at between 225 and 227mph. His best, 227.061mph, was good enough for fourth on the grid.

In the countdown to the race, the Forsythe-Green team excelled in its preparations and planning, winning the $25,000 prize at the pit-stop championship, and running well in practice, during which Jacques continued to impress his own team more and more with his speed, courage and coolness. On one occasion, he was forced to put two wheels off the track and onto the grass at more than 220mph, but reported this incident as if it had been no more than a trifle.

On race morning itself, in front of 450,000 'petrol heads', the anticipation and the atmosphere is electric. Everyone knows that this field of gladiatorial racing drivers is about to embark on a three-hour race, 200 laps of the 2.5 mile oval, a super-speedway, a race distance of 500 miles. Jacques was not flustered by all the trouble, even though the early morning start was enough to put most people off their day long before noon.

Jacques made a slow start, drove in the pack, then stalled at his first pit-stop, lost eight places and was forced to lap for a while in 12th position. By lap 50, he was up to seventh and by lap 62 was into the lead. He could hardly believe it. He was the first rookie to lead the Indianapolis 500, thanks to the clever fuel strategy of the team. Typically, as is the norm for Indycar racing, the lead and the distances fluctuated dramatically, but Jacques remained in touch even when Fittipaldi, in his Penske, powered by a phenomenal Mercedes-Benz engine designed specifically for the event, threatened to demolish the field. For long periods, he was third and relying on his own skill as much as his team's meagre use of fuel to stay there. With 50 laps to go, it looked as if he would have to settle for third as even with his superior fuel mileage, he was unlikely to be able to overhaul the faster Penskes of Fittipaldi and Unser. Then, unexpectedly, Fittipaldi hit a kerb and crashed out into a wall, leaving Unser in the lead, five seconds clear of Jacques who drove a sensible race through the final laps of chaos to finish second. A wonderful result for an Indianapolis debutant.

It was a result that satisfied and thrilled him and put a spring in his step. No longer did he shuffle around the paddock hoping to pass by almost anonymously; he had become a hero and he could puff out his chest, hold his head high and march, with girlfriend Sandrine Gros d'Aillon at his side, as he pleased. And from then on, it was a different Jacques Villeneuve who drove for Forsythe-Green, who stamped his authority on the racing and who reeled off a far more impressive sequence of performances and results. At Milwaukee, in June, he was ninth after running fourth and being pulled in for a stop-and-go penalty, for overtaking under yellows. At Detroit, he was seventh; Portland, sixth; Cleveland, fourth. It was a spell of progress and success.

He continued. He was ninth in Toronto; failed to finish after an accident in Michigan; ninth again at Mid-Ohio and then two more

DNF's followed at New Hampshire and Vancouver (one when he was the victim of an accident, the other when an exhaust failed) before he went to Elkhart Lake and won on the pretty Wisconsin circuit where Cicale and the team decided to run with reduced down-force to maximise speed on the straights and under braking. Again, the tactics worked; preparation made perfect in practice. Jacques rounded off an eventful and impressive first season by finishing seventh at Nazareth and third at Laguna Seca to be declared 'rookie of the year'. He was sixth in the championship in his first year. As Mario Andretti bowed out of racing, signalling, with his retirement, the end of one era, it seemed the arrival of the younger Villeneuve marked the start of another.

Cicale was impressed with his boy. He had defended him against the accusations of being a wild driver. He had seen him impress at Indianapolis. He had seen him perform well in the closing half of the season and he knew, in his bones, that he had a fine prospect in his car for the 1995 season. In terms of commu- nications, their relationship was almost uniquely close and suc- cessful. 'It's incredible,' he said. 'He just listens to absolutely everything you say. He's totally honest with me and I am totally honest with him. I think that's helped with the chemistry between us. At Phoenix, he wanted to know if he could trust the car on his first timed lap. I said "You can trust it in the way you trusted it in practice" and the amazing part is that he took my words at absolute face value and said: "Okay, I can trust it. I'm going to do it." And he just went out and did it.'

Cicale felt he had a very special affinity with Jacques, yet he was often amazed at his qualifying ability. At Mid-Ohio, for example, he recalled that after 15 minutes of a 30-minute session Jacques was on pole by half a second. 'He said "how was that, I'm on pole right? Is that good?" And I said "well, it's good, but in order to really ensure pole position, you're really going to have to go a second faster." And he said, "Okay, I'll do it." And he was a second faster. He somehow has the ability to do almost the impossible things that you ask him to do. And I don't know how he does it, he's a very, very special character.'

In 1995, Jacques proved his character and his ability by winning both the Indianapolis 500, at the second attempt, and by lifting the Indycar World Series drivers' crown. He became an historic hero of his sport, the youngest man to have achieved these successes, the son of a great driver of the past reaching out and doing it for himself. Green knew he had a special talent and admitted he had spotted this as far back as mid-1993 when Jacques did his first Indycar test at Mid-Ohio. 'It was amazing,' he recalled. 'Jacques never put a foot wrong. It was like having a veteran in there. As soon as we ran in him in there, we knew we had the potential to win the championship. We felt Jacques' driving style was suited more to an Indycar than an Atlantic.' He was right.

In his championship year, the Indianapolis-based Jacques achieved four victories, six poles and nine top-five finishes with the help of Green, Cicale, Kim Green, Kyle Moyer and a solid budget of around seven million dollars mostly from Player's. 'We showed that a small team can be successful if you work hard, make good decisions and have the right chemistry,' said Jacques in *On Track* at the end of 1995. 'This championship was built on the chemistry and friendship of our three years together.'

The 1995 season was very different from 1994. It saw nine different winners, four of them for the first time, and it saw the Reynard chassis dominate, particularly that of Jacques, whose car was powered again by a Ford-Cosworth engine. Significantly, among other things, the 1995 Indianapolis 500 was to be the last run as part of the Indycar World Series and Gerry Forsythe left Green to run their team alone as Team Green. It made little difference. He left the old outfit intact and sat back and watched it run like clockwork.

In Miami, on March 5, Jacques qualified eighth, climbed to fourth, profited from slick teamwork during a full-course yellow to go up to third and did the same again to take the lead ahead of Mauricio Gugelmin. 'We got by everyone in the pits,' he acknowledged. 'Our win happened in the pits.'

The victory boosted the confidence of the team at a critical early time and sent them to Australia on March 19 for the second round at

Surfers' Paradise full of hope. There, in Queensland, Jacques qualified second, but retired with a broken transmission. In Phoenix, on April 2, he qualified third, finished fifth and lifted team hopes, which soon deflated when in Long Beach on April 9 he retired with a drive line failure. 'A team mistake,' admitted Green.

Jacques and Team Green bounced back at Nazareth where he started third and finished second, a result which hoisted morale with perfect timing on the eve of the month-long preparations for Indianapolis. This time, of course, Jacques knew just what he was doing and the team planned for it even better than they had the previous year. A famous victory, recorded after he had recovered from a two-lap penalty for passing the pace car, was achieved with a mixture of persistence, planning, good fortune and common sense. Twice, during the race, Jacques, who had qualified fifth, was able to conserve his fuel long enough to be on the end of the lead lap and catch a full-course 'yellow', which allowed him to regain most of that lap. He also kept his cool when under pressure in the closing stages to take advantage of Scott Goodyear's mistake in passing the pace car while leading. It was an error by his fellow Canadian which Jacques was pleased to anticipate when they entered Turn Three and Villeneuve saw from his telemetry that he was doing 180mph.

'I knew he was going too fast and would pass the pace car,' he explained. 'I lifted and then had to brake not to pass it, too. I couldn't believe it. I knew Scott was going to be black-flagged.' He was and Villeneuve won, to revel in a triumph which changed his season, his career and his life. The win lifted him into a points lead in the championship and confirmed beyond any doubt that he was a talent to be reckoned with, too special for just Indycar racing, as Pollock had obviously concluded. The manager of Jacques had already made, by then, his first preliminary visit to Europe to meet with various Formula One teams, and during discussions and meetings at Imola over the weekend of the San Marino Grand Prix had made his first contacts with Frank Williams. His client, Jacques Villeneuve, had only to keep on producing the results to ensure himself a top drive in Formula One for 1996.

The results continued to flow. He took pole at Portland but did not finish due to a broken shock absorber; took pole and won convincingly at Elkhart Lake; grabbed his third successive pole – the first driver to do so in three years – and finished third at Toronto. Then followed an incident-filled race at Cleveland which he won, to stay well ahead in the championship with 138 points to Bobby Rahal's 106, a result which confirmed that with five rounds to go the title was in his sights. It looked to be a comfortable target, but a warning came at Michigan on July 30 where, after qualifying fourth, he suffered a rear wheel bearing failure, pitted for repairs and then slogged round to claim tenth place before flying east to England, for his test at Silverstone with Williams. He still held a lead of 30 points in the drivers' title race and he was in demand on both sides of the Atlantic. Williams wanted him. Bernie Ecclestone wanted him. Team Green wanted to keep him. It was Jacques' call and he chose to make the move.

Chapter Ten

Reporting for Duty: 1995–1996

Soon after he won the Indianapolis 500, Jacques went to New York and appeared on television as a guest in David Letterman's *Late Night* show. He brought the house down. Not literally, only metaphorically. The show opened with Jacques racing around the block of the Ed Sullivan Theater against a New York cab driver, the pair of them driving 'identically prepared New York city taxis', as Letterman described them as he shrieked with excitement. 'No one – and that is the key – no one has a mechanical advantage. But the lights may be a factor, the traffic lights may be a factor.'

They started on 53rd Street. Jacques' yellow cab carried the number 27, while his rival's car merely carried an 'off duty' sign. It was hilarious stuff from the moment the official starter said 'gentlemen, start your meters' through to the finish. The cabbie won to an accompaniment of finger-pickin' country music and a screaming studio audience. Jacques looked partly bemused and partly amused, but it was fun for everyone.

Jacques then made a studio appearance. In coast-to-coast terms, real terms, this was his introduction to America as a public figure and a sporting star. On his introduction, Jacques was asked by Letterman, 'Well, how does it feel now, Mr Big Shot?' And Jacques replied, 'Well, after losing, it never feels great.' Falling easily into the mood, Jacques suggested 'we had a problem with the engine' and had 'got caught in the New York traffic . . . we are not used to the New York traffic yet.' He traced his life history and admitted, 'I had never thought about it. It has always been there. One day I am going to race cars.' He explained that he had grown up always wanting to do things fast, or to jump higher or just to do it more than the other guys and laughed at Letterman's response: 'Well, that's good news for the girl!'

On a more serious note, he talked about the Indianapolis 500 (Letterman admitted he was from Indianapolis) and the tension and the atmosphere. He said that when he walked out half an hour before the start, when the atmosphere is at its most electric in front of 500,000 people, 'it was the moment you have been waiting for a whole month, so you are just thinking "thank God, it is coming". You have been working hard that month and you just cannot wait to start the race. This year it was okay because we had a police escort and we could come in late, but last year I had to wake up at four in the morning and get to the track and to beat the traffic so I was too tired to feel anything last year.'

Asked about the race, Jacques admitted, 'I didn't know I was in the lead and it was the second time this had happened. Last year, when we got into the lead, the team had the board and it had "1" written on it and I thought it might mean I have to come into the pits in one lap and I didn't know. I was not sure. So, the next lap I looked at the big tower and my number was at the top so I thought "Great, I'm leading! Let's not do anything stupid now." This year, the leader pitted just before the yellow flags, so the team was just looking at the meter and telling me "don't use too much fuel, we've got to make sure we don't run out because the pits are closed until all the cars pack up behind the pace car". So, I didn't know I was in the lead, the team didn't know and every time I got behind the pace car, I just went flying by. And that happened twice!'

Jacques was penalised two laps, a punishment which meant he had to do 202 laps to win the 200-lap race. 'A new tradition,' interjected Jacques. 'Yes, I believe it is the first time someone has won from being two laps down. But, I tell you the feeling when the team told me I was two laps down . . . Well, I can't really tell you what I said. I was screaming in the helmet.'

Letterman asked him about the purse for winning. 'It was a million three something,' said Jacques. 'Woah Cool!' said Letterman. 'But the team gets it and then I get my cut,' explained Jacques. 'For any driver, winning that race, it's like winning the Olympics. It means everything.'

'And you got a speeding ticket a couple of days ago?' asked Letterman. 'Yeah,' said Jacques. 'You get penalised on the race track and then on the highway as well. We were driving with another driver, Alessandro Zampedri, and he was racing at Indy as well. And he was in another car and we wanted to get to Milwaukee from Indy and we wanted to beat Chicago's rush hour. It was okay, you know. I was staying under 100mph, so it was pretty safe. But that was not the problem. We stopped to get a burger and fries, and got into the car to eat and drive and just when we got back on the highway there was a police car that just flew by us and so we couldn't go fast any more. So, I was following it and when the police car noticed I was following it, it went up to 85 so I stayed on its bumper and I . . .' ('Just what is wrong with you?' shouted Letterman, as raucous applause drowned out the end of Jacques' sentence.)

On the same show, when asked about his father he said: 'Well, what I know is what I have heard from people and what I have seen on tape. From what I have seen, he was pretty crazy, always sideways and going faster than the car could go. At the time, people loved that. He used to destroy a lot of cars, but they loved him and especially in Italy, which is strange with him being Canadian.'

Finally, Letterman asked about the season. 'Well, we're leading with 22 points and . . .' Jacques could get no further. The show ended and he had been exposed to a wider public than ever before, revealing a zany sense of humour, a broad and relaxed smile and a contentment with himself and his career that had not been seen previously by the outside world. The fans loved him for it. One, Doug Stark from Ontario, said: 'A marketing guy's dream. Wins the biggest race in America. Only man in history to win it when he was two laps down! Young, good-looking, great smile (women love him), fits in with the 18–25 set and gets a bloody ticket four days after winning the Indy 500!'

Winning the Indianapolis 500 at only his second attempt made Jacques Villeneuve a star. Not only the achievement, but the manner of it – and the fact that he was so young (only 24, at the time) – ensured him of massive fame. His family name added the rest. But the incident with the yellows, when he passed the pace car and was penalised after 45 laps, captured the imagination too. Confusion was at the cause of it.

According to his team, he was a lap down and should have passed the pace car, but in fact, as he discovered later, he was leading and should have obeyed the pace car's instructions to stay behind. He had taken the lead when Scott Goodyear, running for Tasman Motorsports, pitted. 'It was a flagrant violation. I think there were three instances when the pace car tried to wave him down. He just didn't slow down,' said Tom Binford, the chief steward.

The incident made history at Indianapolis. While Jacques was out following the pace car, he was also conserving fuel on Cicale's instructions. Cicale had calculated that, at that time, Jacques had only a gallon and a half of fuel left. When the pace car waved other cars, tailenders, by, it seemed Jacques mistakenly understood the signal was intended for him. Confusion reigned. Eventually, it was determined that Jacques was leading – Scott Goodyear and Mario Andretti having pitted – and the field packed up behind him before they opened the pits. Jacques knew he had to come in. It was desperate and he ran out of fuel as he came down the pitlane on lap 42, under yellows.

Cicale was dumbfounded at the chaos. The incident upset him, Jacques and the team, but it determined them to make amends by running as quickly as possible, squeezing the fuel as far as possible and making the tyres last. 'He stayed out longer than the others because we did not worry about the half-tank scenario. He came into the pits only twice more, both times right out of fuel and tyres. We went with a softer Goodyear tyre. It increased our speed, a great deal, in the race and allowed us to get our two laps back.' The team clawed away at their disadvantage.

On lap 80, when the leader Mauricio Gugelmin pitted, Jacques pitted and beat him out. That unlapped him one of the laps. On lap 117, Gugelmin pitted again. On lap 123, Jacques pitted, while the track was under yellows, and managed to squeeze out ahead of the leader to unlap himself once again. He was back in the race, in tenth place, 14 seconds behind Gugelmin.

The rest of the race was then a scrabble with fuel strategy, clever use of the yellows when they were out, and opportunism. Jacques worked his way up to third, obeying his instructions to the letter. Between laps 138 and 141, he moved up to second behind new leader Jimmy Vasser, thanks to not stopping under the yellow. On lap 155, he led for the first time since the penalty when Vasser stopped under the green, but was engaged in a battle with Goodyear and Pruett to the end of the race.

A mistaken effort to pit at the end of lap 163 resulted in Jacques losing two places. Two laps later, he made his final pit-stop. By lap 185, it was Goodyear in the leap ahead of Scott Pruett and Villeneuve. Vasser, in a Ganassi Reynard, clipped a wall. Then Pruett spun into a wall, the yellows came out again and the final dash to the flag lay in prospect once the pace car peeled off.

It was then that Goodyear, full of charging adrenalin, made his mistake. He anticipated the pace car's exit, hit his accelerator hard and passed it before it had reached the pitlane. It was a serious mistake, and he was to be punished severely. A black flag came out. He ignored it and went on to race the distance, but was disqualified from the final five laps and was classified 14th in the result. Jacques, who was second on the track at the time, was the winner. The race was over, the celebrations began with the traditional milk in the pitlane and the championship and Europe beckoned.

'Jacques did a great job of conserving fuel when he had to and driving aggressively when he had to,' said Green. 'We ran the fuel mixture very lean for much of the race and that causes the engine to run hot which robs you of horsepower, so he did a fantastic job to run as quickly as he did.'

Jacques' victory, though widely celebrated, was overshadowed by tragedy as veteran Stan Fox suffered critical head injuries following a crash at the start. But Jacques deserved his triumph and admitted: 'When I heard we were two laps down, I think I swore a little bit. The important thing here is not to lose any laps. I never saw the pace car driver wave at me, so I just kept going the first two times. The third time, he was really waving, so I hit the brakes. I didn't know he was talking to me as I didn't know I was in the lead.'

Green said: 'I guess the strongest memory for me was when we stopped talking for about five or six laps after we had found out about the two-lap penalty. The radio was completely silent and the whole team was completely silent. But then we began to rally ourselves as we realised we could turn the situation around and the whole team, along with Jacques, worked really hard for that victory. It was a great day.'

It was a tumultuous triumph, as is any Indianapolis 500 victory for anyone. It put Jacques on the cover of the *New York Times* and stimulated *Paris Match* to interview his mother, living in Monaco. The French magazine sent reporter Virginie Merlin to La Mascotte. Joann, who watched the race live on her television at home, admitted that seeing him drive in that event was 'a moment filled with emotion and distress' and added that Jacques had telephoned her immediately after the race, just as his father Gilles had always done when he was alive.

Asked about Jacques as a little boy, she said he was '*un petit garçon agite qui ne restait pas en place, qui avait besoin de bouger tous les temps*'. In English, a restless little boy who could not stay in one place for long, but had to keep on the move. Very like his father, she added. 'He wouldn't want to sit at the table to eat when he was in a hurry to get to his games.'

In an interview which ranged across many family matters, Joann said that Gilles had been 'crazy about him and very proud' when asked about his feelings for his son. She recounted the memories of Gilles bringing him presents, particularly little cars which were the only toys which truly interested Jacques, and explained that Jacques had always wanted to be a racing driver. If pressed, said Joann, he would always say that there was nothing else in the world he wanted to do than to become a driver.

She admitted to her continuing migraines and stress related to Jacques' racing. But she made it clear she was deeply proud of him and said he had been an adorable son, '*gentil et sage*'. And, when asked if Jacques was in love, replied 'Yes, for two years. She is Canadian, like him, and she also lives in Monaco. They have known each other since they were young. She is 22 and she is called Sandrine. She is completing her studies in Montreal. They have been together for two years.'

Joann was asked about the ways in which Jacques reminded her of Gilles. 'To begin with, physically, they are similar,' she said. 'They have the same determination, the same courage. Nothing stops him, like his father. And also his calmness. And his air, perhaps, of being a little cold. For those who don't know him well, he doesn't give much away. Gilles was the same.'

In her final answer, Joann revealed how proud she is of Jacques. 'He is *sympathique*. He always has a smile and he is marvellous. He has a natural joy of life, an energy which can explode. I am proud of him.'

After Indianapolis, Jacques went on to win the Indycar drivers' championship. At Milwaukee, the event to which he was hurrying when he was given a speeding ticket, he finished sixth in a race that was something of an anti-climax after the events at Indianapolis. At Detroit, he was ninth, having qualified ninth. At Portland, on June 24, he took pole position for the first time, but retired with a broken shock absorber mount while running second; and at Elkhart Lake, he re-asserted himself with a strong performance – pole position and a convincing win thanks to excellent team spirit and Cicale's decision to run in a low down-force set-up. That put him 22 points clear of Robby Gordon and ready for a smooth run-in to the title.

After that he was third in Toronto; won at Cleveland, after a

controversial race in which there was a certain level of unaccep-
tably rough driving; finished tenth at Michigan (after which he
tested for Williams at Silverstone); took third at Mid-Ohio despite
two crashes in practice; was fourth at New Hampshire (the first
race after it was announced he had signed to join Williams); 12th
at Vancouver after cruising to pole and then suffering gear-box
trouble; and, finally, 11th at Laguna Seca after two left-front
punctures. He was the youngest Indycar champion since 1952.

Canadian magazine *Saturday Night* did a feature after his
second pole. It was an inspired choice. Jacques, it was reported, had never been on pole position, and here he was with
two in succession under his belt. His final qualifying lap was fast
and smooth and set a new record at an average speed of
142.206mph. 'Well, on the last lap, you give it everything you
have,' he admitted. 'Sometimes, you have to go a little bit over
the edge, sometimes you crash and sometimes it works. Today
it worked.'

Green was full of praise for Jacques' ability to work long and
hard hours when needed. 'You know,' he told Jacob Richler,
'Villeneuve was here until 8.30 last night. He was trying to figure
out how he could arrange the gears so that they would better suit
him today. Maybe he picked up pole position today by improving
the car that much. Or maybe we picked up nothing from it. But the
fact that he spent two and a half hours trying to figure it out with
the team . . .'

The sentence was not finished. But it indicated something
special in the bond between Jacques and his engineer Cicale,
the 'father figure', and his team. They were a tight-knit, happy and
loyal bunch together. They worked for each other. All for one and
one for all. And at this time, Jacques was considering Formula
One, but had not made any decision. He had not tested for
Williams. All that was to come. 'As young as he is,' Green went
on, 'to be as fast as he is around this track is quite incredible.
You've got to be really fluid around a track like Road America.
Really smooth.'

Saturday Night carried quotes also from Joann and, of course, from Jacques who, his mother said, grew to dislike watching his father race because of the dangers. 'He was old enough to be aware of the danger and it made him nervous,' she explained. 'But you know, if you are afraid of spiders as a child, it does not mean that you will be afraid of them for the rest of your life. Jacques always wanted to be a race car driver. Part of that comes from having grown up with it. I never discouraged him, but I did try to give him as many different options as I could. He went to a very good private school in Switzerland.'

Jacques admitted: 'In a way, I miss not having gone to university. I was getting good grades at Beau Soleil. I was doing maths and physics and I found that very enjoyable. And it's a fun life when you're with other kids at a boarding school. But when I started racing, the school thought it best to kick me out because it wasn't fair to the other students. And that was it.'

In his feature article, Richler talked also to Pollock about Jacques. He was told that Pollock met Jacques again, after leaving his post as director of sports at Beau Soleil, when he was at the 1991 Monaco Grand Prix and they bumped into one another in the paddock. 'Jacques was dressed in a camel overcoat, looking a real scruff,' said Pollock, who took him out that night, according to Richler. 'He was a bit lost.' He introduced him to some of his Formula One friends (Pollock, by then, had become active in motor sports promotion). Within a short time, after each had gone their separate ways – Pollock to Switzerland, Jacques back to Italy – the young driver was turning up in his offices to persuade him to become his manager.

Pollock told Richler he agreed to take the job and soon after moved Jacques to race in Japan, a comment, if accurate, which would confirm that Pollock was installed as Jacques' manager before 1992. 'It was the most competitive F3 series at the time,' he said. 'Basically, it was going to be good for his maturity both as a person and as a race driver.' Richler's research throws light on to how and where Jacques met Sandrine, who was at a race meeting, sitting in a 'big, plush chair halfway down the motorhome, engrossed in one of Anne Rice's vampire chronicles'. Gros d'Aillon now studies communications at Concordia University in Montreal, but she lived in Monaco for ten years, where the two met at the Canadian Club, at a Canada Day party, of all things.

Villeneuve talked to Richler over his usual lunch of pasta and tomato sauce. 'I love this sport,' he told him, 'because I like being on the edge. I like speed. But not any kind of speed. You could be in a plane and going very very fast and that's nothing. But speed when you feel the limits and when if you go over the limit, you're going to crash or something is going to go wrong. It can be on skis or on a motorbike. And in a car, well, Indycar racing is so competitive you have to push yourself sometimes beyond the limit. It's great. This has always been what I wanted to do. I never thought about doing anything else.'

Later, he added in a discussion about his future that he was interested in Formula One and felt there was a good chance he would make that move. 'But if I got to F1, it won't be because my father was there and I want to do everything he did. I'm really proud to be his son, and he will always be a legend. He will always be up there whatever I accomplish. But the reason I'm racing is not because he died and, for example, he didn't win a championship so I have to do it instead of him. No, that has nothing to do with it. The reason I'm racing is because I want to.'

After his test with Williams, Jacques talked to a few of his closest and most trusted friends and colleagues in the motor racing world. Then, he agreed to join them. Green was upset to see him going and Jacques was happy to be moving, but not so happy at leaving his friends behind. It was a wrench after three happy years.

'I think Jacques is his own person and lives his own life in his own right except when he is racing,' said Green. 'He worked really hard for our team and was completely focused. So focused. He was very good at figuring out situations and problems. He would never step into the unknown. If he only had a car that was good enough for tenth, he would finish tenth. If he had a car good enough to win, he would win. I will remember the whole thing with him. The three years were planned with Jacques, his manager and myself and the fact that it worked really well, better than any of us thought, was absolutely fantastic.'

'I wanted to go with a top team and now I have the opportunity,' said Jacques, when he was asked to explain his decision to switch from Indycars to Formula One and Williams. 'If I had decided to stay in Indycars, it would have closed doors to me in Formula One down the road. So, we decided that now was the time to do it. I'm sure I'll miss Indycars and Team Green quite a lot.'

He won the Indycar title at Laguna Seca on September 10 and was in Europe, testing for Williams at Monza, on September 13 three days later. It was a big show for him and for the Italians. They flocked to see the son of their hero. Jacques did 38 laps, clocked a best time of 1:27.11 and eased himself into it. 'Once we got going, it went pretty well,' he said.

He talked of the challenge ahead, the changing of series and continents, as if it was all part of a seamless flow of life for him. And it was. He talked of the learning process he faced and the newness of everything that lay ahead, but he did so with a quiet confidence that made the Formula One world sit up and listen.

He went on to test at Imola, at Magny-Cours in France, at Estoril in Portugal, all the time gaining more and more experience, including his first running in wet conditions. He practised and he tested until he understood the car, the challenge and some of the circuits well. Then, he was ready. He had completed the apprenticeship and he was reporting for duty as team-mate to Damon Hill for what was certain to be an exciting 1996 season in Formula One.

Michael Schumacher, the double world champion, had moved to Ferrari. Jean Alesi and Gerhard Berger had gone the other way to Benetton. Hill was rising strong in reaction to his disappointments of the previous season and Jacques Villeneuve had arrived.

Chapter Eleven

The Kid's First Year: 1996

March 9 1996. Melbourne. The day before the opening race of the season and Jacques Villeneuve is driving his Rothmans Williams Renault FW18 fast, with precision and with commitment and he secures pole position for the Australian Grand Prix. It is a performance of verve and it makes everyone talk. Pole on his debut! Hey, this is something. The talk is about him and his father. It may be the start of the kid's first year, but his old man is the subject on the lips of so many who have yet to allow the son to rise that Jacques' own achievements take many people by surprise.

They should not have done. In his brief career, particularly in his three years in America, he had made a considerable impact – especially when you think of that Indianapolis 500 triumph – and he was well prepared for his opening Formula One race meeting in every respect.

Jacques had been testing throughout the winter, spending many hours at Estoril, many hours with reporters who wanted to find out about the new Villeneuve and many hours learning his way around the circuits, the cars and the people of Formula One. He did 6,000 miles of testing. In the Williams team, he was quickly nicknamed 'Mr Smiley' and then 'Kermit' and later 'Bambi'. Patrick Head, the team's booming-voiced technical director, said Jacques practised 'high grunge' when he first took serious note of his new driver's tastes in civilian clothes. Everyone at Williams seemed to like him. He was the new pet.

When Ann Bradshaw, the team's press officer, was asked how Jacques was settling in, her reply was instantaneous and affectionate. 'He's mad! Totally bonkers,' she exclaimed. 'He has quickly become part of the family.' For Jacques, it was a busy and pressurised period in his life. He had to work hard, learn fast and perform at a high standard. He stayed in close touch with his family, his mother Joann and sister Melanie, and listened to the advice of manager Craig Pollock.

Joann said: 'Gilles was very competitive with a lot of drive. When he was struggling, and after he died, I also needed a lot of determination to carry on. Jacques has that determination and drive. I'm basically a calm person and he may have inherited that from me. He also has an analytical mind which I think he got more from me than Gilles, who was a lot more impulsive as a person. Jacques is very mature for his age. He's been through a lot, learned a lot and now he's very much his own man. He doesn't want to be seen as a replacement for his father. Jacques wants to be seen as Jacques.'

This maturity was manifested in his work. He concentrated hard. He clocked good times. On the eve of the season, he was being talked of as a possible championship challenger, certainly capable of coping with the speed and experience of Damon Hill, his Williams team-mate and 11 years his senior. In an interview with *F1 Racing*, Jacques made it clear he felt he could be champion in his debut year. 'I don't think it is out of the question. I know I can be quick, so that means I can fight with the quickest. That's my personality. You're in there because you are a competitive person in anything you do. You want to win and you want to beat everybody.'

In the same interview, he said he felt that the Williams team offered him the family atmosphere he wanted. 'Once you get involved with the people who work on your car, and you get a close relationship, then it's just the same. You work with human beings, and communication is what counts. Frank Williams is very much like that, and I think it's one of the reasons he's had so much success. The relationship has been great so far, but I'm sure if we had a few bad races, it would be different.' He denied, again, that he was carrying on his father's legacy. 'I'm not racing because my father left too early and I have to carry the name and the tradition. I don't really care about tradition. I'm racing because I have fun and I enjoy it.'

As always, there were hints at the private and personal side of his character, but no tangible pieces of information. Jacques revealed that he enjoyed reading Tolkien, fantasy books, playing the piano (when the time permitted) and writing his own songs. He said he felt Damon Hill was a very nice guy. 'He's fast, too. I will have equal number one status with him and I think we'll get along quite well,' he said. Talking more about books, he added: 'I read a lot, especially books like *Lord of the Rings*. I don't want to read about something that happens every day. I want to escape into something completely unreal. But it makes sense when you put yourself into that other world, and I like that.'

The build-up period had also revealed a well of confidence in him at Williams. Head admitted that the team had signed him after seeing him in action in the test in August 1995 and after receiving quite a lot of information about him. 'A lot of top drivers have adequate skills,' he admitted. 'It's a question of whether they have the motivation and all the other things that go together to make a good Grand Prix driver. He has the necessary determination to succeed.' Talking to *Autosport*, Head added: 'I would be surprised if he doesn't win some races, but it would be fanciful for anyone to expect him to be in a position to win the championship.' As to pressure, and his ability to deal with it, Head said: 'I think he'll be quite good in that way. He's quite good at isolating himself from those pressures and if they become too heavy he's got one or two people around him who'll make sure that he's isolated a bit from them anyway.'

Jacques himself was confident from the start. The test at Silverstone had told him what he wanted to know about Williams and Formula One. 'Yes, it was important to do the test, not that I could adapt to Formula One, or to show that I could, because personally I felt like I could, but to see how the team works, to see how the human side of it was, and it was very positive. It looked like you could get a great chemistry going on and that is what it takes to win. That is what we had in the States and to me that was important. If you have got to spend most of the year with the same people, working hard, you need a human relationship.'

By the time they got to Melbourne, everyone at Williams, Hill included, knew that Jacques was serious about winning races and about challenging for the title. It might take time, but it would happen. There was a certainty about him and it. In Australia, it was hot, but after taking a close look at the circuit, by jogging and roller-skating, Jacques felt cool about the whole thing. His debut was not going to be such a big deal for him as it was for the media masses. He was fast throughout, dealt adroitly with attention he received, secured pole in a style to send a frisson through the paddock and then missed out on victory in the race only after leading, recording the fastest lap and succumbing to pressure from Hill. He hit a kerb and damaged an oil pipe, causing the loss of oil pressure which prompted the team's Renault engineers to request him to slow down. But second, on his race debut, was enough to create headlines about a star being born and talk of Jacques as a new Senna even if he could not emulate the record of Giancarlo Baghetti, who was the only previous driver to have won on his debut, back in 1961, at Reims.

In the *Sun* newspaper in London, former Grand Prix winner and *Eurosport* commentator John Watson was quoted as saying: 'Jacques is so much like Ayrton, it's uncanny. The way he drives and his tremendous confidence reminds me of Ayrton. There's no doubt he is going to take the sport by storm and Damon will have no easy rides if he is to win his first world title.' Bernie Ecclestone, who had pulled off the move that brought Jacques to Formula One and Williams, was just as confident. 'He will do whatever he has to do at the time to get the result,' he said. 'He is like Senna as a person and Prost as a driver.'

In Brazil, however, after a besieged stay at the beach house of the late Ayrton Senna's family in Angra dos Reis where Jacques could hardly even spend an hour on the beach, he found it more difficult. Jackie Stewart had said that Jacques' debut in Australia was the best he had seen by a Formula One driver and, in Brazil, the new Villeneuve reportedly flew into the track in a helicopter laid on by Ayrton Senna Promotions, organised by Julian Jakobi. But, on another circuit he had never seen before, he found it more difficult too. Interlagos was physically tougher, he qualified in third place on the grid, and it rained.

Jacques spun out after 26 laps of the race on the last Sunday in March. Hill won for the second Grand Prix in succession and added a third a week later in Buenos Aires when he dominated the Argentine Grand Prix. Jacques finished second. From three fly-away races, it was a promising start for the newcomer. He followed it with victory, in his fourth Formula One race, at the Nurburgring in the European Grand Prix on April 28, but then endured a disappointing San Marino Grand Prix at Imola where he was among the non-classified runners at the finish. 'I made a mistake in Brazil and at Imola, I was a little on the edge with the components,' he admitted. 'A wishbone broke. But that could have been due to my first-lap collision with Jean Alesi. My start was a bit hairy and all the banging wheels with Jean was a bit useless, as well.'

In these opening races of the year, several interesting things emerged. One was that Jacques took a very different route on set-up with his car to that taken by Hill; another was that he preferred to remain outside and independent from the rest of the drivers and the way things had traditionally been done. (He declined to join the Grand Prix Drivers' Association, for example; and he also elected to stay as remote from media relations as possible, a decision that was promoted by his manager Pollock, designed to protect him from over-exposure. It did not make him universally popular.)

On set-ups, however, Jock Clear, Jacques' race engineer, said: 'Their set-ups [Jacques' and Hill's] are as different as they could be, chalk and cheese. Jacques is more of the Schumacher/

Hakkinen school, which likes oversteer. In effect, he says "get the front end to turn in really well for me, and I'll catch the back end before it comes round." Each probably couldn't drive the other's set-up, but for Jacques, his own approach seems to be bearing fruit.'

The set-up talk did nothing to disturb Hill as Jacques gathered experience and steam during the first half of the season, before building up pressure in the second. He always remained in contention for the title, even when he was 17 points behind Hill as they flew to Montreal for the Canadian Grand Prix in June. After Imola, he had retired from a difficult rain-swept Monaco Grand Prix following an accident and then followed world champion Michael Schumacher of Germany home in his Ferrari at the Spanish Grand Prix. That race, in tempest-like conditions, had seen Hill retire ignominiously and early, and given Jacques a chance to cut the gap, but few observers felt he could raise his performance level sufficiently to stay the pace.

By the time the circus reached Montreal, the local hero was the inspiration of a phenomenon known as 'Jacko Mania', a cult movement which seemed to have swept through every shop, store, bar, pub and restaurant. The emotional wave was unlimited, but Jacques himself seemed suitably unimpressed when he strolled into the Museum of Fine Arts to participate in a pre-race media conference. Jacques, quite simply, did not want to be there. 'We are doing this today so there will be no pressure this weekend,' he explained. 'For sure, it will be a special race because it's in Canada and in front of the fans, but all that means is that there will be a lot more pressure outside the race car.'

The fact that the Canadian Grand Prix was to take place on the circuit named after his father did nothing for him. 'He died when I was 12 [sic] and then I went to boarding school in Switzerland and I didn't spend the rest of my life crying and thinking that my daddy wasn't with me. It's just that life goes on. Racing here in Canada is special because it's in Canada, but the fact that the track is named after my father is not very special, partly because he didn't design the track, because the track was designed and named after him. If it had been designed by him, then it would have been special.'

In Montreal, Jacques missed out on pole by just two-hundredths of a second in front of a huge crowd. It was a critical advantage for Hill, who started from the front, won the battle for the first corner and took the race. Jacques was disappointed, but not despondent. He had given his best and only narrowly missed out on claiming what would have been a stirring victory.

A fortnight later, on June 30, it was the French Grand Prix and the result was the same: a Hill victory after Schumacher had taken pole position, with Jacques second; but this time Jacques had had to recover from a very heavy crash during qualifying. He described it graphically in his own column in London's *Daily Telegraph* newspaper: 'Coming out of one of the fastest corners on the circuit at about 140mph, the car went a little bit wide, but not wanting to lose the lap, I chose not to lift off. The car went over a kerb for a moment and the wheels were off the ground. When they touched down, it was on wet grass, which made the braking useless and the steering difficult. Any hope of regaining control was lost when a dip in the ground launched the car into the air just before it ploughed into a tyre barrier.

'The angle of the car at the point of impact was not particularly severe, but, instead of sliding along the barrier, the tyres grabbed the car with great force, stopping it dead, then bouncing it back onto the track. The car was wrecked and my helmet hit either the steering wheel or the windscreen and there were also paint marks on it from hitting the tyres. Still, it could have been worse. Throughout the accident, I kept my hands on the steering wheel which, I'm convinced, helped absorb some of the impact. Normally, it is thought that drivers should take their hands off the wheel in these situations, but keeping my hands on the steering wheel had helped me in a couple of heavy crashes in Indycar racing. All that force has to go somewhere and, if you don't deflect it by gripping the wheel, a lot of it will be transferred into your shoulder straps, which could break a collarbone, or even your neck.

'As it happened, my neck was stretched enough to cause some

pain, but not enough to prevent me from using the spare car and finishing qualifying with a lap time as quick as the earlier one.'

Intense physiotherapy from Erwin Goellner, the Williams team physiotherapist, and a long night shift from the Williams mechanics, ensured Jacques took part in the race and managed to score six points for second place. This feat, coupled with the accident and his machismo in dismissing it as nothing very much, impressed many observers, and Jacques, far from being viewed solely as a talented man of the future, began to be studied more closely. After all, he was the same man who had taken up piano lessons earlier in the season, as a recreation, and who had been offered a job by a computer shop in Monaco when he revealed he had bought a collection of component parts to make his own computer and had built it in just three hours.

After France, Jacques went to Silverstone determined to exact some revenge on Hill for beating him at Montreal. He wanted to give him some of his own medicine and, with luck in the form of a mechanical failure on one of Hill's wheels, he achieved it. He may have qualified second, but he won the race and he clocked the fastest lap at the British Grand Prix. The start, however, was decisive. 'We had the same weapon here as Damon,' admitted Jacques. 'The same engine, same car and basically the same refuelling strategy . . . And we were very close anyway. We knew it was important to get him then, and, of course, he didn't have a very good start. But then it was close with Alesi – who got a very good start – and it was close into turn one.' Asked about Hill's poor start, he said: 'I don't know. I was concentrating on my own start and I didn't care why he had a bad start . . . I was just happy about it.'

Jacques' Silverstone victory kept his title hopes alive. He had gone into the race 25 points behind, but he came out of it only 15 down and with six races remaining. His win also gave him an opportunity to refute rumours that had been circulating in some parts of the paddock, suggesting he was to be replaced in the Williams team for 1997. 'I know what my situation is, so that's just it . . . All you need is one person in the paddock to open his mouth and invent a story and the 20 other papers will write it,' he said. 'It's bull.'

Commendably, he rejected the notion – put forward as a possibility – that he might make the most of Hill's alleged problems with coping under pressure by 'playing with that'. The answer from Jacques was honourable and unequivocal. 'No. Not outside of the car,' he said. 'I think those are stupid games. Mentally, that's outside the car. There's no point in that. He will put pressure on himself. I don't have to play those stupid games.' Pressure certainly did begin to build up on Hill in the second half of the year, particularly in late July when rumours circulated that his seat at Williams was under threat and that Heinz-Harald Frentzen was being recruited to replace him. He answered the rumours by taking pole, winning and recording fastest lap in the German Grand Prix at Hockenheim, where Jacques finished third after Gerhard Berger had retired with a blown Renault engine in the closing laps in his Benetton. Jacques suffered from problems with a broken front damper, solved after the warm-up, but never found his best set-up for the race.

This left him, with five races remaining, still attempting to find the big rush from behind to claim the crown and become the first man to win an Indycar World Series drivers' title and the Formula One championship back to back. He would, if he was successful, also become the first newcomer to win an F1 title at the first attempt. The gap was 19 points when they went to Hungary, where Jacques remained hopeful. 'We can fight very hard and we will do that   we will try to beat him,' he said.

In qualifying, it was a resurgent Schumacher on pole, Hill second and Villeneuve third. But in the race, the order was changed and Jacques won. Hill, after some tactical problems following a poor start, was able to recover and storm back to second. The Williams' team triumph, another one-two in a season of six such successes, earned them the constructors' championship for a record-equalling eighth time. 'That means we don't have to think about that any more,' said Jacques. 'We had a good lead in the constructors' championship, so we knew we had to be careful for that, but now we can fight hard with Damon.'

The Budapest triumph was a significant one. It showed that Jacques could learn and shine on a tight and twisty circuit on which he was driving for the first time, resist heavy media pressure and speculation – he had been urged by Bernie Ecclestone to take part in a television documentary with Clive James, but had refused; after which James, in a throwaway line, described him as 'the Greta Garbo of the pitlane' – keep himself out of trouble and take advantage of any opportunity that arose. (In this race, he effectively passed Schumacher in the pits to seize the initiative.)

After this victory, which many believed was built out of Villeneuve's success in persuading the team to permit him to pursue his own personalised set-ups following a successful test at Nogaro in France while Hill was on holiday, events moved quickly on to the classic Belgian Grand Prix at Spa-Francorchamps in the Ardennes. A sweeping circuit of majesty and high speeds, it was a venue loved by everyone and widely expected to offer Jacques a massive challenge on his first time there. It was a big challenge, but he met it and overcame it easily by grabbing pole position with the help of some typically capricious wet weather. The race, however, was a different matter, with Schumacher stamping his authority on proceedings on his own favourite track to claim a marvellous victory for Ferrari. Jacques was second, Hill fifth and the championship, once looking almost like a foregone conclusion in the Englishman's favour, suddenly seemed to be wide open again.

'It's a great track,' said Villeneuve, for whom radio communications problems led to a messed-up pit stop. 'More like the old-fashioned circuits. We don't have enough of these. Because it is so long, by the time you get to the end of a lap, you have almost forgotten what it was like when you started.'

On the same weekend, John Watson, the winner of the fatal race at nearby Zolder in 1982, recalled his relationship with Gilles Villeneuve and compared him with his son, Jacques. 'Gilles was a natural driver with phenomenal instincts and reactions and he liked to have a car that you could throw around with oversteer,' recalled Watson. 'He could only drive one way and that was flat out.'

For Watson, it was a tragedy in itself that Gilles drove only for Ferrari (a team which, he said, treated drivers badly by throwing them against one another in those days) and never for a team like Williams, as Jacques did. 'Perhaps Ferrari were the worst team for Gilles Villeneuve,' he explained. 'The gift and the talent he had as a racing driver were misused at Ferrari because they, as a team, loved the caricature of the racing driver that Gilles was. Had he been signed up by McLaren or Williams, Brabham or Ligier, those were the teams that had really begun to capitalise on the ground effects at that time and had Gilles gone there he would have learned things that he was totally ignorant of. Gilles' potential was exploited as the result of the adulation and mythology that grew up around him. It was wasted because the natural talents and gifts that he had never got the results. It didn't half build up a myth, but the sad thing is that the man died – and he died because he made a decision in a particular set of circumstances which were very charged by emotion from the Grand Prix at Imola. It was a waste of a driver, a waste of a life, and a waste of a charismatic man and a family man as well. If he had been in Ligier or Brabham, what they would have taught him about being a Grand Prix driver, rather than just getting in and driving it to death, he would have won more Grands Prix, he would have been world champion and he would probably be living today.'

Watson was grieved by the death of Gilles Villeneuve, particularly in the way he died, but he saw much to encourage him in his son. 'Jacques is establishing his own identity,' he said. 'He is a product of his mother and father and he has had a very good European education and I would say he is much cleverer and brighter than his father was. He is not Gilles Villeneuve, he is a facsimile of Gilles Villeneuve on the race track. He will take on his father and combine it with his own personality. They have a different talent. Jacques has used his talent to win races. He is a thinking racing driver, developing speed, where his father had raw speed, but that's because they grew up in a different place. Jacques had no checks on him. No restrictions. Gilles would do things driving from Monte Carlo to Fiorano that you would get ten years in jail for. No respect for other cars or other road-users, self-belief, and driving at speeds that were just ridiculous. Totally reckless.'

He went on to suggest that Jacques could be very like his father, but using his own education to try and 'cap' the explosive nature of his personality, keep it under control within him. 'He thinks he might be sitting on a time bomb, he thinks he might have his real father in him, and he might be capping it because he has had an education and an upbringing which has given him better intellect to cope with the situation,' said Watson. It was a hint that the competitive side of Jacques' personality lay mostly hidden from view.

Asked about his relationship with Hill, Jacques said: 'We are competitors. We don't hate each other's guts. There's no reason for that. He is a nice guy and we get along pretty well. But that's where it stops.' This was not a hint at tension below the surface, but a statement of fact. Just as it was purely factual for him to explain that he had learned his way around Spa in advance by 'checking out a new video motor racing game (Microprose 2). The tracks are actually quite close to real life which gives you a good idea of where you should be going. When you come out of the pits, it just gives you an idea of which way the track goes.'

At Spa, he also talked about the famous Eau Rouge corner and compared it to the Indycar ovals and hinted that his style of starting, using left-foot braking and a hand-clutch, would suit him better for the uphill grid. But once he had finished, he was disappointed. 'It was a good opportunity to put up a lot of points against Damon, so in that respect I am disappointed. We partly lost the race through lack of communication at the moment when the flag came out . . . We didn't understand what we were saying to each other.'

After the Belgian Grand Prix, it was clear the championship showdown was alive and well, even if Hill's hopes were waning.

He was told the following week that his services were not required by Williams for 1997 and, after the furore had died down, arrived at Monza for the Italian Grand Prix intent on regaining some of his lost leadership over Jacques. Hill was composed, took pole position ahead of Jacques, but lost the race again when after a mediocre start and a scrap to regain the lead on the opening lap, he hit tyres installed to provide a temporary safety measure at the chicane and was forced to retire on lap six. Jacques also had problems after running over the chicane on the opening lap, damaging his steering, and he finished seventh. Schumacher won. The title race for the drivers' championship went on to Portugal and Estoril on September 22.

There, again, Hill took pole, dominated the weekend and scorched away. But Jacques, second on the grid, steadily worked his way back after a poor start, passed Schumacher on the outside of the final Parabolica corner – causing an uproar in the process – and won brilliantly to cut Hill's lead to nine points with one race, in Japan, remaining. And there, at Suzuka, on a warm, perfect sunlit afternoon on October 13, it was decided by the combination of a return to his best form by Hill and an errant wheel, which worked itself loose off the right rear of Jacques' car and bounced into the second safety net at the first corner with 15 laps to go. It was all over. Jacques had needed a victory, with Hill out of the points to do it, but the result he wanted had been reversed.

Hill was champion, but in his first year, the kid had proved himself strong enough to cope and fast enough to win. 'Jacques has been an absolutely outstanding newcomer,' said Hill. 'I'm certain that he is a future world champion. He's taken to Formula One like a duck to water. I've really been impressed with him this season.'

And Jacques? At the end of a tumultuous first year, he was satisfied with his effort, if disappointed not to have succeeded at the last gasp. 'I'm feeling very comfortable for next year,' he said. 'I'm happy because when I came across here, everyone was telling me that you can't overtake and that F1 is boring. That's not true. I've had fun this year. It's not only in the last race that you have to look at the championship. Damon did a better season than we did. But I have learned a lot, driven aggressively, and it should be better next year.'

As Hill celebrated and Jacques wondered what might have been, Rickard Rydell mused on life on the other side of the world. He had been dealt the poorer cards after their year together in Japan. While Jacques shot for the Formula One drivers' title, Rydell was in his third season with Volvo in the British Touring Car Championship. 'He's got a famous name and that's made it easier for him,' he suggested. 'And he's got a very good manager in Craig Pollock, but I don't resent him for what he's done. It's just a shame that there are so many other F1 drivers who are there just because of money or connections. But that's how motor racing is – you need the money, or you need the lucky break. Looking at it, I'm one of the few drivers who has won Macau, but hasn't got a drive in F1.'

In Japan, during the course of that final weekend, Bernie Ecclestone sat still long enough to reflect on the first year of Jacques in Formula One. Looking back, he recalled: 'I had not seen him drive and I had never been to an Indycar race. I just had the same hunch as when I got Benetton to take Schumacher. I said he would be a world champion. You just get a feeling when you've been around a long time. You see these guys and you know this guy is a winner. He's dedicated and he has got what it takes to win races. I am not surprised how well he has done this year. I am disappointed. I thought he was going to win the championship. I think he was unlucky because Damon has raised his game so much this year. If Damon had been driving this year as he had last year, then Jacques would have won it easily.'

As to how he coped with the new environment of Formula One and Europe, Ecclestone, in typically direct and opinionated style, said: 'From his point of view – and you have to remember who his father was – it has not helped him to have that name. He has got where he is for himself not because of his dad.

'He has been brought up in a different environment and I think if his current managers will allow him to do what he does well – and that is to speak to people, speak to the press and to become more accessible – he will be an enormous asset. He speaks three languages well, which is good, and he is a young guy and he is attractive to a different audience, perhaps, than Damon would attract.

'That's it. His management has made it more difficult for him. I think they have really, really – and I have got to speak to them about it – been short-sighted. And I think they are bad for Jacques because what they are taking away from him is his sort of individuality and he's not like that. I mean he is an approachable guy. Normally, when somebody does something there is a reason behind it. If you can see a good reason, you think well, fine. But I personally at the moment cannot see a reason. I think their biggest hang-up is that they're thinking someone is making some money out of him and we're not seeing any of that and that's just a stupid way of approaching things because they need him up front as much as anything.'

The final word on Jacques . . . from Jacques, in an interview used in advance of the German Grand Prix by the race organisers. 'Unless you are 100 per cent sure of something, or only if something is as important as life to you, you should be diplomatic. Apart from that there is no point in pissing people off. Most times, if you say something you know what you mean, but you also know that if you say it the way you think there are ten different ways of understanding it. So, you have to be careful with stuff like that. I don't want to get involved in games which were played over the media like we have seen it with a few drivers last year. That's not part of the work. That takes too much energy.'

After our Hockenheim meeting, Jacques did not speak to me, personally, again during the 1996 season, but through watching him closely and studying him through the research for this book, it was possible to see humour, sympathy and humanity were there, in strong supplies, alongside his hard-headed talents as a racing driver. He handled his disappointment at Suzuka like a gentleman and the final indications, as the sun set on 1996, were that he would start 1997 as a better-understood driver and man than in July six months before.

Chapter Twelve

Claiming the Champion's Crown: 1997

There was no Damon Hill at Williams any more in 1997. After his championship success, Damon moved on and became the lead driver for the Arrows Yamaha team, leaving Jacques to take his place at the head of Williams' driver line-up for Renault's final fling. The French manufacturer, a hugely successful engine supplier to Williams and Benetton throughout the 1990s, had announced its intention to withdraw from Formula One at the end of the year. It wanted to go out with a bang, too, by claiming another world title to add to those won during its unprecedented years of glory. Jacques, therefore, was expected to steer his Williams Renault through a triumphant season with his new team-mate Heinz-Harald Frentzen alongside him. The expectation brought pressures, of course, but in the end they were pressures which were to break his chief rival, Michael Schumacher. Not Jacques. Michael, attempting to realise Ferrari's ambition to end 18 barren years without the drivers' crown, steered into Jacques' car in a spectacular collision, during the decisive European Grand Prix at Jerez. It was the last race of the season, the 'showdown', and was dubbed a shameful act of road rage, bringing shame upon Schumacher, but delivering Jacques with his, and Canada's, first FIA Formula One World Drivers' Championship. In one second of sublime sporting justice, the entire year was settled. But what happened before that race, throughout a full season of attrition and stress, was instrumental in the making of the man. For Jacques' champion year saw him also emerge as a champion in many other ways . . .

Twelve hours after the defining moment of his season, Jacques Villeneuve was doing his best to forget it. Along with dozens of other regular members of the Formula One paddock, he was in the Discoteca Pantalan K, down by the yacht club in Puerto de Santa Maria, joining friends, team-mates, colleagues and rivals in a party to celebrate the end of the season, Renault's departure from the sport and his first Formula One World Drivers' Championship. Like everyone else, Jacques had a broad smile on his face. The drinks were free, the music was good and he had the sweet taste of success on his lips. It was the end of a long and tough 17-race season which had seen him experience the full roller coaster of Formula One's ups and downs. It was a loud, busy and fun party. It was a memorable night . . . and a short one. The next day, he started a new job – as Canada's first world champion. And that meant talking, talking and talking, as interview upon interview carried his grin around the planet.

By abruptly ending his participation in the 1997 European Grand Prix (the final and decisive race of the year), in a gravel trap on the outside of the *Curva del Expo 92* at the cramped race circuit at Jerez de la Frontera, Schumacher had brought infamy and ridicule upon himself, and given Jacques a clear run to his first title.

Schumacher's failed 48th lap assault on Villeneuve's car resulted, not in the destruction of the Canadian's bid for glory, but his own. His Ferrari, steered in a fit of jealous road rage into the sidepod of Jacques' FW19, rebounded away from the collision and into ignominious retirement. Schumacher's face, inside his helmet, must have matched the crimson paintwork of his car. His attempt to take a third world drivers' title in four seasons had perished along with his reputation and, despite the lack of action by the race stewards, he was called to face an extraordinary meeting of the ruling body of the World Motor Sports Council, the FIA. Jacques, commendably, resisted the temptation to crow. All year, he had been painted as the rebel without a cause and a man whose views brought him into direct conflict with the FIA but, in his hour of glory, he was the embodiment of good sportsmanship and dignity. There were no cheap shots. And Jacques was hailed as a more-than-worthy champion.

Despite all the pre-race hype, no one truly expected it to end the way it did. The 1997 season began in uproar, and ended in uproar, for Formula One and for Jacques. Billed as the pre-season favourite for the title – the best man, in the best car, with the best chance of cutting himself a slice of Formula One history – Villeneuve had struggled to wear the mantle with comfort. In Melbourne, where he took a dazzling pole for Williams Renault, he crashed out together with Eddie Irvine and Johnny Herbert on the opening lap. It was to be a portent of what was to come . . . a year of living and racing dangerously, particularly when Irvine was around. Despite his experience, his position as team leader and his standing in the sport, Jacques continued to court controversy and attention. He had accidents, haircuts and bleaches, conflicts with the authorities, and brushes with other drivers, all the way from pre-season testing to Melbourne, from Monaco to Montreal, and from Silverstone to Spain. But in the end, throughout a chaotic year of unpredictable twists and turns, a kind of justice prevailed, and the man with most wins took the title on a hot and dusty afternoon in southern Spain.

Back at the start of the year, it had all seemed so different. The Williams FW19 was one of the last cars out of the blocks and had less razzmatazz around it, when it was unveiled, than any of its rivals. Ferrari, with Marlboro's help, had invited hundreds of reporters to Maranello for a snow-shrouded glimpse of their latest challenger for glory; McLaren Mercedes-Benz, with West's assistance, hired The Spice Girls and Alexandra Palace; Mild Seven Benetton Renault took over Planet Hollywood in central London. The Rothmans Williams Renault team, in their typically English way, merely lifted a blue sheet off their car at an informal gathering in their old Didcot factory. No theatres, no banks of seats and no fanfares. Just a smiling Frank Williams and a serious-looking Jacques alongside his new team-mate Heinz-Harald Frentzen.

'It would be great to feel like the favourite for the championship and I'm looking forward to being up there, but you never know what's going to happen,' Jacques admitted. 'A lot of people say it's already finished and that's dangerous. It's my plan to win the title. I'm very excited about it and I hope it goes well. That's the reason you're racing: to be competitive, to win and to fight for the championship . . .'

At only 25 (he was not 26 until early April), he sounded like a veteran campaigner. He sounded confident too. However, in his views on safety and the future of the sport, he knew he courted criticism because he did not follow the trail of conventional thinking. He wanted to find some excitement, and he wanted his cars and his racing to take him to the edge of his talent. 'I know everything now,' Jacques explained, to a table surrounded by reporters. 'There is nothing for me to learn. I just have to adapt a bit and improve on what I've learnt so far . . . the mentality, the drivers and all that. And F1 in general. But knowing the tracks will help a lot because I'll be able to work on the set up of the car with Jock [Clear] right from the start.' Talking about safety and in particular the proposed 1998 technical regulations, he added 'When you look at all the changes that are being made to the rules and the tyres, it's becoming scary to see how low F1 can go just to make it more spectacular. But it's a false, manipulated way of making it more spectacular. It would become more a circus than a sport. F1 doesn't feel fast enough already, so I don't see the point in making it slower.' It was the first shot in an increasingly angry dialogue with the ruling body which was to overshadow much of the first half of Jacques' season.

In its February issue, the respected *Autosport* magazine ran a front cover heading which asked 'New Williams — Best F1 car ever?' The same edition, of course, gave evidence for the question by reporting that Villeneuve, in his first test in the new car, had lapped the *Circuit de Catalunya* at Barcelona in just one minute and 18.86 seconds. That time was 1.8 seconds faster than Damon Hill's pole time for Williams in the previous year's Spanish Grand Prix. It was a warning to the rest of the teams – and a signal to Williams – that they had got it right. Unfortunately for Jacques, it encouraged the Williams men to relax more than usual, to focus on 1998 earlier than expected, and to allow the opposition to catch up during the first half of 1997 when, in more normal circumstances and without such profound rule changes lying ahead, they would have remained focussed on the challenge at hand.

Not that it really seemed to matter. To be more than two seconds clear of his nearest non-Williams rival in qualifying, indicated that Jacques was in such good shape he should have little trouble coping with anything. Anything, that is, other than the brake problems which caused Frentzen to spin out in Melbourne. Or errant Ferraris handled by the much-criticised Eddie Irvine. Jacques' view of his late start, and early finish at the first corner, in the Melbourne race (which was won with some comfort by David Coulthard in a McLaren) blamed the Irishman squarely for the incident that ended his race. 'I let the clutch slip too much, but I was still okay and I was second or third. Then Eddie just braked way too late on the inside of the track. I saw him when I was turning, which was still okay. But Eddie was going too fast and he couldn't turn . . . We had the quickest car out there and we just threw the weekend away.'

Disappointed and, perhaps, a trifle disillusioned, Villeneuve's emotions were understandable. But, as always in Formula One, there was not much time for sorrow. After Australia, the next race in Brazil was only three weeks away. The shimmering heat of São Paulo, the smog and the anti-clockwise tough-on-the-neck track at Interlagos were on the other side of the world, too, and the drivers needed perfect preparation to ensure peak fitness. Jacques rested well, cleared his mind and dominated the weekend, but still needed a generous slice of luck, after another chaotic first corner accident, to give him a chance not only to win the race, but also to take the lead in the Driver's Championship. Once again, Villeneuve took pole. Once again, he made a less-than-impressive start. And, once again, he found himself sliding into the gravel within seconds of the start.

This time, luckily, Rubens Barrichello's Stewart Ford was stranded on the grid and the race was red-flagged to a halt. Jacques, slow off the grid, had attempted to fight the flying Ferrari of Michael Schumacher going towards the first corner and ended up, on the outside, sliding off on the slippery surface, onto the grass and out. 'There was all sorts of stuff going on down there,' said Damon Hill, who was only a short distance behind. 'Jacques was on the grass and, the next thing I knew, I was on two wheels doing a kind of stunt driving balancing act . . .' Behind them, Herbert and Irvine had collided for the second race running. The race was restarted, with Schumacher screaming into the lead, only to be passed by Villeneuve as they rushed down the straight at the start of the second lap. Apart from during pit-stops, Jacques stayed in front from then on until the finish, but it was never easy as Gerhard Berger, in his Benetton Renault, was in close pursuit. 'At the start, it felt like Australia again and so I was glad to see the red flags,' said Jacques. 'Also, my seat was not very comfortable because of the gravel in it. But, at the second start, I could see that Michael was running a lot of wing, so I figured I could get past him quite easily.'

Jacques was right. He did. And he won relatively comfortably. For him, it was also an important victory because it helped to relieve the pressure that was mounting as a result of his non-scoring finish in Australia, Frentzen's intensifying problems and the media-stirred furore over his views on safety in which the FIA were taking serious interest. In order to clear the air and clarify the issues, he talked to *Autosport* again. 'What I said about safety has been interpreted as if I was saying that people have to die and we want crashes,' he explained. 'But that's not what I was saying. If you want that, you just put walls in the middle of the straight. But you do need that small element of danger that tells you where the edge is, so you have to push yourself to reach it. If you take that edge away, it's easy for anyone to be quick because, if you spin off, you go in a sandtrap and that's it. When you go around an oval and you see the wall there, it's not fear, but there is something that takes your foot off the throttle by itself and you have to concentrate to make sure you do it flat. You have to push yourself as a human being.' Asked if he could understand why the rule makers were trying hard to make the sport safer, Jacques replied 'Yeah. Because Ayrton Senna died and it got many people on their backs, because it's not right anymore to hurt yourself on TV. But what made F1 popular ten years ago was that the drivers were not normal human beings. Now, we are presented as athletes but not anything special. You take more risks driving on the roads. F1 has to be the ultimate or else why should it be called Formula One? You need to be proud when you finish a quick lap. That's the human nature side of it: the fighting. If you take that away, you take a lot of the racing away.'

In the same interview, Jacques was invited to explain why he did not agree with the proposed regulation changes which meant the introduction of grooved tyres and narrower cars for 1998. 'The new rules are for safety, but the major point is that it's an artificial way of making racing better and I don't believe it would make the racing better anyway . . . If anything, I would go back to wider rear tyres, because mechanical grip is always better than aero grip. It allows you to fight better and stay closer to someone. If you get sideways you can catch the car.'

He also brushed aside the critics – including Damon Hill – who had ascribed his views to a quasi-death wish, or some sort of thrill-seeking curiosity. 'I read stuff saying that I should grow up and Damon wrote that, when I said the edge, I meant paralysis or death. That's not what I meant. And he should know that. He comes from bike racing and he knows what risk is about. You're on a knife edge and you know that if you make a mistake, you're going to pay for it. But that doesn't mean you want something blatantly dangerous that's going to kill you. That's the other extreme.'

It was an interview which did not pull any punches. It raised the pulses of some people, too, particularly when Jacques added a few personal views on other issues. 'I think a lot of people are a little bit annoyed by how far it [the changes] went, so I hope so [people will listen],' he went on. 'But I've noticed that the key people don't seem to listen much to what the drivers think. Drivers don't have weight but we're the ones with our butts in the car. So, we should have something to say. A lot of people agree with me but they're not allowed to say it. I say what I think about what is important to me and I don't care if it might not be politically correct. But how many drivers are allowed to talk and will be listened to? Not many. Just the few in the top teams who win races. The only problem is that the three of four major ones – and I am not naming names – do not race any more for the love of the sport, or the speed, or the edge or the excitement you get out of it. Making money has become more important, so they don't want to risk their lives. They want to make sure they go home so they can look at and use their money . . . I'm not afraid of death. It's natural. You're born and then you die. Death is part of the wheel of life, although there is no point in making it come quicker on purpose . . . Racing is dangerous. There's that risk and this edge of pushing yourself, and always pushing it more. That doesn't mean you want to do it just because it is dangerous. That's stupid, like jumping off a cliff. It's a danger you are in control of and that's okay.'

These were classic Villeneuve words in print and they grew to dominate his racing in the first half of 1997. His views appeared to attract as much interest as his driving, particularly when they were published by a German magazine, together with unsavoury descriptive allegations, which led Jacques into difficulties with the FIA – and with Max Moseley in particular. But all this lay in the future when the F1 circus flew into Buenos Aires for the Argentine Grand Prix early in April, with Jacques' opinions still hot on the gossip trail. It was also believed, at this time, that he was discussing the renewal of his contract with Williams (they held an option on him for 1998), and also talking to both Prost and the planned Reynard team. The talking, it seemed, was to go on and on, and on, but the majority of close observers felt that the lack of any official confirmation indicated that Villeneuve had agreed to remain with Williams.

It may have been the talking, or it may have been the food, but neither did Jacques' health much good in Argentina. He went down with a severe stomach upset which required him to make rapid and regular visits to the upstairs toilet outside the media centre, before he blitzed the opposition once more in qualifying and then winning the race, ahead of Irvine's Ferrari. Again, he was on top of the track – making a good start and leading all the way, bar a brief spell after his second pit stop. Severe dehydration was the greatest problem for Jacques in what he later described as being the 'toughest race of his Grand Prix career'. He explained 'After the first stop, the gear lever was getting stuck and it was really difficult to change gears – sometimes it was soft and sometimes it would shift by itself. That was giving me some problems so I slowed down a bit until I realised that Ralf [Schumacher] and Eddie [Irvine] were doing less stops than me, and that gave me a hard time.'

Victory helped him to recover. But it did nothing to modify or moderate his views on the 1998 rule changes, and his headlong rush into conflict with Mosley and the FIA. Soon after returning from Buenos Aires, he was back in action, testing for Williams at Barcelona . . . on grooved tryes and in a new narrow-chassis car. 'What they are proposing scares me,' he said afterwards. 'It is not going to be Formula One anymore. It will destroy racing as it exists. It is a joke. It will not be pure anymore. They may as well tell us to buy Formula Three cars and to pretend it is Formula One.'

It was evident by now that Jacques was on collision course with the FIA and that prospect became more clearly visible when he was reprimanded in Imola for ignoring a yellow flag during qualifying for the San Marino Grand Prix. Yellow flags were to play a major part in his year. Frentzen also passed through the yellow flags in Italy. Both men were given a one-race ban, (suspended for two races) but this reaction was almost nothing compared to the one Villeneuve provoked by repeating his views on the 1998 regulations, during a news conference at the Emilia Romagna circuit. There, in his best form, he took a coruscating pole position, led the early laps of the race but fell back to third during the pit-stops. For a spell, he pressurised Schumacher's Ferrari but retired after 40 of the 62 laps with gearbox problems, as Frentzen broke his Williams duck and took an accomplished victory at last.

The next race was at Monaco but, before that, Jacques was back testing in Barcelona and managed, for a change, to avoid any further controversy. The car did the talking as he topped the times, suggesting that he and Williams were well-prepared to take on anyone on the streets of Monte Carlo. For Jacques, of course, it meant a weekend at home . . . and a weekend to forget. Not only did Frentzen continue his high form of Imola by claiming the first pole of his career, but Villeneuve also admitted he messed up his last-gasp effort to snatch pole away by making mistakes on a wild lap, including one lurid slide on the final corner. This left him third on the grid and in the hands of the Gods or, to be more accurate, in the hands of the weathermen.

For the second time in a year, Williams failed to gather the right intelligence on the rain that lay ahead shortly before the race and sent their men out on slicks – on a track covered in puddles. It was a wet race day. But during the pre-race period, the team were so busy poring over printouts and traces in the trucks that they forgot to look out of the windows and draw common-sense conclusions. A dismal failure to communicate properly made it worse and that, added to the team's belief that the circuit would dry very quickly, ensured a Grand Prix which began full of high promise but ended in disarray. After only a few laps in the wet wake of Schumacher (who was running in his prepared 'wet' car), both Williams men pitted for inter-mediates on their dry setups. Jacques lasted only to lap 16 when he crashed into the rails at Ste Dévote, Frentzen to lap 39. Worse still for them both, Schumacher's spectacular victory lifted him four points clear in what was to become an increasingly close scrap for the World Drivers' Championship and Jacques' point-less return was his second in succession.

For Villeneuve, too, the weekend was marked by a singularly

brusque confirmation by Mosley of the FIA's intention to go ahead with the 1998 rule-changes. Jacques declined to be drawn in but it was clear from the manner in which Mosley spoke that their divergent views on the matter could cause further trouble. For his part, Jacques said little more on the subject during the following week's Barcelona test – where he bettered the times again – before he travelled back to Catalunya to win the Spanish Grand Prix. Second fastest on Friday, behind Jean Alesi's Benetton, he bettered the qualifying session on Saturday and the warm-up on Sunday. Then, he drove to a comfortable race victory, controlling the contest from the front with a two-stop strategy designed to minimise the risk of blistering tyres. The win put him back on top of the Drivers' Championship, three points clear of Schumacher, who finished fourth.

'I'd planned on stopping only twice,' explained Jacques afterwards. 'If you make three stops, you have to push like a maniac all the time so you don't lose the lead when you come in. With tyre wear a problem here, I didn't want to have to do that.'

After Spain, there was a welcome two-week gap in the calendar, interrupted only by testing at Magny-Cours and Silverstone, before the Canadian Grand Prix, Jacques' home race. It should have been a quiet period of rest, recuperation and preparation, but for Villeneuve it was thrown into turmoil by the late notice that he was being summoned by the FIA to appear before the World Motor Sports Council in Paris, in order to explain his outspoken criticism of the 1998 rule-changes. The final straw, for Mosley, after several outbursts, was an interview published by the German magazine, *Der Spiegel*, in which he was quoted describing the regulations, in language unacceptable in normal families.

The announcement called him to Paris on June 11, which meant that he had to return from Canada to Europe for the hearing and suffer the inevitable consequences. Jet lag, which he had hoped to avoid by flying out more than a week early, became a nuisance once again. 'Jacques is quite happy to go and talk to the FIA, but he's not particularly pleased about the risk of jet lag – the timing is relatively dangerous,' warned Craig Pollock, Jacques' manager. He also denied that Villeneuve had used the word ascribed to him by the German magazine. He claimed that Jacques had been misquoted through translation. Jacques, as outspoken as ever and determined not to be 'gagged', continued to talk freely. 'I don't think people should stop saying what they believe if they truly believe it. But if the choice is to speak out and maybe get disqualified, or shut up and say nothing, the choice is easy, isn't it? I said what I had to say. The message is out and people can do what they want with it. Next year, we'll see if I was right or wrong.'

The hearing itself resulted only in a reprimand for the driver who promptly turned around and flew directly to Montreal, arriving tired and disappointed on the eve of his home event. At a news conference the following day, looking bleary-eyed, but nonetheless mentally alert, he denied that he would allow the remprimand to stop him speaking as he felt. 'I haven't been asked to change my views,' he said. 'They just want me to use better words. As long as I don't say the regulations are stupid or something like that, then it's okay. Instead of talking when I first get out of the car and you're all excited and you don't really think straight, it's better to take a deep breath and think about what words you use.'

If this misdemeanour and the attendant publicity were not enough to spoil Jacques' weekend at home in Canada, the outcome of the race made certain he flew back to Europe feeling disillusioned. Never quite his normal dominant self, he qualified second behind Schumacher but appeared below par in the warm-up on Sunday morning. He switched to his spare car when his regular race car developed a starter problem, but pointed out that this was routine, the car felt great and was handling better on full tanks. None of it mattered. In the race, in front of a vast crowd of Canadains expecting a Canadian victory, he lasted only one complete lap. On his second lap, he spun off at the final chicane after making an elementary error.

'It was a beginner's mistake,' he said. 'The car was so good that I wasn't pushing at all, just following Michael, as he was eating up his tyres and I was trying to conserve mine. The track was incredibly slippery and it took me by surprise – I certainly didn't think I was going into the last corner too fast . . .' It was a shock for Jacques and a shock for the fans. Many, silenced by what they saw, began to head for the exits. What happened then was tense and eventful – Schumacher ran on to win, but only when the race was halted early after 54 laps following a severe accident in which Olivier Panis broke both his legs. Victory gave Schumacher a seven points lead over Jacques, who was as unimpressed by that as he was by the mournful reactions of several of his fellow drivers at the Frenchman's crash.

If it was a huge disappointment for the people of Montreal to see their hero leaving early, it was an even bigger disappointment to Villeneuve himself. Before the race, he had indicated reasonable pleasure at his start to the year. 'I'm pretty happy,' he said. 'Three wins in six starts is as much as I had last year in 16 races . . . The only big black note was Monaco where we screwed up on the strategy. We took a big gamble and it didn't pay off. The last one to decide the strategy is the driver. He makes the final call. But, you're sitting in your car, under trees, you cannot see the sky, there's an umbrella . . . It was not really wet at the start/finish line. But it was wet at Casino Square . . . We were in a 50-50 situation and I was tempted to go with intermediate tyres, but then the rain stopped. When we left for the formation lap, it started to rain again so I knew we were screwed . . . it was too late. In the race, it was dreadful. There was nothing you could do. It was just sliding and sliding. Most of all, I knew that it was a big mistake. But you cannot turn back time . . .'

This was the toughest time of the 1997 season for Villeneuve and for Williams. The team needed a boost, but it was not to come in the following French Grand Prix at Magny-Cours where Schumacher secured another victory and outright control of the title race. With Irvine third, behind Frentzen, and Jacques fourth, the result also lifted Ferrari clear in the Constructors' Championship. Doubters began to emerge and point at Villeneuve's contribution to the Williams season, his outspoken views, his clash with the FIA and his, some said outrageous, decision to bleach his hair before the French race. 'Of course, I am worried about the championship,' he admitted. 'But it is still open.'

According to some, Jacques' dyed hair did not make him popular with team sponsors Rothmans. Nor did his decision, after his delayed arrival at the circuit on the Thursday, to criticise other drivers for their play-acting in reaction to Panis' accident in Montreal. 'If you think about it,' he said. 'Two broken legs is nothing very bad. That happens to everybody in their lifetime. How many skiers hurt themselves like that in winter? So, just relax a little bit.'

His suggestion that fellow drivers' reactions were contrived brought Jacques into more controversial waters. The team were not happy with his form, the sponsors were not happy with his words and he was not happy with his championship position. 'If I had a serious accident, or if I died during a race, I would not want the race to be stopped,' he said. 'I think we have to accept the risk.'

Many pundits, at this time, began to question Jacques' state of mind. A crash in Canada? A row with the FIA? Crazy views? and now a strange hair-colour . . . The French race did nothing to quell these concerns. Fifth in free practice, he was fourth in qualifying after a heavy crash on Saturday morning and finished fourth in the race, after a last-ditch effort to pass Eddie Irvine within sight of the finish. Having selected a set up for the wet conditions he anticipated, Jacques was never in contention.

By now, the pressure was mounting on Jacques. Yet, it was at this time, in early summer during the approach to the British Grand Prix at Silverstone, that he seemed also to be most relaxed. He had been in contact with the Williams team physiotherapist and fitness trainer Erwin Goellner, requesting some additional work on his own preparation. And he was happy also to put the past, including his disagreement with me over this book, behind us. A nod and a handshake in Buenos Aires had helped heal the rift. An interview, conducted in haste in Berne airport in early July, did the rest.

'I think we were too competitive in the first race, when we were on pole by more than a second-and-a-half,' he explained. 'It sounded too easy. I think we relaxed too much after that and now it has come back to bite us. We started to work too much, too early, on next year's car. Now, I think we need to start work again on this year's car . . .' It was a warning to the team, not to meddle in the wrong areas at the wrong time, but to keep their eyes on this season's priorities. Jacques knew he needed a win. He also knew the team needed one. And, at Silverstone, he duly delivered again, his fourth win of the season, the team's 100th, a result that lifted him back into contention, just three points behind Schumacher, and Williams back within three of Ferrari. This win, however, was not a straightforward affair – it was lucky.

Jacques took pole, again with a last minute dash. He led the early laps and then had to overcome a loose left front wheel which upset his steering. A 33-seconds-long pitstop left him seventh, but he worked his way back and took advantage when Schumacher's Ferrari underwent a wheel bearing failure while leading, and then Mika Hakkinen's McLaren Mercedes-Benz suffered an engine failure. 'I think I could have got him, he was sliding around more and more, and I was just waiting for the last few laps,' said Jacques.

Testing at Monza followed and then the German Grand Prix at Hockenheim, where Jacques spun out after 33 laps of a race in which Williams were never a force. Gerhard Berger, on his emotional return to the Benetton team after missing three races, won ahead of Michael Schumacher, leaving Jacques trailing by ten points again. Poor balance was the official explanation for his Hockenheim disappointment (where he qualified only fifth), but Jacques put it behind him with a determination to improve quickly and win again in Buadapest at the Hungarian Grand Prix.

As usual, it was hot at the Hungaroring. And, as usual, it was eventful. The big surprise, however, was not in the paddock this year, but on the track where Damon Hill performed with all the *élan* and speed of 1996. He was fast in qualifying, behind a front row of Michael Schumacher and Jacques, and he nearly won the race by claiming a maiden victory for Arrows Yamaha. A gearbox hydraulics problem intervened, however, as he led with four laps remaining and allowed Villeneuve to beat him home on a day when Hill deserved the triumph, even if Jacques took the points. With Michael Schumacher fourth in his rubber-eating Ferrari, the Championship scrap closed up again. In the drivers' title race, there were just three points in it and in the constructors' the same, with Schumacher and Ferrari leading each. Jacques knew, however, that his fifth win of the year was a lucky one and he owed it as much to Hill's misfortune as to his own intelligent drive, conserving his tyres as much as possible

Next stop for what was rapidly becoming one of the tightest title-tussles in years was Spa-Francorchamps and the Belgian Grand Prix. As always for Jacques and the rest, the big danger was another inspired drive from Schumacher . . . and that is how it turned out. He seemed to understand the weather in the Ardennes forests better than anyone and be able to predict each shower. Outpaced during qualifying, which was run in the dry, Schumacher wound up third behind Jacques and Jean Alesi's Benetton on the grid where, as at Monaco, Schumacher studied the skies and chose to race on intermediate tyres, while all around were on wets. He ran an extra familiarisation lap, was last on the grid and first to the chequered flag. Jacques had pole, fastest lap and then came sixth, just one point to show for his efforts until Hakkinen's subsequent disqualification for fuel irregularities granted him fifth place and two points. It was another defeat as much by the weather as by the double champion. It meant that Schumacher had a comfortable 12-point lead, reduced to 11 by Hakkinen's DQ, but still a luxurious advantage to carry to Monza and the Italian Grand Prix in September.

There, on another weekend of high drama, Jacques ran into more problems with yellow flags . . . and had to endure a race in which he finished fifth, only one place ahead of Schumacher. It meant he trimmed the German's lead by a point, to ten, at a circuit where Williams had hoped to do better. Second behind Frentzen in Friday's free practice, Jacques was unable to leapfrog him on Saturday and wound up fourth on the grid, two-tenths of a second slower. At the start of the race, he lost another place to the eventually victorious David Coulthard's brilliant start and was never able to improve. 'I really pushed hard,' said Jacques. 'But I was a bit stuck behind Fisichella. I could run quicker than him. But as soon as I got up close behind him, I lost downforce and I couldn't fight . . .'

Equally serious a threat to Jacques' title dream was another one-race ban, suspended until the fourth race of the 1998 season, which he collected on Sunday morning for failing to slow down for yellow flags during the warm-up session. The stewards said they had given him a harsh penalty because it was the third time this year that he had committed the offence – a decision which prompted a furore among the teams because Michael Schumacher had driven past a red flag during testing at Monza two weeks earlier and had not been punished at all. Jacques, having experienced one serious brush with the authorities earlier in the year, opted for a diplomatic approach to this problem when asked to comment. 'It's a little annoying. I find it severe. But I don't make the rules. That's the way it is and you just have to accept it. Even though I wasn't pushing at that corner when the yellow flags were there, one of these laps was quicker than the other one, so it was decided that I didn't slow down enough.' It was a decision, of course, that was to have a dramatic effect on the final unfolding of the championship itself.

By this time, also, it was clear that Jacques and the team needed to find something extra if they were to maintain their challenges for the two titles. Jacques was busy commuting between racing, testing and his home in Monte Carlo with little time for any life in between, but he did manage to embark on a far more specific fitness programme created for him by Goellner and to squeeze in a flying visit to Canada to see Sandrine, his girlfriend. 'It is good for Jacques to cut himself off completely from his racing,' said Pollock. 'He does need to clear his head. Usually, he goes back to Monaco, trains, gets onto his computer and into his music, something intellectual and unrelated to racing . . . Obviously, it's also important for anybody to see their girlfriend.' The Williams team also recognised that it was necessary to ask Frentzen, third in Monza, to agree to accept team orders, when the need arose, to assist Jacques' push for the Drivers' Championship.

The next race was at the A1-Ring at Zeltweg in Austria, a rebuilt circuit returning to the calendar for the first time in a decade, but only as a pale shadow of the old, classic and high-speed Osterreichring. With four races remaining, 40 points available and Schumacher 10 points ahead, the momentum appeared to be with him and Ferrari, but Jacques had no intention of allowing it to remain so.

'Jacques is an intelligent chap and he'll be able to work out for himself what he has to do,' said Williams' technical director Patrick Head before the trip to Austria. 'It's still pretty much wide open, I would say. In truth, maybe it will be a reliability thing either way that might make the difference . . . Anything can happen. I'd rather predict a horse race, actually. You're not just looking at how well the team and driver get their car set up for the cricuit, but you're also looking at first corner incidents that may shunt people off – so many different factors. All I can say is that Jacques has got to raise his game a bit – which he's capable of doing.'

Asked to talk about Jacques' position in relation to the yellow flags, and his suspended suspension, Head said 'It seems to me to be very severe, but the officials said they did that because it was not the first incident – but the third time it's happened this year. If he is wise, he'll take note of it . . .' This was before they went to Austria where, in a race of unexpected drama in the Styrian Alps, Villeneuve scored a much-prized victory and Schumacher was left to finish sixth after, of all things, finding himself entangled in difficulties over a yellow flag, which he claimed he did not see. He was punished with a costly ten seconds penalty, as he saw his championship lead trimmed to a single point.

Jacques, starting from pole, lost out to Mika Hakkinen's McLaren Mercedes-Benz, Jarno Trulli's Prost Mugen Honda and Rubens Barrichello's Stewart Ford at the start, but kept his cool. He passed Barrichello on lap 24, Trulli at the pit stops and then, with some clever racing, worked his way ahead of the field – Hakkinen having blown his engine on the opening lap – to secure a badly needed triumph. No wonder he was smiling afterwards. 'Only one point down now,' he said. 'And next it's the Nurburgring . . . I won there last year and I think it is a track which suits our car much better than this one.'

Villeneuve's hunch was proved right when the teams reached the Nurburgring just one week later. He was squeezed out of pole by Hakkinen and out paced in teh race by both Hakkinen and his McLaren team-mate David Coulthard, before both of the Meredes-Benz powered cars suffered engine failures. This gave Jacques a second successive victory he could scarcely have expected but one that was very welcome, particularly as Michael Schumacher had bounced into early retirement after an opening lap collision with his brother Ralf's Jordan Peugeot. The outcome was that Jacques had a nine-point lead and needed only to outscore Schumacher by a single point in Japan to lift the title.

'There are two races to go and I don't want to think about it until it's done, although hopefully it will be,' he said. 'But I am looking forward to the next race because we have put 19 points on Michael in two races and I'm sure that he will remember that going into Suzuka.' And, of course, he did. So, too, did Ferrari. They worked around the clock to improve their car and they worked just as hard on team preparations, on tactics and pit stops, for what they perceived could be their last gamble. It was going to need something special.

Jacques attempted to stay relaxed and work on his training again before the long flight to Japan. 'When Jacques gets into a situation where there is pressure on him as soon as he gets out of the car, he goes into another kind of mode,' said his manager Craig Pollock. 'He started doing this a couple of months ago and he stepped everything up. He does not want to have to make any excuses.' His race engineer Jock Clear remained convinced Jacques was handling the pressure well and was prepared to take the crown. 'He is dealing with it all very well now, as he has been since August. The race at Spa was a real kick in the guts,' he said. 'He was devastatingly quick there and if it had not rained he would have blown Michael away. It was very different to Canada. He was at his weakest in Montreal, he put in his weakest performance of the season in terms of having his mind on the job and he never really got it together.

'But now, leading the championship again, I don't think we will have a repeat of that. He is confident the car is capable of doing the job and he is psychologically quite strong too – he feels Michael is struggling a bit under the pressure now. He had identified Michael as a human being. And he believes he can beat him in a straight fight.'

By the time he arrived in Suzuka, a place that is always a bit of a walk on the wild side, Jacques had enjoyed a few days' relaxation in some of his old haunts in Tokyo and was very relaxed. He was reading a biography of Jim Morrison and appeared to be perfectly tuned into what was required of him. He made it clear he had no intention of being invovled in any unsporting activity, but could have had no idea of just what lay ahead. Not only were Ferrari planning a team effort to thwart his bid for glory, but he was also to run through the yellow flags again, find himself excluded from the race, reinstated to run under appeal and then, with his concentration badly affected, consigned to finish fifth.

The two points won were virtually worthless and still proved to be a week later when Williams withdrew their appeal. Instead of being a single point ahead of Schumacher, who secured a vital strategic victory in Suzuka, he found himself a point behind him again with one race remaining. The circumstances were too similar to those of 1994 (when Schumacher led Damon Hill by a single point on the approach to the final race in Adelaide) for anyone to ignore them, or the way in which that year's Australian Grand Prix settled the championship. 'The man who goes into Jerez in the lead is in a position where, as we've seen a number of times previously, he can be very aggressive with the person behind and if both cars don't finish . . .' said Head, musing on the possibilities. It was, clearly, a cat-and-mouse situation.

The position had been created, as it had throughout 1997, by yellow flags. This time it happened during Saturday morning's free practice when the marshalls were attempting to remove the Tyrrell Ford of Jos Verstappen, which had stopped on the straight before the flat out 130R corner. Six drivers ignored the flags, because they believed they could see the situation clearly and thought it was safe. One of them was Jacques. The others were Johnny Herbert, Michael Schumacher, Ukyo Katayama, Rubens Barrichello and Heinz-Harald Frentzen, all of whom were given one-race suspended bans. Although the offences took place in the morning, it was curious that Jacques was not called in to see the stewards until after he had qualified on pole position – and he was not told of the decision to ban him until after nightfall that evening. The result was chaos and there was much media furore even before Williams announced their appeal.

For Jacques, it took the edge off what had promised to be one of his most memorable weekends on a circuit he knew well and loved. He consequently lost concentration and motivation, and made a poor start, resulting in Ferrari not only controlling the race, but also dominating it. He was not part of the show. 'I'm really disappointed at what has happened,' he said at the end of the weekend, as he stood outside the cramped temporary team offices at the back of the garages in Suzuka. 'It would be easier to accept this kind of thing at the beginning of the season. But when the stakes are so high, at the end of the season, it becomes hard to accept it's being played like that. But there are rules and I am not the one making them. I believe we have a good reason to appeal because it's a very important race. There was no question of not racing. I never give up. It was frustrating to race knowing that there was a good possibility of being disqualified, but there was nothing I could do. It was a very difficult weekend, knowing I could be suspended in a week. It's been the most difficult season of my career.'

Later, when the appeal was withdrawn, no doubt after detailed discussions of all possibilities with all parties involved, Jacques was pragmatic about the loss of the two points he won at Suzuka. 'There was no point in risking being disqualified from Jerez as well,' he said. 'Had we won in Japan, then you'd risk trying to keep the points, but for two points, it's better to make sure we are in Jerez.'

This thinking and the Williams' team's actions fell in line with FIA president, Max Mosley, who had previously warned that Jacques risked 'not only the loss of his two points from Japan, but suspension from Jerez' if he proceeded with his appeal. It was, therefore, a wise move all round. And, for Formula One's box office, of course, it meant a second successive Championship showdown in two races.

Once again, between races, Jacques did his best to relax. He flew home from Japan, retreated to his flat in Monte Carlo and trained, took it easy and did little else, apart from some weekend media work for Renault, before travelling down to southern Spain. Geollner helped again on the final preparations. When Jacques arrived in the interview room at Jerez on the Thursday afternoon before the race billed as the Spanish showdown, he looked as smiling and happy as possible. Tension, however, lay below the surface and Schumacher, arriving 20 minutes late and in off-duty gear, tried his best to provoke it further with a mixture of languid and haughty styles of behaviour. Much of the focus was on deliberate collisions that might settle the outcome and Jacques, forthrightly, said he could not live with himself if he did such a thing. It was a good remark. Schumacher, who won the 1994 title in acrimonious and controversial circumstances following the crash with Hill at Adelaide, blanched only slightly – but enough. The hype had started and the phoney war was happening.

It stayed that way. Both men kept to themselves. Both worked hard within their teams. The weather was hot and the pressure unrelenting. A huge crowd, by Jerez standards, came to the circuit each day. Normally used only for motorcycling, the dusty and twisty Andalusian track was hosting Formula One for the first time in three years – and it could barely cope.

As the temperatures rose throughout the weekend, so did the excitement and the tempers. By Saturday morning, Jacques was feeling ragged and tired of the Ferrari games. Blocked repeatedly by Eddie Irvine during free practice he chose to jump from his car and approach the Ulsterman, still sitting in his Ferrari, and give him a piece of his mind. 'We all know he is a clown,' said Jacques. His words also included one adjectival oath and a reference to Irvine's intelligence. Irvine responded with a typically unworried, almost indolent, casualness which was to characterise his drive on Sunday. Having played the lead role in Schumacher's success in Suzuka, this time he was left to start from a distant seventh on the grid, while Schumacher, second, was surrounded by Villeneuve, Frentzen and Hill. It was a sandwich he would have preferred to avoid.

The race, when it began, was sensational. Schumacher started superbly, followed by Frentzen and Jacques. Frentzen let Villeneuve through on lap eight and he stayed second, apart from brief moments in the lead due to pit stops, until lap 48. In that time, he was sometimes close enough almost to touch Schumacher's car but found passing it a difficult proposition. Then, the most unexpected opening appeared on the inside of the German's car as they went into the Dry Sack curve, a long right-hander at the end of the back straight. Jacques saw it, considered his chances, made his decision in a flash and went for it.

By the time Schumacher realised what was happening, the front left wheel of the Williams was ahead of the Ferrari. Too late. He may not have made his move in an entirely premeditated fashion but it was certainly calculated. Schumacher pulled the wheel to the right and his front right whell rammed into the sidepod of the Williams, sending the pair into a collision which was as dangerous and hazardous, as it was spectacular. Every spectator at the circuit who could see in the incident, as well as the estimated 400 million watching the race worldwide, was stunned. There was a roar of astonishment. But, unlike Adelaide in 1994, this time it was Schumacher who suffered. His car bounced out and into a gravel trap. He was out of the race, the title was lost and so was his reputation. Jacques drove on in front, eventually allowing the two McLarens to pass him, and finished third, seizing the points he needed for the drivers' crown.

'Trying the move was a big risk,' said Jacques. 'I knew Michael was capable of just deciding to take me off, which he tried to do. So, I wasn't really surprised when he finally decided to turn in on me. But there was no point in just being second. It was better for me to try, and to finish in the gravel, than finish second with very heavy shoulders. The hit was very hard and I was surprised that I was able to finish the race. I couldn't go more to the inside. I was actually on the grass. So either Michael had his eyes closed, or somehow his hands slipped on the wheel or something.

'I think the move surprised him a little bit because when he looked in his mirror I was way behind him and suddenly I was ahead of him. It's good I caught him out because otherwise we would have been off. I was surprised he hadn't already closed the door but it was only a matter of time before he decided to turn in on me. But he didn't do it well enough because he went off and I didn't . . .'

It was the defining moment of the year for Jacques. Schumacher was pilloried in the media by his own fans, in Italy and in Germany, and by many former champions. Hill, the Adelaide '94 victim, said 'Michael showed his true colours and got what he deserved. I didn't think he would do anything because it would destroy his reputation, but what he has done has underlined in people's minds just what his antics and tactics are. At least, he is consistent.'

Jacques emerged as the Champion and a sporting victor. His success was popular. The world recognised his achievement and Canada rejoiced. After the race, he was emotional when he thought of the land in which he was born and grew up, and he paid a warm tribute to his people. He went out on the grid to celebrate with Jock Clear, the pair of them cavorting before a Canadian flag. His engineers wore yellow wigs in a mark of affection for the boy they had dubbed Billy Idol in June at Magny-Cours. Jacques went round and thanked them all. 'Jacques is a quick driver, obviously, and he is a very determined person,' said Patrick Head. 'He's carried himself very well – a man only in his second year of Formula One and then under heavy pressure in the middle of the season, when things weren't going well and the car was quite difficult. He's shown himself to be a real fighter and a good sportsman.'

Jacques smiled, and smiled and smiled. It was over. It felt good. Not only had he won the title, but he had also won it well. Everyone was satisfied – not least those whose faith in the Villeneuve tradition – that the individuality he brought with him to Formula One had been tested during the year. He deserved his celebrations, his party and his installation as a very worthy World Drivers' Champion.

JACQUES VILLENEUVE FACT FILE

Italian Formula Three Championship 1990

April 1	Vallelunga (I)	Reynard Alfa Romeo	DNF
April 15	Pergusa (I)	Reynard Alfa Romeo	sixth
April 29	Magione (I)	Reynard Alfa Romeo	eighth
May 12	Varano (I)	Reynard Alfa Romeo	DNF
June 17	Imola (I)	Reynard Alfa Romeo	5
June 24	Monza (I)	Reynard Alfa Romeo	DNF
July 8	Levante (I)	Reynard Alfa Romeo	second
July 28	Misano (I)	Reynard Alfa Romeo	DNF
September 2	Monza (I)	Reynard Alfa Romeo	18
Sept 16	Varano (I)	Reynard Alfa Romeo	10
October 7	Vallelunga (I)	Reynard Alfa Romeo	10
October 21	Vallelunga (I)	Reynard Alfa Romeo	14

Tenth in championship

Italian Formula Three Championship 1991

March 31	Monza (I)	Reynard Alfa Romeo	DNF
April 12	Levante (I)	Reynard Alfa Romeo	DNF
April 21	Enna Pergusa (I)	Reynard Alfa Romeo	eighth
May 5	Vallelunga (I)	Reynard Alfa Romeo	23
May 19	Magione (I)	Reynard Alfa Romeo	fourth
June 1	Imola (I)	Reynard Alfa Romeo	fourth
June 15	Varano (I)	Reynard Alfa Romeo	DNQ
June 30	Monza (I)	Reynard Alfa Romeo	second
July 14	Mugello (I)	Reynard Alfa Romeo	24
Sept 1	Monza (I)	Reynard Alfa Romeo	third
Sept 15	Mugello (I)	Reynard Alfa Romeo	25
October 6	Vallelunga (I)	Reynard Alfa Romeo	third
November 24	Macau GP	Reynard Alfa Romeo	eighth
December 1	Fuji (J)	Reynard Alfa Romeo	eighth

Sixth in championship

Japanese Formula Three Championship, 1992

March 8	Suzuka (J)	TOM'S Toyota 032F	sixth
March 29	Tsukuba (J)	TOM'S Toyota 032F	fourth
May 3	Fuji (J)	TOM'S Toyota 032F	third
June 14	Nishi-Sendai (J)	TOM'S Toyota 032F	first
June 28	TI Circuit (J)	TOM'S Toyota 032F	third
July 12	Mine (J)	TOM'S Toyota 032F	first
Sept 13	Sugo (J)	TOM'S Toyota 032F	fourth
Sept 27	Suzuka (J)	TOM'S Toyota 032F	second
October 25	Suzuka (J)	TOM'S Toyota 032F	DNF
Nov 15	Suzuka (J)	TOM'S Toyota 032F	first
November 22	Macau GP	TOM'S Toyota 032F	third

Second in championship

Formula Atlantic Championship 1993

April 4	Phoenix (US)	Ralt Toyota	DNF
April 18	Long Beach (US)	Ralt Toyota	Second
May 9	Road Atlanta (US)	Ralt Toyota	first
June 6	Milwaukee (US)	Ralt Toyota	DNF
June 12	Montreal (CAN)	Ralt Toyota	first
June 20	Mosport (CAN)	Ralt Toyota	second
July 11	Halifax (CAN)	Ralt Toyota	DNF
July 18	Toronto (CAN)	Ralt Toyota	third
August 8	New Hampshire (US)	Ralt Toyota	second
August 15	Trois Rivières (US)	Ralt Toyota	DNF
August 28	Vancouver (US)	Ralt Toyota	DNF
September 11	Mid Ohio (US)	Ralt Toyota	first
September 18	Nazareth (US)	Ralt Toyota	DNF
October 2	Laguna Seca (US)	Ralt Toyota	first
October 3	Laguna Seca (US)	Ralt Toyota	first
November 21	Macau	Ralt Toyota F3	DNF

Third in Championship

PPG Indycar World Series, 1994

March 20	Surfers Paradise (AUS)	Reynard Ford 941	DNF
April 10	Phoenix International (US)	Reynard Ford 941	DNF
April 17	Long Beach (US)	Reynard Ford 941	Fifteenth
May 29	Indianapolis (US)	Reynard Ford 941	second
June 5	Milwaukee (US)	Reynard Ford 941	ninth
June 12	Detroit (US)	Reynard Ford 941	seventh
June 26	Portland (US)	Reynard Ford 941	sixth
July 10	Cleveland (US)	Reynard Ford 941	fourth
July 17	Toronto (US)	Reynard Ford 941	ninth
July 31	Michigan (US)	Reynard Ford 941	DNF
August 14	Mid-Ohio (US)	Reynard Ford 941	ninth
August 21	New Hampshire (US)	Reynard Ford 941	DNF
Sept 4	Vancouver (CN)	Reynard Ford 941	DNF
Sept 11	Elkhart Lake (US)	Reynard Ford 941	first
Sept 18	Nazareth (US)	Reynard Ford 941	seventh
October 10	Laguna Seca (US)	Reynard Ford 941	third

Sixth in championship

PPG Indycar World Series, 1995

March 5	Miami (US)	Reynard Ford 951	first
March 19	Surfers Paradise (US)	Reynard Ford 951	DNF
April 2	Phoenix (US)	Reynard Ford 951	fifth
April 9	Long Beach (US)	Reynard Ford 951	DNF
April 23	Nazareth (US)	Reynard Ford 951	second
May 28	Indianapolis (US)	Reynard Ford 951	first
June 4	Milwaukee (US)	Reynard Ford 951	sixth
June 11	Detroit (US)	Reynard Ford 951	ninth
June 24	Portland (US)	Reynard Ford 951	DNF
July 9	Elkhart Lake (US)	Reynard Ford 951	first
July 16	Toronto (CDN)	Reynard Ford 951	third
July 23	Cleveland (US)	Reynard Ford 951	first
July 30	Michigan (US)	Reynard Ford 951	tenth
August 13	Mid-Ohio (US)	Reynard Ford 951	third
August 20	New Hampshire (US)	Reynard Ford 951	fourth
Sept 3	Vancouver (CDN)	Reynard Ford 951	twelfth
Spt 10	Laguna Seca (US)	Reynard Ford 951	eleventh

Indycar Champion

F1A Formula One World Championship 1996

March 10	Melbourne (AS)	Williams FW18 Renault	second
March 31	Interiagos (BR)	Williams FW18 Renault	DNF
April 7	Argentina (Arg)	Williams FW18 Renault	second
April 23	Nurburgring (D)	Williams FW18 Renault	first
May 5	Imola (I)	Williams FW18 Renault	eleventh
May 19	Monaco (F)	Williams FW18 Renault	DNF
June 2	Catalunya (Esp)	Williams FW18 Renault	third
June 16	Montreal (Cnd)	Williams FW18 Renault	second
June 30	Magny Cours (F)	Williams FW18 Renault	second
July 14	Silverstone (GB)	Williams FW18 Renault	first
July 28	Hockenheim (D)	Williams FW18 Renault	third
August 11	Hungaroring (H)	Williams FW18 Renault	first
August 25	Spa Francorchamps (B)	Williams FW18 Renault	second
September 8	Monza (I)	Williams FW18 Renault	seventh
September 22	Estoril (P)	Williams FW18 Renault	first
October 13	Suzuka (J)	Williams FW18 Renault	DNF

Second in Championship

F1A Formula One World Championship 1997

March 10	Melbourne (AS)	Williams FW19 Renault	DNF
March 30	São Paulo (BR)	Williams FW19 Renault	first
April 14	Buenos Aires (Arg)	Williams FW19 Renault	first
April 27	Imola (I)	Williams FW19 Renault	DNF
May 11	Monaco (F)	Williams FW19 Renault	DNF
May 25	Barcelona (Esp)	Williams FW19 Renault	first
June 15	Montreal (Can)	Williams FW19 Renault	DNF
June 29	Magny-Cours (F)	Williams FW19 Renault	fourth
July 13	Silverstone (GB)	Williams FW19 Renault	first
July 27	Hockenheim (D)	Williams FW19 Renault	DNF
August 10	Budapest (H)	Williams FW19 Renault	first
August 24	Spa Francorchamps (B)	Williams FW19 Renault	fifth
September 7	Monza (I)	Williams FW19 Renault	fifth
September 21	Zeltweg (Aus)	Williams FW19 Renault	first
September 29	Nurburgring (Lux)	Williams FW19 Renault	first
October 12	Suzuka (J)	Williams FW19 Renault	fifth
October 26	Jerez (Eur)	Williams FW19 Renault	third

Index